ACT!® 2005

FOR

DUMMIES®

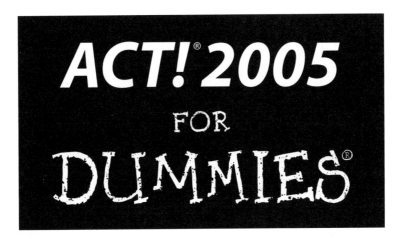

by Karen S. Fredricks

**ACT! Certified Consultant, ACT! Premier Trainer, and
Founder of the ACT! Users Group of South Florida**

WILEY

Wiley Publishing, Inc.

ACT!® 2005 For Dummies®

Published by
Wiley Publishing, Inc.
111 River Street
Hoboken, NJ 07030-5774

Copyright© 2004 by Wiley Publishing, Inc., Indianapolis, Indiana

Published by Wiley Publishing, Inc., Indianapolis, Indiana

Published simultaneously in Canada

For general information on our other products and services or to obtain technical support, please contact our Customer Care Department within the U.S. at 800-762-2974, outside the U.S. at 317-572-3993, or fax 317-572-4002.

Wiley also publishes its books in a variety of electronic formats. Some content that appears in print may not be available in electronic books.

Library of Congress Control Number: 2004107898

ISBN: 0-7645-7532-5

Manufactured in the United States of America

10 9 8 7 6 5 4 3 2 1

1O/RQ/QZ/QU/IN

WILEY

About the Author

Karen S. Fredricks began her life rather non-technically growing up in Kenya. She attended high school in Beirut, Lebanon — where she developed her sense of humor while dodging bombs. After traveling all over the world, Karen ended up at the University of Florida and has since been an ardent Gator fan. In addition to undergraduate studies in English and accounting, Karen has a Master's degree in psycholinguistics. Beginning her career teaching high school English and theatre, Karen switched to working with the PC in its inception in the early '80s — and has worked as a full-time computer consultant and trainer ever since.

Karen is an ACT! Certified Consultant, an ACT! Premier Trainer, and a QuickBooks Premier Certified Advisor. She is the author of many training manuals and a contributor to numerous newsletters. A true ACT! FanACTic, she founded the ACT! Users Group of South Florida and served as the official host for the ACT! 6 Launch Tour in Florida.

Karen resides in Boca Raton, Florida, with her long-suffering husband Gordon, over-achieving daughters Andrea and Alyssa, and her little white dog Carolina. Her company, Tech Benders, provides computer consulting, support, and training services. In her spare time, Karen loves to play tennis and write schlocky poetry. Feel free to send your comments about the book to dummies@techbenders.com.

Dedication

In loving memory of Betsy Fredricks Levine (1959-2000).

I know you're still making friends out of strangers and asking questions along the way. We miss you!

Author's Acknowledgments

I have been blessed with so many wonderful people in my life that I hardly know where to begin.

The people at Wiley Publishing have been the greatest to work with and have made writing this book a true pleasure! Special thanks to my Acquisitions Editor, Terri Varveris, for discovering and having faith in me. Thanks for going that extra mile, Terri!

Thanks also to the entire ACT! Certified Consultant community for their willingness to share and to Best, CRM for their continuing support. Susan Clark — you are one, class ACT!; Lon Orenstein and Steve McCandlish — you are my idols among ACT! Certified Consultants!; Melissa and Ted — thanks for all your effort and hard work.

I'd like to also thank my marketing guru, Norma Wolpin, who qualifies as a true ACT! FanACTic — even if her coffee skills are no better than mine! Hugs go to Cecelia Alvarez, my wonderful assistant and ACT! Certified Consultant, for being my right hand — and for letting me steal her terrific layouts! Special greetings go out to my Wednesday, Saturday, and Sunday games at the Swim and Racquet Center of Boca Raton and to the CLAWS of Boca for your continuing support, love, and friendship. You guys rock!

When I grow up, I want to be just like my mom and dad! Mom is 87, has fewer senior moments than I do, volunteers at church several times a week, and has one of the most active social lives in South Florida. At 83, Papa Carl plays tennis, takes his boat out on Coast Guard patrols, and still does tax returns. You two are inspirational!

Words can't describe how special my daughters are to me. You have brought such joy to my life and are a constant source of pride and support. Love and thanks go out to "Dr." Andrea Fredricks and the very theatrical Alyssa Fredricks for putting up with my lack of presence over the last few months. Although we have all pursued very different paths in life, the three Fredricks women all share a single-minded devotion and dedication to the things — and people — we love!

And finally Gordon, my best friend, husband, and partner, deserves special recognition for being the #1 Dummy in my life — and I mean that in only the best of ways! He proofread, stapled, offered suggestions, and kept me supplied with red licorice as I typed away. He's also remained relatively sane despite living with his Type A wife for the past 27 years. T.B., I know you're now capable of writing *Grocery Shopping For Dummies*. I couldn't have done it without your help. I love you!

Publisher's Acknowledgments

We're proud of this book; please send us your comments through our online registration form located at www.dummies.com/register/.

Some of the people who helped bring this book to market include the following:

Acquisitions, Editorial, and Media Development

Project Editor: Pat O'Brien

Acquisitions Editor: Terri Varveris

Copy Editor: Rebecca Senninger

Technical Editor: Roy Laudenslager

Editorial Manager: Kevin Kirschner

Media Development Manager: Laura VanWinkle

Media Development Supervisor: Richard Graves

Editorial Assistant: Amanda Foxworth

Cartoons: Rich Tennant (www.the5thwave.com)

Production

Project Coordinators: Adrienne Martinez, Courtney MacIntyre, Erin Smith

Layout and Graphics: Andrea Dahl, Lauren Goddard, Joyce Haughey, Stephanie D. Jumper, Michael Kruzil, Jacque Roth, Heather Ryan

Proofreaders: Laura Albert, Carl Pierce, Charles Spencer, TECHBOOKS Production Services

Indexer: TECHBOOKS Production Services

Special Help: Teresa Artman, Andy Hollandbeck

Publishing and Editorial for Technology Dummies

    Richard Swadley, Vice President and Executive Group Publisher

    Andy Cummings, Vice President and Publisher

  Mary Bednarek, Executive Acquisitions Director

    Mary C. Corder, Editorial Director

Publishing for Consumer Dummies

    Diane Graves Steele, Vice President and Publisher

    Joyce Pepple, Acquisitions Director

Composition Services

    Gerry Fahey, Vice President of Production Services

    Debbie Stailey, Director of Composition Services

Contents at a Glance

Table of Contents

Part VI: The Part of Tens 339

Introduction

*A*CT! is the best-selling contact manager that's used by more than 4 million professionals and 11,000 corporations worldwide. For many of these users, ACT! represents their first foray into the area of contact relationship management (CRM). Contact management software is a little more complex to understand than other types of software. With a word processor, each document that you create is totally separate; if you make a mistake, you need only to delete your current document and start fresh. Contact management, however, builds its way into a final product; if you don't give a bit of thought as to what goal you wish to achieve, you could end up with a muddled mess.

I am a *fanACTic*. I'm not ashamed to admit it. I use ACT! at work. I use ACT! on the road. I use ACT! at home. I've even inspired my friends to use ACT!. I'm excited about the product and know that by the time you learn to unleash the power of ACT!, you'll be excited, too.

So what am I so excited about? I've seen firsthand how ACT! can save you time and help make you more efficient in the bargain. To me, accomplishing more in less time is an exciting thought — it allows more time for the fun things in life. Best of all, ACT! is a program that's very easy to master in a very short time. You'll be amazed not only at how quickly you can set up a database but also at how easily you can put that database to work.

Maybe by the time you finish this book, you, too, will have become a fanACTic!

About This Book

ACT! 2005 For Dummies is a reference book. As such, each chapter can be read independently and in the order you want. Each chapter focuses on a specific topic, so you can dive right in, heading straight for the chapter that interests you most. Having said that, however, I must say that I've tried to put the chapters into a logical sequence so that those of you who are new to ACT! can just follow the bouncing ball from chapter to chapter. More experienced users can use the Table of Contents and the index to simply navigate from topic to topic as needed.

Essentially, this book is a nuts-and-bolts how-to guide for accomplishing various tasks. In addition, drawing on many of my own experiences as a full-time ACT! consultant and trainer, I've included specific situations that should give you a feeling for the full power of ACT!.

Conventions Used in This Book

Like in most Windows-based software programs, you often have several different ways to accomplish a task in ACT!.

For the most part, I show you ways to perform a function by using the ACT! menus. When an instruction reads Choose File➪Open, you must access the File menu (located at the top of the ACT! screen) by clicking it with the left mouse button and then choosing the Open option from the subsequent menu that appears. In most cases, you can access these commands from anywhere within ACT!, although I generally advise new ACT! users to always start a task from the Contact Detail view which is the first window you'll see when ACT! opens. If you must be in a particular area to complete a task otherwise, I tell you where.

I also present you with shortcuts here and there. Generally, ACT! shortcuts are triggered by simultaneously pressing the Ctrl key and another key on the keyboard. For instance, the shortcut for recording a history is Ctrl+H.

At times, you need to access one of ACT!'s hidden menus, which you do by clicking an appropriate area of the screen with the right mouse button and then choosing from the menu that appears. In these instances, I simply say *right-click* when you need to right-click.

What You Should Read

Of course, I'm hoping that you're going to sit down and read this entire book from cover to cover. But then again, this book isn't the Great American Novel. And, come to think of it, the whole reason why you bought this book in the first place is because you want to get your ACT! together (no groans, please!) as quickly as possible because you're probably finding yourself with too much to do and too little time to do it in.

For the time being, I'm going to let you get away with just reading the parts that interest you most. I'll let you read the last chapter first and the first chapter last if you'd like because this book is designed to allow you to read each chapter independently. However, when you find yourself floating in a swimming pool, soaking up the sun, and wondering what to do with all your spare time, you might want to go back and read some of those chapters you skipped. You just might discover something!

What You Don't Have to Read

This book is intended for both new and existing ACT! users. Most of the instructions apply to both groups of readers. Once in a while, I include some information that might be of special interest to more advanced readers. Newbies, feel free to skip these sections! Also, any information tagged with a Technical Stuff icon is there for the truly technically inclined. Everyone else can just skip this info.

Foolish Assumptions

One of my least favorite words in the English language is the word *assume,* but I've got to admit that I've made a few foolish — albeit necessary — assumptions when writing this book. First of all, I assume that you own a computer and that ACT! is installed on it. Secondly, I assume that you have a basic knowledge of how to use your computer, keyboard, and mouse, and that ACT! isn't the very first application that you're trying to master.

I've also assumed that you have a genuine desire to organize your life and/or business and have determined that ACT! is the way to go.

Finally (and I feel quite comfortable with this assumption), I assume that you'll grow to love ACT! as much as I do.

How This Book Is Organized

I've organized this book into six parts. Each part contains several chapters covering related topics. The following is a brief description of each part, with chapter references directing you where to go for particular information:

Part I: The Opening ACT!

In Part I, you get an introduction to the concept of a database and why ACT! has become such a popular choice of database users (Chapter 1). In this part, you read about what to expect the first time you fire up ACT! (Chapter 2) and how to set the main preferences in ACT! (Chapter 3).

Part II: Putting the ACT! Database to Work

Part II focuses on putting your contacts into ACT! (Chapter 4) and, more importantly, how to find them again (Chapters 6 and 7). I show you how to view all the details about one contact, how to pull up a list of all your contacts, and even how to create an easy list report.

After you master organizing your contact information, Part II helps you organize your day. ACT! makes it easy to take notes (Chapter 8) so that you start relying on ACT! more and your memory less. You find out how to schedule appointments, calls, and to-dos — and other important events in your life. And, you discover how to view those activities in the daily, weekly, and monthly calendars (Chapter 9). Your life can become complicated, but have no fear because ACT! does its best to help you navigate through the maze. The History, Documents, and Secondary Contacts tabs allow you to accumulate lots of information about each and every one of your contacts (Chapter 5).

Part III: Sharing Your Information with Others

Corporate America lives for reports, and ACT! is up to the challenge. Whether you want to print labels or telephone directories on commercially printed forms or prefer to utilize the ACT! built-in reports (Chapter 11), Part III shows you how. I even tell you about building your own reports from scratch (Chapter 12).

One of the best features of ACT! is the ability to communicate easily with the outside world. Part III shows you how to work with templates to automate routine documents as well as how to send out mass mail merges — whether by snail mail, fax, or e-mail (Chapter 13). You also discover the advantages of using ACT! for your e-mail client (Chapter 14).

Part IV: Advanced ACT!ing

We're all different and often like to do things in our own unique way. ACT! understands that concept and allows you to customize it to your heart's content. At first glance, ACT! may seem like just an over-the-counter piece of software, but by adding fields (Chapter 15) and placing them on customized layouts (Chapter 16), you can make it perform as well as an expensive piece of proprietary software.

Every database needs an Administrator. If you're elected to the job, you need to know how to perform administrative tasks, such as adding users, checking for duplicate data entry, and performing routine maintenance (Chapter 17). If you have remote users that need to access all or parts of your database you need to know how to synchronize your database (Chapter 18).

Part V: Commonly Overlooked ACT! Features

Part V focuses on four of the most frequently overlooked ACT! features:

- **Microsoft integration:** Synchronize your ACT! and Outlook address books and calendars; attach a Web site in Internet Explorer directly to an ACT! contact; and explore the various ways that you can use ACT! and Excel together (Chapter 19).
- **Sales opportunities:** Track your prospective sales, prioritize them, and analyze what you did right — or wrong — in making the sale (Chapter 20).
- **Groups:** Group your contacts together to add a new dimension to your database (Chapter 21).
- **Companies:** This is an exciting new feature of ACT! 2005. The Company feature enables you to view and edit contacts that all "belong" to the same company (Chapter 22).

Part VI: The Part of Tens

With apologies to David Letterman, you have three of my favorite ACT! lists. First, in Chapter 23, I give you a list of the major differences between ACT! 2005 Standard Edition and ACT! 2005 Premium Edition. Then in Chapter 24, I list my favorite new ACT! 2005 features — which is specifically designed for anyone who has used a previous version of ACT!. In Chapter 25, I give you ten of my favorite ways to customize your layouts.

Icons Used in This Book

The Tip icon indicates a special timesaving tip or a related thought that might help you use ACT! to its full advantage. Try it; you might like it!

The Warning icon alerts you to the danger of proceeding without caution. *Do not* attempt to try doing anything that you are warned *not* to do!

The Remember icon alerts you to important pieces of information that you don't want to forget.

The Technical Stuff icon indicates tidbits of advanced knowledge that might be of interest to IT specialists but might just bore the heck out of the average reader. Skip these at will.

Where to Go from Here

For those of you who are ACT! old-timers, you might want to at least skim the entire contents of this book before hunkering down to read the sections that seem the most relevant to you. My experience is that the average ACT! user is probably only using a portion of the program and might not even be aware of some of the really cool features of ACT!. You might be surprised to discover all that ACT! has to offer!

For the ACT! newbie, I recommend heading straight for Part I, where you can acquaint yourself with ACT! before moving on to other parts of the book and of the ACT! program.

Part I
The Opening ACT!

The 5th Wave
By Rich Tennant

"We can monitor our entire operation from one central location. We know what the 'Wax Lips' people are doing; we know what the 'Whoopee Cushion' people are doing; we know what the 'Fly-in-the-Ice Cube' people are doing. But we don't know what the 'Plastic Vomit' people are doing. We don't want to know what the 'Plastic Vomit' people are doing."

In this part . . .

You're excited about all the possibilities that ACT! has to offer and want to dive into the program as soon as possible. Here's where you'll find an overview of some of the cool features that you'll find in ACT!. You'll also become familiar with the many faces of ACT!; after all, you wouldn't want to get lost along the way. But first you have to do a bit of homework and whip ACT! into shape by fiddling with a few preference settings to ensure that ACT! will produce the type of results that you're looking for.

Chapter 1

An Overview of ACT!

So what is ACT!, anyway? I find that one of the hardest things that I have to do with ACT! is to explain exactly what it is. I like to initially explain ACT! by using very politically correct terminology. For example, ACT! 2005

✔ Is a Customer Relationship Management (CRM) Software Package

✔ Provides users and organizations with powerful tools to manage their business relationships

✔ Is a packaged software product that can be customized based on your company's requirements

✔ Is the world's leading CRM software

Feel free to use these points to impress your friends. If, after telling all this to your friends, they still look at you rather blankly, at least you know that your knowledge of computing is equal to — if not greater than — theirs. At that point, you may want to list some of the wonderful features of ACT!, which I do in the first section of this chapter. I also describe the typical ACT! user and give you a brief primer on some pertinent ACT! terminology. Finally, I end the chapter with a few ground rules that I've established over the years. I've watched new users wrestle with certain aspects of using ACT!, and I want to save you the trouble.

What Does ACT! Do?

Using ACT! allows me to have more free time — which means that I have more playtime. Because I want you to enjoy the benefits of using ACT!, I've put together a little shopping list of features so that you can see all that ACT! can do for you, too. In parentheses after each item, I include a chapter reference where you can find more information about a particular feature (if you're so inclined).

ACT! is a multifaceted personal management tool that

- Stores complete contact information, including name, company, phone numbers, mailing addresses, and e-mail addresses. (Chapter 4)

- Comes with over 50 predefined fields for each contact that you add to your database. If you want to add new ones to meet your specific needs, go right ahead. (Chapter 15)

- Records an unlimited number of dated notes for each of your contacts so that you can easily keep track of important conversations and activities. This feature is particularly useful for those of us who, unlike our friend the elephant, do forget things on occasion. (Chapter 8)

- Keeps more than a boring old calendar. Your scheduled activities are cross-referenced with the appropriate contact so that you have a full record of all interactions that you have had — or will have — with that contact. In addition, you can set an alarm to remind you of the important stuff, and roll over the less important things until the next day. (Chapter 9)

- Prints out anything from simple phone lists, or address books, to detailed reports on activities, notes, leads, and sales opportunities. You can print reports of your reports if you feel so inclined. (Chapters 11 and 12)

- Creates mailing labels and envelopes. Or, if you prefer, perform broadcast faxes and e-mails with ACT!. (Chapters 13 and 14)

- Manages your sales pipeline with built-in forecasting tools. If you're so inclined, print a few sales reports — or create a graph showing your open, won, or lost sales. (Chapter 20)

- Synchronizes data with remote users. (Chapter 18)

- Lets you design and activate a series of activities so that you're reminded of your tasks — assuring that none of your contacts "fall through the cracks." (Chapter 10)

The Typical ACT! User

So just who is the typical ACT! user? Well, with more than 4 million users and 11,000 businesses currently using ACT!, you are safe to assume that nearly every industry is represented among its user base. Although ACT! started as primarily a tool for salespeople wanting to follow up on their prospects and customers, ACT! has evolved into a tool used by any individual or business trying to organize the chaos of daily life.

I think it's only fair to warn you about one of the possible side effects that you might develop if you use ACT!. If you're anything like me, you'll become addicted to ACT! and eventually use it to manage all facets of your busy existence. You might just become a fanACTic. Quite simply, a *fanACTic* is an ACT! user who has become addicted to using ACT!.

So just who is using ACT!? Everyone.

- ✔ The CEO uses ACT! because he wants to know what his salespeople are doing and how his customers are being treated.
- ✔ The administrative assistant is using it to automate routine tasks and to keep a schedule of various tasks and activities.
- ✔ A salesperson is using ACT! to make sure that she's following up on all her prospects.
- ✔ The disorganized person finds that using ACT! can help him become more organized.
- ✔ The smart person uses ACT! because she knows that she'll have more time to play by working more efficiently.
- ✔ The lazy person uses ACT! because he knows it's more fun to play than to work.

So what kinds of businesses use ACT!? All kinds.

- ✔ Large businesses that want to improve communication among employees
- ✔ Small businesses that have to rely on a small staff to complete a multitude of tasks
- ✔ Businesses of all sizes looking for software that can automate their businesses and make them more productive in less time
- ✔ Businesses looking to grow by marketing to their prospects
- ✔ Businesses looking to retain their current customers by providing an excellent level of customer service and developing lasting relationships

So who's *not* using ACT!? Okay, I just said that simply *everyone* is using ACT!, but a few stubborn folks remain out there who aren't looking to organize their lives, such as

- Workaholics who live to spend every waking moment at work
- People who don't use even a paper address book to keep track of their contacts
- Hermits who don't need to schedule any appointments or remember to make follow-up phone calls
- Individuals with photographic memories who retain all information and never need to take a note
- Companies that require no paperwork
- Businesses that do no marketing or that have no interest in expanding their customer base

Terms You Need to Know

Nobody likes technical jargon, but in the course of showing you how to use ACT!, I might end up lapsing into Geek Speak and use a handful of somewhat technical terms; I just can't avoid it. Becoming familiar with them now just may be less painful in the long run.

ACT! is a database program. A *database* is a collection of information organized in such a way that the user of the database can quickly find desired pieces of information. You might want to think of a database as an electronic filing system. Although most ACT! users create a database of contacts, some users develop ACT! databases to collect information about things other than contacts. For example, you might create an ACT! database to catalog all the CDs and DVDs in your collection.

Traditional databases are organized by *fields, records,* and *files:*

- A *field* is a single piece of information. In databases, fields are the smallest units of information. A tax form, for example, contains a number of fields: one for your name, one for your Social Security number, one for your income, and so on. In ACT!, you start with 50 separate fields for each individual contact. You find out how to add information into these fields in Chapter 4. And, in Chapter 15, I show you how to change the attributes of existing fields and how to add new ones to your database if you're the database administrator.

✔ A *record* is one complete set of fields. In ACT!, all the information that you collect that pertains to one individual contact is a *contact record*.

✔ A *file* is the entire collection of data or information. Each database that you create in ACT! is given a unique filename; creating more than one file or database in ACT! is possible — head to Chapter 3 to find out how.

The Basic ACT! Ground Rules

Sometimes you just need to learn things the hard way. After all, experience is the best teacher. Luckily for you, however, I've compiled a list of rules based on a few mistakes that I see other ACT! users commit. You're not going to find these rules written down anywhere else. And they may not even make a whole lot of sense to you at the moment. But as you become more and more familiar with ACT!, these rules will make all the sense in the world. You might even want to refer to them from time to time.

Karen's Four Rules of Always:

✔ Always log in to ACT! as yourself.

✔ Always strive for standardization in your database by entering your data in a consistent manner.

✔ Always input as much information into your database as possible.

✔ Always compress and reindex and perform a backup of your database at least once a week!

The Two ACT! Flavors

New to ACT! version 7 are two separate editions. Everything I cover in this book applies to both versions of ACT!:

✔ ACT! Standard Edition 2005.

✔ ACT! Premium Edition 2005.

The Premium Edition contains some features not found in the Standard Edition; I do not cover those additional Premium features in this book.

All users sharing the same database must be using the *same* edition of ACT!.

You can read more about the differences in the two editions in Chapter 23 but for now, I want you to be aware of the basic differences between the two versions.

ACT! Standard Edition 2005

- ✔ Utilizes the Desktop Edition (MSDE) version of SQL
- ✔ Is designed for individuals and small workgroups
- ✔ Allows a maximum of 10 active named users per database
- ✔ Can be purchased at any of the major retail chains
- ✔ Can't open a database created using ACT! Premium Edition 2005

ACT! Premium Edition 2005 for Workgroups

- ✔ Includes MS SQL Server 2000 Standard Edition but can also work with MSDE if preferred
- ✔ Is designed for the corporate "enterprise" user
- ✔ Does not place a limit on the number of database users
- ✔ Can only be purchased through volume licensing distributors
- ✔ Can open a database created using ACT! Standard, or can save a database to a Standard format

So what are you waiting for? Boot up your computer, grab the book, and get going. After all, it's time to ACT! (pun intended).

Chapter 2

The Various Faces of ACT!

*A*fter getting the hang of maneuvering in ACT!, you'll find that it's an amazingly easy program to master. The key is to become familiar with the lay of the land *before* you start building your contact database. By doing so, you avoid playing hide-and-seek *later.* To that end, I show you how to log into and open an ACT! database. Although initially getting around in ACT! is pretty easy, you might become lost in the maze of views and tabs that ACT! is divided into. I help you navigate through that maze by taking you on a tour of ACT! so that you can become familiar with the various ACT! screens. Finally, you discover the places that you can turn to if you need additional help.

Locating the Correct Database

When you open ACT!, by default, ACT! opens up the database that was last open on your computer. Easy enough, huh? If, however, you stumble into the incorrect database by mistake, you need to know how to find the correct one. If you're lucky enough to have inherited a database that someone else developed (someone who maybe even placed that database on your computer for you), be sure to ask where that database is located — before that person walks out of your life.

In Chapter 3, I show you how to change the *default database location;* that's the place on your computer that ACT! uses to store any new databases that you create and look in to open any existing database. If, by chance, your database isn't in the default location, you have to change the default location (as I discuss in Chapter 3), move your database to the correct location, or browse to the location of your database.

The first screen that you see when opening ACT! each and every time is the Contacts Detail window. If you click around and end up in any of the other ACT! screens, don't panic. One of the nice things about ACT! is that you're able to execute most commands from any ACT! screen (unless I tell you otherwise). And I promise that pretty soon the various screens become so familiar to you that you'll navigate through ACT! with the best of them.

To open a database, make sure that ACT! is open and then follow these steps:

1. **Choose File⇨Open Database from the ACT! Contact Detail window.**

   The Open dialog box appears (see Figure 2-1).

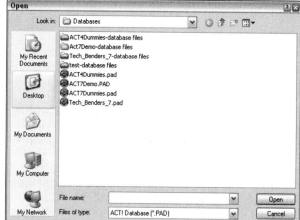

Figure 2-1: Opening an ACT! database.

2. **Click the drop-down arrow to the right of the Look In box.**

3. **Double-click to expand the folder that contains your database.**

4. **Select the name of your database and then click Open.**

   If you prefer, double-click the name of the database that you want to open.

When you open an ACT! database, you are actually using a "shortcut"; these shortcuts all end with the .pad file extension. ACT! actually stores three different groups of data:

✔ **Main database:** The main database consists of all of your contacts' information, activities, notes, histories, and so on. The database files are stored on your local machine by default. You can move the database and all associated files to another location or even over to a network drive if you so desire.

✔ **Database supplemental files:** These files and folders are automatically created when you create a new database and include layouts, templates, e-mail messages, and any attachments associated with a contact record. You cannot change the location of these files in the database; they are automatically stored as part of your database.

✔ **Personal supplemental files:** These files are saved to your local computer, and include files such as word processing documents not associated with a contact, newly created layouts, and templates. E-mail messages and attachments not associated with contacts are also saved as personal supplemental files.

The ACT! Login Screen

If more than one person is sharing your ACT! database, ACT! presents you with a login screen each time that you attempt to open your database. Essentially, the login screen, as shown in Figure 2-2, asks you for your user name and your password. Your user name and password are not case sensitive (that is, you can enter your name by typing either lowercase or UPPERCASE letters). You also need to make sure that you enter your user name and password information correctly. For example, if my user name includes my middle initial with a period, I must type that middle initial — including the period — to gain access to my database.

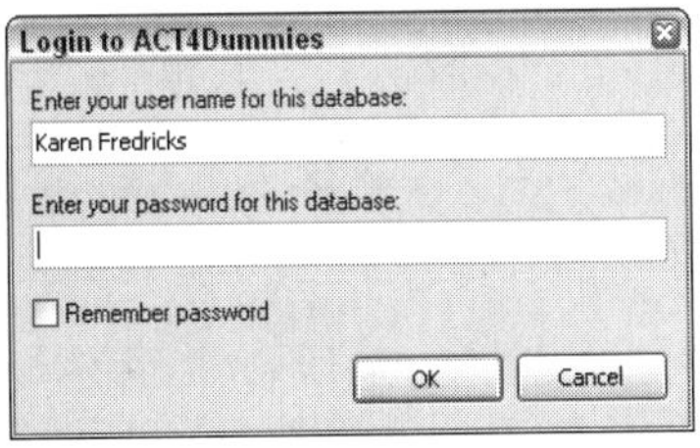

Figure 2-2:
Logging in
to ACT!.

Generally, the administrator of your database determines your password. The *database administrator* is the person responsible for making major changes to the database and for performing routine database maintenance. Although several users may all have access to an ACT! database, ACT! doesn't require that each user have a password. So if the database administrator didn't assign you a password, just leave the password area blank.

If you are assigned a password, notice that asterisks appear while you type it in. That's normal. Just like when you type your ATM card PIN, your ACT! database password is hidden while you type it to prevent any lurking spies who might be watching from learning your password. You're able to change your own password; see Chapter 3 to find out how.

Figure 2-2 shows that ACT! gives you the option of saving your password (an option automatically selected by default). Although this option helps you to log in to your database in the future, you may want to rethink this decision. First of all, what good is a password if it always magically appears anytime that you attempt to access your database? Secondly, by having ACT! remember your password, you may eventually forget it yourself!

The Importance of Being My Record

The first contact that you see when opening an ACT! database is your own — that's your *My Record*. My Record is nothing more than a contact record that is associated with a user of the database. Your My Record stores all your own information, which automatically appears in some of the preset templates that come with ACT!. For example, a fax cover sheet includes *your* telephone and fax numbers; a report has *your* name at the top; and a letter has *your* name at the bottom. If, for some reason, someone else's information appears as the first contact record that you see when you open your database, explore these three possibilities:

✔ Did you log in as yourself? If not, do so. Then, when you open ACT! again — logged in as yourself — your My Record appears.

✔ Did you inadvertently change your own contact information? If that's the case, change it back.

✔ If you're 100 percent certain that you logged in as yourself and haven't changed your contact information, your database is likely corrupted. I'm not trying to scare you, but I recommend that you turn to Chapter 17, where I show you how to perform a little CPR on your database.

Taking the time to enter in all your own contact information is very important. If you don't, you may find that you're missing key information when you start to work with templates and reports. For example, if you never enter your own fax number, your fax number doesn't appear on the Fax Cover Sheet template, which means you have to fill it in every time that you send a fax. Save yourself the trouble and fill in your My Record right off the bat.

Your My Record also allows you to use a few other important ACT! features:

✔ Permission to perform various functions is based on the security level of your My Record.

✔ Contacts, notes, histories, activities, and opportunities marked as "private" can only be viewed by the Record Manager who created them.

  ✔ Every time that you enter a new contact, your name appears as the creator of that contact.

  ✔ When you delete a contact, a history of that deletion appears in the History area of your My Record.

  ✔ Every time that you add a note to a contact record, your name appears as the Record Manager of that note.

  ✔ When you schedule an activity, your name automatically attaches to that activity.

Finding Your Way Around in ACT!

The purpose of this book is to serve as a reference book for both new and existing ACT! users. I certainly don't want to lose anyone along the way. New ACT! users might be somewhat intimidated when they encounter ACT! for the first time. Be assured that this experience is akin to the first time you drive a new car at night in the rain: momentary panic sets in. After you've driven the car for a week or so, the location of the light and windshield wiper controls becomes second nature. I guarantee you'll have the same experience with ACT!.

Navigating through ACT! is fairly easy. However, to make the navigating even easier, I highlight throughout this section a number of pitfalls that you want to avoid.

The title bar

The title bar provides you with several pieces of key information:

  ✔ The software name

  ✔ The database name

  ✔ The user's name

Don't overlook the importance of this wealth of information! If your title bar reads `Free Cell`, it's a good indication that you've stumbled into the wrong piece of software. If the database name indicates `ACT7demo`, chances are pretty good that you're in the wrong database and may be adding hundreds of new contacts to the wrong place. And if the user name is not yours, you may not be getting the appropriate credit for all your hours of hard work. You can see the title bar, along with other key areas of ACT!, in Figure 2-3.

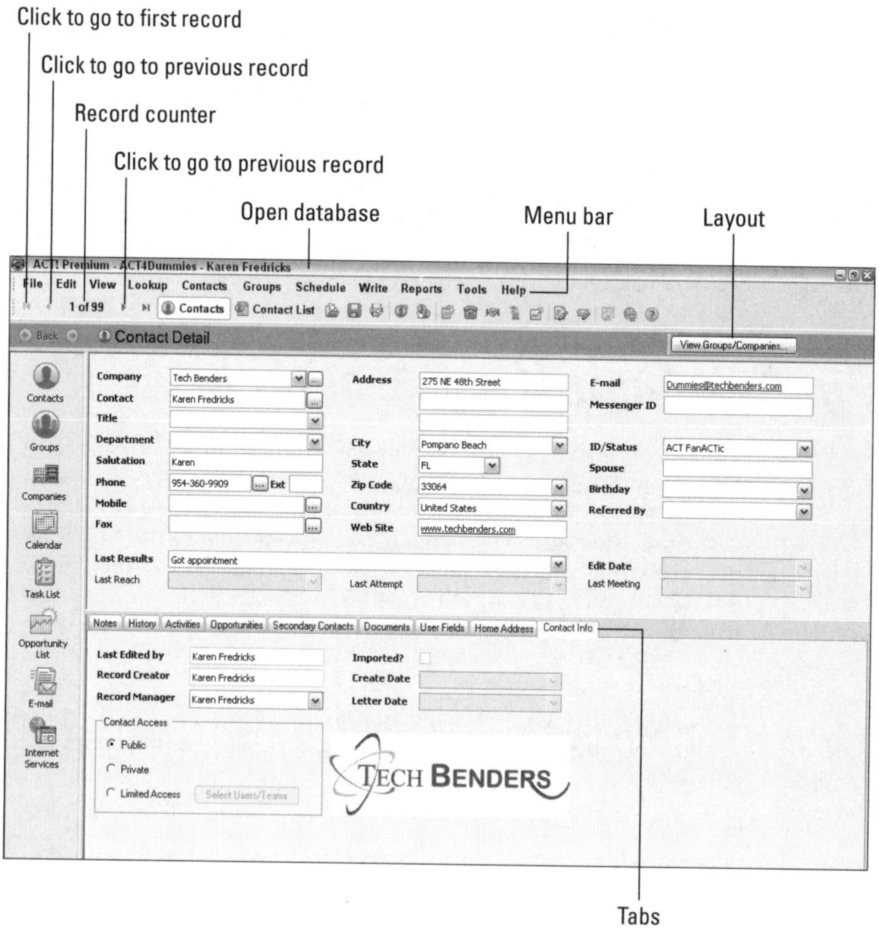

Click to go to first record

Click to go to previous record

Record counter

Click to go to previous record

Open database   Menu bar   Layout

Figure 2-3:
The opening
ACT!
screen.

Tabs

The record counter

ACT! supplies you with a record counter in the top-left corner of the Contact
Detail window (refer to Figure 2-3). The first number indicates the number of
your record as it relates alphabetically to the other members of your current
lookup. This number changes when you add or remove contacts. The second
number supplies you with the total number of contacts in either your entire
database or your current lookup. (A *lookup* refers to the contacts in your
database that you're currently working with. You can find out everything that
you ever want to know about a lookup in Chapter 7.)

I recommend getting into the habit of checking the total number of contacts in your database each time you open ACT!. If the total number of contacts changes radically from one day to the next, you just might be in the wrong database. Worse yet, a dramatic change in the number of contacts may indicate corruption in your database.

To the left and right of the record counter is a set of left- and right-pointing triangles. You can click these triangles to navigate through the contact records. For instance, to go to the previous record, you simply click the left-pointing triangle. Refer to Figure 2-3, which shows how to use these triangles.

The layout

One of the biggest sources of confusion to the new ACT! user is the use of layouts. The *layout* refers to the order in which fields appear on the ACT! screens as well as the colors, fonts, and graphics that you see. You can specify the colors, fonts, and graphics in the layout as well as the position and order of fields. If the database administrator created new fields for the database, these fields must then be added to a layout.

✔ You can modify the contact, company, and group layouts or create your own layouts to suit your needs.

There's no right or wrong layout — only the layout that you prefer. For example, the Sales Department may need to see one set of fields, but the Customer Service Department may need to see an entirely different group of fields — and want them to appear in a specific order.

✔ You can remove fields that you don't use or move fields to other tabs.

✔ You can add your own tabs to the bottom of a layout.

Renaming and reordering the tabs to your liking helps you organize your fields. For example, you might want to keep all the personal information about a customer on one tab and the products that he's interested in on another tab.

You can find the name of the layout by clicking the Layout button in the lower-left corner of the ACT! screen, as shown in Figure 2-3. If you inadvertently switch layouts, you might not be able to see all the information in your database, or you might see your information arranged in a different order. At this point, panic often sets in. Don't worry — your data is most probably alive and well and viewable with the help of the correct layout. To switch layouts, click the Layout button to access a list of all layouts; from that list, choose a different layout. In Chapter 16, I explain how you can create your own customized layouts.

Make sure you take the time to acquaint yourself with the name of the layout that you're using. You might find yourself the victim of one of those random, drive-by clickings you've been hearing so much about and end up in the "wrong" layout. If you know the name of your preferred layout you can easily "find" it again.

The menu bar

Like most software programs, ACT! comes equipped with a *menu bar* that appears at the top of every ACT! screen. These menus include all the options available for the current view. Unlike most other software programs, however, ACT!'s menu options are dependent on the view that you are currently in. If you are in Contact Detail window, the various tab options appear in the Edit menu; if you're in the Contact List, however, the tab options are *grayed out,* indicating that that option is not currently available.

You're able to customize all menus to fit your needs; check out Chapter 3 for the details.

A quick way to familiarize yourself with ACT! is to click each and every one of the menu items. Doing so may seem like a waste of time at first but you might see something that piques your interest. You might click the Schedule menu and notice the Activity Series option. Hopefully, curiosity overcomes you, and you have an overwhelming desire to find more about that feature. Or you might notice the Sort choice listed in the Edit menu and think hmmm, maybe I can sort my database in a different order than alphabetically by company.

The toolbar

ACT! also features a *toolbar* at the top of each window. The toolbar includes the most commonly used tasks of the current view. Toolbars work in much the same way as the menu bars. You can customize each toolbar to include the tasks that you use most frequently. And, like the menu bars, toolbars vary depending on the current view that you're looking at. For example, the toolbars that you see in the calendar views include a Show Filter/Hide Filter icon to change the view settings on your calendar, and the toolbar that you see in the Group Detail window include icons for creating groups and subgroups.

The Back and Forward bar

Lurking just below the toolbar is the *Back and Forward bar.* The Back and Forward bar provides you with a road map of sorts by letting you know the exact area of ACT! that you're currently working in. And, like your Internet browser, the Back and Forward bar has handy-dandy left- and right-pointing arrows that allow you to return to the previous window you were viewing.

The Contact Detail window

When you first open up ACT!, you land in the Contact Detail window, which allows you to see all the information about one specific contact. You can use the Contact Detail window to enter, modify, and view information about your contacts. Each contact record displays as a single page that is divided into a top and bottom half:

✔ The top half of the screen contains generic fields that are probably used by just about all ACT! users everywhere. Many of these fields are used extensively in the templates (that is, reports, letters, fax cover sheets, and labels) that ACT! has already set up for you.

✔ The tabs at the bottom provide additional fields for each of your contacts.

You can — and should — customize the bottom half of the screen to better serve the needs of your business. You can click through the page tabs in the middle of the screen to get an idea of some of the fields suggested by ACT!. I show you how to add contact information into your database in Chapter 4 and how to modify those tabs in Chapter 16.

The Divider bar

One of the fast food chains used to have a jingle about "having it your way" a number of years back and you might want to hum a few bars of that tune each time you open ACT!. A point in case is the Divider bar that separates the top half of the Contact Detail window. Got a lot of fields in the top half of your screen? Grab the Divider bar and drag it down. Want to have more room to view some of the tabs along the bottom? Grab that bar and drag it up a bit.

The Navigation bar

ACT!'s Navigation — or *Nav* — bar is the column of icons located along the left side of the program. The *Nav bar* allows you to move quickly between the various areas in ACT!. For example, maybe you want to view all the information about one particular contact by clicking the Contacts icon, or maybe you want to see a list of all your groups by clicking the Groups icon.

The ACT! tabs

Because ACT! comes with approximately 50 predefined fields, and because your database administrator might add another 50 or so customized fields, placing those fields where you can see them clearly is important. Plunking 100 fields on one half of your screen gives you a jumbled mess. I suppose that you could lay out those fields by using a smaller font, but the result — although neat — is impossible to read!

ACT! solves this dilemma in a rather unique fashion. The top half of the Contact Detail window displays the most basic fields that are fairly typical to all contacts. In this portion of the screen, the fields include places for the name, address, and phone numbers as well as a few miscellaneous fields. The bottom half of the ACT! screen displays additional information about your contact that's divided into categories, which you access by clicking tabs located across the middle of the Contact Detail window.

The first seven tabs (refer to Figure 2-3) — Notes, History, Activities, Opportunities, Groups/Companies, Secondary Contacts, and Documents — are called *system* tabs. The system tabs are actually *tables;* they don't hold single fields with a single piece of information in each one. Rather, you can add an unlimited number of like items to the same tab. For example, you can add multiple notes about your contact using the Notes tab, or you might have numerous sales opportunities that involve your current contact displayed on the Opportunities tab.

Because the system tabs contain tables rather than fields, you can't customize them in the same way as the other tabs. However, you can remove a system tab or change their order. Chapter 16 shows you how to fix the order.

Depending on the layout you're using, you probably see several additional tabs after the system tabs. These tabs generally display less frequently used information about your contact, such as these:

- ✔ The User Fields tab displays ten user fields; these fields are just waiting for you to customize them.
- ✔ The Home Address tab reveals your contact's home address, personal e-mail address, and phone number as well as the spouse's name.

You can find out how to customize the user fields in Chapter 15 and the layouts in Chapter 16.

All the tabs are dependent on the layout that you're currently using. If you switch layouts, your tabs change as well.

Some of the ACT! add-on products add new tabs to your ACT! screen. For example, the ACT! QuickBooks link draws information from QuickBooks and plops it into a brand new tab called QuickBooks.

Getting Help When You Need It

In addition to the information that I provide in this book, ACT! 2005 comes with a very good — and quite extensive — online Help system that supplies step-by-step instructions for just about any ACT! feature that you might want to explore.

You can access the ACT! online Help system in one of two ways:

✔ Press the F1 key on your keyboard.

✔ Choose Help from any ACT! menu bar.

When you access ACT!'s Help menu, you're treated to several options. All these Help options provide a wealth of information, and you shouldn't be afraid to use them.

✔ **Help Topics:** This option supplies you with lots of information based on the currently open window. Use this option when you find yourself scratching your head about something and you'll probably be rewarded with just the answer you're looking for.

✔ **"How to Use Help":** This area of help provides you with the most information. In fact, you can find so much good information that this section is further subdivided into three tabbed areas:

  • **Contents:** Think of the Contents tab as the Table of Contents in a book. The Contents tab presents you with the major topics covered in ACT!. If you click the plus sign next to each topic, you find a more detailed listing of the subject.

  • **Index:** As its name implies, the index is just like the index you find at the back of a book. It provides you with an alphabetical listing of every feature found in ACT!. You can either scroll through the list of features or type in the first few letters of the feature that you are looking for.

  • **Search:** The Search tab provides you with the most in-depth information about the various ACT! features. This feature is particularly helpful if you aren't sure of the exact name of the feature that you're trying to find. For example, you may be looking for instructions on how to force a field to display only capital letters. A search of the Index tab doesn't help you (the feature is actually called Initial Capitalization), but you can find the information by typing **capital** in the Search tab. Figure 2-4 gives you an idea of all the help you can find in the Search window.

✔ **Online Manuals:** ACT! comes with two nifty PDF files. One is a Quick Reference card that you can print to help you with the most common of ACT! features. The other is a rather large document that you can refer to — or print — when you need extra help.

✔ **Getting Started Wizard:** In your zealous haste to start working with ACT!, you might have chosen to ignore the wizard that pops up immediately after you first fire up ACT!. The Getting Started Wizard insures that your word processor and e-mail preferences are set correctly and help you to either convert an existing database or create a new one.

✔ **ACT! Update:** As much as you may want to think that the software you purchase is perfect in every way, it's not. Very often, users like you discover "bugs" or little errors in the software. Sometimes, major changes such as the release of a new operating system may cause your software to exhibit some bad behavior. An update patch generally corrects these problems. The ACT! update insures that you have the latest and greatest release of ACT!; best of all, there is no charge for this service!

✔ **Service and Support:** Ever wonder how to find help when you really need it? Three great options can provide a bit of extra handholding:

  • **Contact information:** Includes a link to the various fee-based support options offered by Best Software.

  • **Knowledge Base:** Includes articles written by ACT!'s tech support about commonly asked questions and procedures.

  • **ACT! Consulting:** Most of you know a brother, buddy, or colleague that "knows" ACT!. As the old saying goes, a little knowledge is a dangerous thing. In reality, these well-intentioned folks probably know ACT! as it pertains to their business — not yours. Unless they are earning a living by consulting in the ACT! program, they are probably not your best source for accurate information.

  Your best source of help for ACT! is the ACT! Certified Consultant. These consultants (or *ACCs*) earn their livelihood by working with people like you. They are certified ACT! fanACTics who spend a great portion of their day working with any and all things ACT!. They can help you with anything from converting to ACT! from another program and customizing your database to training your employees. Most ACCs even make house calls. Clicking the ACT! Consulting option takes you for a field trip out to an Internet site that contains a listing of all the local ACT! consultants.

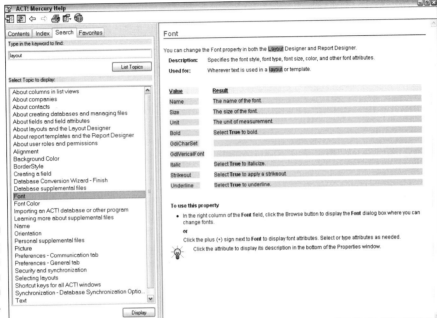

Figure 2-4:
Using the
Search
window in
ACT!'s Help.

Chapter 3

Getting Your ACT! Together

I could easily have titled this chapter "Have It Your Way" because here's where I show you how to set up a new database and add a couple of users to it. You discover some of the preference settings that you can change in ACT!, especially if you're sharing your database across a network. Finally, if you're a real power user, you'll be excited to know how to change your menus and toolbars.

Creating a New ACT! Database

If your initial meeting with ACT! entailed looking at the Act7demo database that comes with ACT!, you know that it's a great database to use for learning purposes *before* actually starting to work on your own database. After playing with the demo for only a short time, you're probably eager to start working on your very own database. The easiest way to create your first database is by using the Getting Started Wizard. In addition to setting you up with a new database, the wizard helps you to set a few of the most basic preferences needed for ACT! to work correctly.

Follow these steps to set up your new ACT! database with the Getting Started Wizard:

1. **From any ACT! screen, choose Help⇨Getting Started Wizard.**

   The first of the five Getting Started Wizard screens appears.

   At this point, feel free to put your feet up on the desk, answer a few questions, and let ACT! do the grunt work for you.

2. **On the wizard's introductory screen, click Next to get started.**

   Quick as a flash, the Getting Started Wizard - Word Processor screen appears. Here's where you get to choose your word processor. It's an either/or proposition; you have only two choices (see the next step).

3. **Choose Microsoft Word (if Word is installed on your computer); otherwise, choose the ACT! word processor. Click Next.**

   In the next screen, you get to tell ACT! which e-mail client you're using. (For information on determining which e-mail client you need to be using, scurry over to Chapter 14.)

4. **Select the e-mail program of your choice and then click Next.**

   If you prefer, you can even tell ACT! that you prefer to skip the e-mail setup for now.

   By now, I'm sure you realize running a wizard means clicking the Next button a lot. Smart reader! However, the next step in the wizard gets a wee bit more challenging because you have to decide to either create a new database, convert an existing database from a prior version of ACT! into ACT! 2005 format, or to just skip the database setup. I've made the assumption that you are setting up a brand new ACT! database; that's the direction the steps take.

5. **Select Set Up Database Now and then click Next.**

   In this step of the Getting Started Wizard, you get to make a couple of decisions about the future of your database as you can see in Figure 3-1.

   - **Database Name:** You might want to give the database a really cool moniker, such as the name of your company, so that you can easily identify it later.

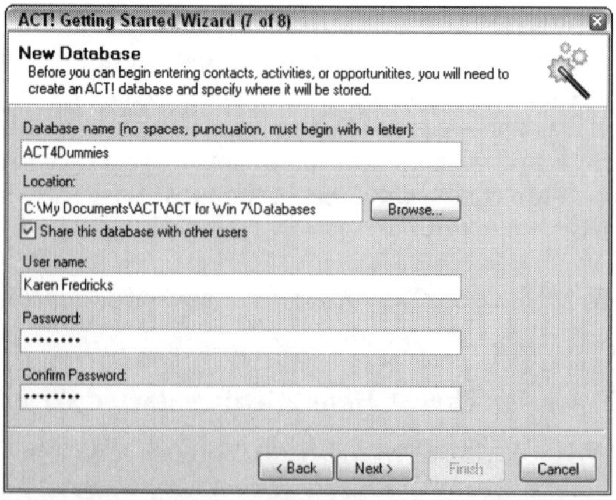

Figure 3-1:
Setting up a
new ACT!
database.

- **Location:** By default, the database is saved to the default database folder. Unless you change that preference, the default location is `C:\My Documents\ACT\ACT for Win 7\Database`. You also can indicate whether you want to share this database with other people with whom you might be networked.

- **User Name:** Most of the time the person setting up the database is also one of the database administrators. Keeping this is mind, indicate the name of the database administrator.

- **Password:** The good news is that as you type your password, each letter appears on-screen as an asterisk just in case someone is lurking over your shoulder trying to nab your password. The bad news is that because you can't see what you're typing, you might just type something you didn't intend to. ACT! demands that you retype your password to ensure that you didn't misspeak the first time.

6. **Fill in the appropriate information and then click Next.**

   The final screen of the Getting Started Wizard appears, recapping all the important decisions that you just made about your new database. If you made a mistake or simply changed your mind, now's the time to click the Back button and fix things!

7. **Double-check your answers carefully, make the appropriate changes (if any), and then click Finish.**

If you need to create another database, simply repeat the wizard or check out the next section, where I show you how to make a copy of an existing database. When you're ready to add contacts to the database, head to Chapter 4.

If you have already set your preferences, you don't need to use the wizard to create a new, blank database. Just do the following:

1. **Choose File⇨New Database from any of the ACT! views.**

   The New Database dialog box appears. By coincidence, it is identical to the New Database screen of the Getting Started Wizard (refer to Figure 3-1).

2. **Fill in the database name, location, user name, and password, and then click OK.**

Copying an Existing Database

Each time you create a new database by using either the Getting Started Wizard or by choosing File⇨New Database you are creating a new, pristine database based on ACT!'s original "out of the box" fields. After you use ACT! for a while, you might want to create a new database based on a database that you or someone else has customized.

If you make an exact copy of your database, you want to be careful how you use it. If you merely want to place a database on another computer for reference, making an exact copy by following these steps is fine. However, if your intention is to create a database for a remote user for purposes of synchronization, read Chapter 18 to find out how to create a database for a remote user. If you're creating a copy of a database for backup purposes, check out Chapter 17, where I show you how to create an ACT! backup.

1. **Choose File⇨Save Copy As from any of the ACT! views.**

   The Save Copy As dialog box opens (see Figure 3-2), where you decide what type of database you want to create.

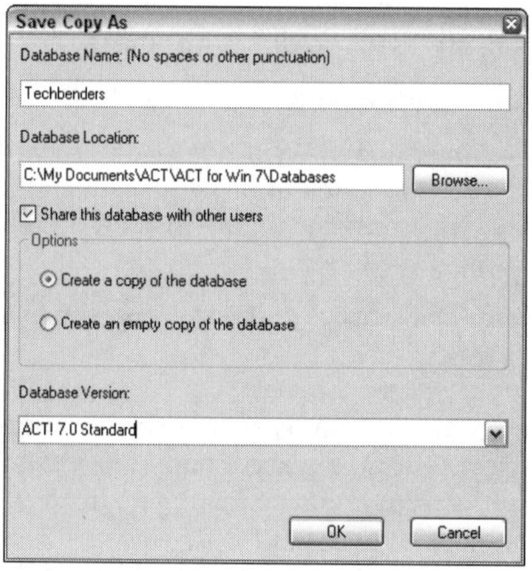

Save Copy As

Database Name: (No spaces or other punctuation)

Techbenders

Database Location:

C:\My Documents\ACT\ACT for Win 7\Databases   Browse...

☑ Share this database with other users

Options

⦿ Create a copy of the database

◯ Create an empty copy of the database

Database Version:

ACT! 7.0 Standard

OK   Cancel

Figure 3-2:
Creating a
copy of a
database.

2. **Type a name for the copy of the database.**

   Do not make the mistake of assigning the same name to the new database that you have already used for your existing database. Even if you save the database copy to an entirely new location, there's a good chance that you'll accidentally use the "wrong" database. By default, whenever you open ACT!, it opens the last database that you used; ACT!'s title bar tells you the *name* of the currently opened database but not its *path*. If two databases have the same filename, you may end up working in the incorrect database — without even realizing it.

3. **Specify the location for the new database.**

   By default, the new database is saved to `C:\My Documents\ ACT for Win 7\Databases`. You can also indicate whether you want to share the database.

4. Specify the type of database you're creating.

Although creating a copy of your existing database is easy, you must understand the consequence of your decision at this point. Consider your choices:

- **Create a Copy of the Database:** This option creates an *exact replica* of your currently opened database. After you create a new ACT! database and customize it by adding many new fields, you may want to duplicate it for use by other offices or for other businesses that you might own. The new database copies the field structure of your existing database as well as all the actual contact records within the database.

- **Create an Empty Copy of the Database:** This option creates a blank database that contains all the customized fields that you created in your existing database, but it does *not* contain any of the contact records from your original database.

5. Click OK.

A dialog box appears asking you to insert the name of the primary user of the database, as shown in Figure 3-3.

6. Fill in the user name and password for the primary user of the database.

As you see in Figure 3-3, you're also given an option to select a name from the current database, which is what you want to do if the primary user is already one of the contacts in the database that you are copying. You are now ready to start entering contact records into your new database. Chapter 4 contains the details about adding contact records to a database.

Figure 3-3:
Selecting
the main
user of the
new ACT!
database.

Save Copy As

Choose Contact:
Fredricks, Karen

User Name:
Karen Fredricks

Password:
Supersecret

Confirm Password:
Supersecret

OK   Cancel

Adding Multiple Users to a Database

A *Record Manager* is a contact in your database who is also a user of your database. If several people are entering data into your ACT! database, I highly recommend setting up each person as a Record Manager. If you and Jane are both set up as users of the database, you need to make sure that you log in as you and Jane logs in as herself. ACT! automatically enters several key pieces of information based on the way that you log into the database. For example, you're recognized as the *record creator* of each new contact you add to the database. Likewise, if Jane enters a note, that note is associated with her name. If you generate a document from one of ACT!'s templates, your name — not Jane's — appears as the generator of that document. Most importantly, your name is associated with any meetings, calls, or to-do's that you schedule in ACT!. Having unique, identifiable users in a database allows you to view your own activities on a calendar. Otherwise, you might find yourself driving to Podunk to visit Jane's mom on her birthday!

Only the database administrator has permission to add new users to the ACT! database.

To add a new user to your database, follow these steps:

1. From any of the ACT! screens, choose Tools⇨Manage Users.

The User Management dialog box opens, as shown in Figure 3-4.

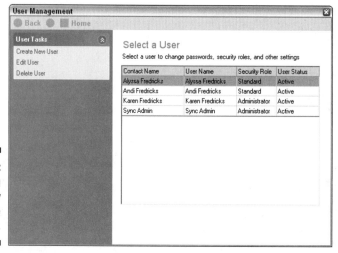

Figure 3-4:
Adding
a new
database
user.

2. **Click Create New User.**

   In the next window that appears, you are given a choice to create the new user from an existing contact, or to create a brand new user who isn't currently a member of your current database. In earlier versions of ACT! this option was buried away, often resulting in an "evil twin" situation in that although you only know one John Smith, he is represented twice in your database — once as a user and the other time as simply a member of your database.

3. **Choose either Existing Contact or New Contact and click Next.**

   If you chose the Existing Contact option, you see a list of all the contacts in your database. You can sort the list alphabetically by either contact or company by clicking the corresponding column heading. After you sort the list, type in the first couple of letter of the contact's last name or company (depending on how you sorted the list) in the Look For text box and ACT! magically takes you to that name. Click Next to continue.

   If you chose the New Contact option, a dialog box opens that is similar to the User Management dialog box. (Refer to Figure 3-4.)

4. **If the new user you added is also new to your database, you need to type in his/her name.**

   If you already indicated the name of the user in Step 3, his/her name is sitting there waiting for you.

5. **Fill in the user name.**

   The user name is not case-sensitive. Just make sure you remember what name you decide on. If you are setting up multiple users for the same database you just might want to stick to a set naming convention: "Gary Kahn" or "gkahn" are good choices; you might want to avoid "Gary B. Kahn" or "Gary Kahn, Esq."

6. **Fill in the password.**

   By now you know the drill: You type in the password once, and because that was so much fun, you type it a second time.

7. **Choose the security role of the new user.**

   ACT! provides you with five levels of security, and because you are the Administrator, you set those levels for all subsequent users.

   - **Browse:** This user has the most limited role; he or she can view contacts, view calendars, and add activities. The Browse user cannot add, modify, or delete contacts; or modify or add any other data.

     The Browse role is typically assigned to users who need to look up calendar details and schedule activities. In the real world, the database administrator typically assigns a user Browse level access if he has serious doubts as to the user's ability to add data.

- **Restricted:** This role allows users to access only areas of the application to which he or she is granted permission. The Restricted role is typically assigned to users working in a support capacity or acting in a Standard or Manager role. A Restricted user can access all data that he or she creates but cannot delete any data, even if he or she created it. This role also doesn't allow users to create companies or groups.

- **Standard:** A Standard user is the default user role assigned to new users. The Standard user can see the records in a database that he creates or is given explicit access to. Standard users can add, delete, and modify records; and synchronize data. What a standard user cannot do is add new users to the database, perform database maintenance, back up the database, import and export data, or modify database fields and layouts.

- **Manager:** A Manager role is the second most powerful user role. Typically Managers are people, such as sales managers, who manage the various users of the database and control the types of data that is entered into the database. Managers generally don't have the time — or sometime the technical knowledge — to use the various maintenance tools that I describe in Chapter 17. The manager can access nearly all the areas of ACT! except for database maintenance and user management. The manager is also restricted from viewing, editing, or deleting the private records of other individuals.

- **Administrator:** The Administrator can perform any database function and is the chief, the head honcho, the Big Guy — the person everyone blames if something goes wrong with the database. When a user creates a database, he or she is automatically assigned the Administrator role. This role is the most powerful role in ACT! with access to all areas of the application and all data in the supplemental files folders. The only thing the Administrator can't do is access, edit, or delete records marked as private by another user and get out of speeding tickets when caught doing 50 in a 35 mph zone.

Be sure to note which users you give the Administrator user level. These users are the only ones who can add users, create a backup, and perform routine maintenance on the database.

Assigning two users as Administrators of the database is always a good idea. Not only do two people feel extra special, it can save your little rear end. As hard as it might be to believe, the Administrator may leave the company suddenly, and without warning — taking the keys for the rest room and the password for the database with him. This means you might not be able to access the database, to perform routine maintenance, add users, or make field changes. You may also find yourself looking for a new job. *Remember:* No password, no entry!

8. **Select the Active check box.**

   This option enables the new user to access your database. If, for some reason, you do not want a user to have access to your database, feel free to clear this check box. I show you how to delete and disable (but hopefully not maim!) your database users later in this chapter.

9. **Select additional options that the user might be able to access.**

   • Allow user to synchronize with handheld devices

   • Allow user to perform Accounting link tasks

10. **Click Finish.**

Deleting Login Users

After you master adding new users to your database, you need to know how to delete users when they leave. After all, easy come, easy go. The first thing that you need to do is to determine whether you're going to actually delete the user or just deny him or her access to the database. There is a slight difference.

If you are the database administrator and you simply want to stop someone from accessing the database, you can do so without having to actually delete that person as a user. You can simply shut off her login privileges (a very simple process).

One of the reasons why you add users to the database is so that they can perform various functions, such as scheduling appointments and creating notes. The user's name is also associated with any contact that he may create. Opting to shut off a user's login privileges, rather than delete that user entirely, eliminates the possibility of losing this information. Here's how you shut off a user's access to the database:

1. **Choose Tools⇨Manage Users.**

   The User Management dialog box opens (refer to Figure 3-4).

2. **Select the name of the user for whom you wish to change the access rights.**

3. **Click Edit User.**

4. **Click Next to bypass the Password window.**

   If you're removing a user's ability to log in to the database, he no longer can use a password.

5. **Select Inactive and then click Finish.**

If you are using ACT! 2005 Standard Edition, you are limited to ten *active* users. When someone is no longer working at your company — or no longer needs access to the database — make sure you change the user information to reflect his or her inactive status.

Some of you are still determined to permanently erase all traces of past users from both your database and your mind. The only users you can safely remove from your database are those users who never added contacts, activities, notes, or histories. You might also have other users who no longer need to be associated with specific contacts, activities, notes, or histories. ACT!, being the smart program that you've grown to know and love, allows you to delete a user while preserving the information (notes, histories, and so on) associated with him by reassigning those items to another user.

Follow these steps to remove a user from your database:

1. **Choose Tools⇨Manage Users from any ACT! view.**

   The User Management dialog box appears (refer to Figure 3-4).

2. **Select the name of the user who you want to remove from your database.**

3. **Click Delete User.**

   A dialog box appears giving you two options:

   • **Delete Records Belonging to This User:** If you choose this option, you are in essence saying adios to all contact records and associated data including notes and history — no matter who entered that data.

   • **Reassign Records to Another User:** Although you retain all the contacts, notes, histories, and activities created by the user, the other user's name is now assigned to them.

   ACT! searches through your database and reassigns every record, note, and contact one at a time. This time may be good to perfect the art of thumb twiddling; the larger your database, the longer reassigning takes.

After you reassign contact records to a new user, you can't reverse the process. From here on, the notes, histories, and contacts that the deleted user created appear to have been created by the new user. However, if you simply delete a user without reassigning his records, you risk losing a lot of contact information. If you don't want that to happen, I recommend simply removing the former user's login privileges.

Rather than deleting a user of your database, you might also consider changing the Record Manager field for all contacts that are now associated with the new user. Skip over to Chapter 17 to find out how you can change the field data for a whole bunch of contacts at once.

Working with Passwords

If you're the only user using your ACT! database, or if your clients love you and would chop their arms off at the wrist before turning to one of your competitors, security might not be an important issue for you. But if you're like most people, you probably prefer not to share every tidbit of information in your database with anyone who wanders into your office. Whether you want to prevent certain personnel from changing the basic field structure of your database or adapt a "look but don't touch" attitude with the unfortunate computer-challenged among your employees, ACT! has two security methods that can help you accomplish your security goals. You can either

- ✔ Assign a specific security level to each user as I discuss earlier in the section, "Adding Multiple Users to a Database."
- ✔ Password-protect your database; I discuss this option throughout the rest of this section.

Unless a contact record is marked as *private,* ACT! 2005 Standard Edition has no way of allowing someone access to only a portion of the contacts in a database. If you want to limit the contacts a particular user sees, you have a couple of options. You can upgrade to ACT! 2005 Premium Edition, which allows access to user records, based on your "team" preferences. You can also supply the user with his own database and synchronize just those contacts that he has access to from the main database as I show in Chapter 18.

Setting a password

Both the database administrator and the individual database user can set a password for the user. The theory for this is that the individual can pick a password that has some meaning to him — and so, hopefully, he doesn't forget it. (If a user does forget his password, however, the administrator can reset it.)

If you have access to a database and are afraid that some nasty person might use your name to gain access illegally, I recommend assigning a password to yourself, which is ridiculously easy. Here's what you do:

1. **From any of the ACT! screens, choose File➪Set Password.**

   The Change Password dialog box appears, as shown in Figure 3-5.

2. **Enter your current password in the Current Password text box.**

3. **Type your new password in the New Password text box and then for added excitement type, it once more in the Confirm New Password text box.**

4. **Click OK.**

Change Password ⊠

Current Password:

****

New Password:

****

Confirm New Password:

****

OK   Cancel

Figure 3-5:
Changing
a user's
password.

Resetting a password

You might not know your password because you don't have one, so before tracking down your administrator to change a password for you, try leaving the password field blank. (I frequently get phone calls and e-mails from ACT! users who have no idea what password is assigned to them. Guess what? They often don't have one!)

But if you've tried every password that you can think of — and even have tried using no password at all — and still can't gain access to the database, you might have to bribe the database Administrator into resetting your password. I find that chocolate chip cookies work the best, but feel free to pick the bribe of your choice. Then, make sure the Administrator follows these steps:

1. **From any ACT! screen, choose Tools⇨Manage Users.**

2. **Select the name of the user whose password is being changed and then click Edit User.**

3. **Type in the new password in the text box and then retype it in the Confirm Password dialog box.**

4. **Click Finish.**

Changing a password

From time to time, you might want to change your password. Perhaps you feel that a former employee compromised your security, or maybe you've just been watching too many James Bond movies. Whatever the case, remember the new, improved password, or you may be forced to chase the database administrator around with another batch of cookies!

1. **Choose File⇨Set Password from any ACT! view.**

   If you're going through this chapter section by section, you already know that you can do this from within any of the ACT! screens. I don't mean to sound like a broken record here; I just want you to get used to the idea.

2. **Enter the current password in the Current Password text box.**

3. **Enter the new password in the New Password text box.**

4. **Enter the new password in the Confirm New Password text box.**

5. **Click OK.**

Giving ACT! the Preferential Treatment

After you install ACT! on your computer, becoming familiar with various preferences is a good practice. If you're the sole user of the database, these settings likely save your sanity. If you share the database with other users, these
settings probably save you all a lot of head scratching.

If you created your original database by using the Getting Started Wizard,
some of your preferences are already set. However, reviewing your work
never hurts! Your preference settings are the place to turn to if you're the
kind of person who likes to have things your own way. You might routinely
store all your documents in a specific location and want ACT! to follow that
same example. Or you might have a fondness for fuchsia and orange and
want to have your ACT! screens coordinate with this color scheme.

Here's how to change several of the most basic preference settings. Feel free
to flip through the various preference tabs to get an idea about additional
preference settings that you might also want to tweak. You can find the ACT!
Preferences dialog box, as shown in Figure 3-6, by choosing Tools➪Preferences.
The Preferences dialog box is arranged into six tabs, each of which I discuss in
the following sections.

General

As the name implies, you find an assortment of preferences on the General tab.
General preferences allow you to specify settings for your database, such as
how names and salutations display on your contact records, whether checking
for duplicate records is enabled or disabled, and where files associated with
your database are stored. ACT! automatically stores your database in the My
Documents folder. Your database contains all your basic contact information
as well as supplemental files such as layouts, templates, and saved e-mail messages. In addition, you might want to have your own set of "personal" supplemental files; this area is where you can tell ACT! where you prefer to have them
saved.

If you're not the Administrator, you can't change the history or duplicate
checking options.

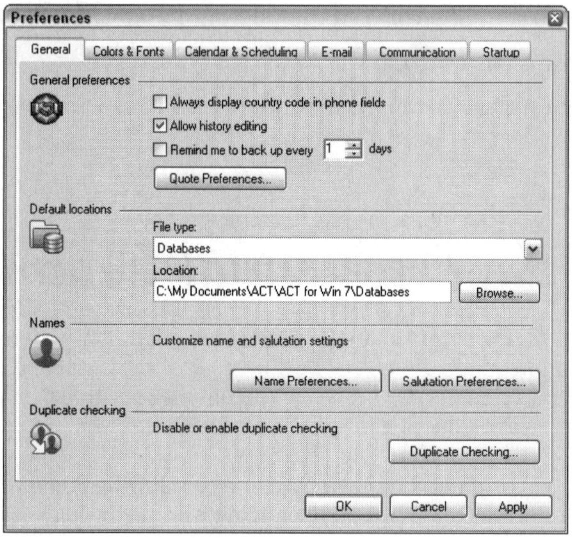

Figure 3-6:
The ACT!
Preferences
dialog box.

Colors & Fonts

You can set the colors and fonts for almost any area of ACT! including all list views, tabs, and calendars. However, there isn't a global color setting; you must set the colors and fonts for each item separately in the Colors & Fonts tab, as shown in Figure 3-7. To set colors and fonts, follow these steps:

1. **On the Colors & Fonts tab, select an item to customize from the Customize list.**

   In the Customize list, you find a list of all the lists, calendars, and system tabs. You'll also notice in Figure 3-7 several items in the list with the words "detail composition;" these indicate areas in ACT! in which you can write in extra details when necessary.

2. **In the Appearance section, select the text and background color for the item you selected on the Customize list.**

3. **Click the Font button.**

   The Font dialog box appears.

4. **Select the font, style, and size of the font.**

5. **Click OK.**

6. **To change the appearance of another item, select the item from the Customize list, and repeat Steps 2 through 5.**

7. **Click OK to save your color preferences.**

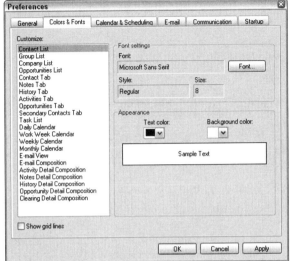

Figure 3-7:
ACT!'s color
and font
preferences.

Calendars & Scheduling

The Calendars & Scheduling tab is nothing more than a gateway to the heart of the matter: changing the calendar and scheduling preferences.

When you click the Calendar Preferences button, you can set

- ✔ The days of the week you want to appear on your "work week" calendar
- ✔ The minute intervals for your daily and workweek calendars
- ✔ Various calendar options, such as whether or not you want to see "pop ups" when you hold your mouse cursor over a scheduled activity
- ✔ How you want to banner all-day events

When you click the Scheduling Preferences button, you can get the Activity Type Settings dialog box. From this dialog box, you select the activity type for which you want to set options. You can set options for each activity type, but you must set the options one activity type at a time. The options you can include for each activity type are

- ✔ The priority level you want to display automatically when the activity type is scheduled
- ✔ How long before the activity you want the Ring Alarm to ring for the activity type
- ✔ The default duration for the activity type
- ✔ The fields for which you want to display drop-downs lists for the activity type

E-mail

Exactly as advertised, the E-mail preference tab is the area where you tell ACT! exactly how you want to handle your e-mail. The preferences you might want to set include

- ✔ The e-mail system you want to use with ACT!: Microsoft Outlook, Outlook Express, or Internet Mail

- ✔ Composing options including signatures, dealing with forwarded and replied messages, and even how you want the recipients name to appear when composing a new e-mail message

- ✔ How often you want ACT! to notify you about newly received messages

- ✔ How you want to handle attachments that you receive

Communication

The Communications tab lets you choose your word processor and fax preferences including

- ✔ The word processing and fax software you want to use with ACT!

- ✔ How you want ACT! to check your spelling in e-mail messages and word processing documents

- ✔ The Quick Print header and footer options when printing the Company, Group, Opportunity, and Contact lists

Startup

The Startup options dictate both the default settings for each new contact added to your database and how ACT! starts up every time you run the program.

- ✔ The Record Creation setting lets you set the default to Public or Private for each new contact, group, and opportunity you add to the database, and whether you want to automatically link each new contact to their company record.

- ✔ Startup Database lets you specify the database you want ACT! to open automatically as well as how often you want ACT! to check for new software updates.

Customizing the Navigation Bar

One of the things you might find the most endearing about ACT! is your ability to mold the program to the way that feels the most comfortable to you. You might decide that for whatever reason you don't like the way the Navigation bar look (those big icons that run down the left side of ACT!). No problem — all you have to do to have it "your way" is follow the next few steps:

1. **Right-click the Navigation bar.**

   Note the menu that appears is divided into three sections. You actually get to choose one option from both the top and middle sections.

2. **Chose from the following options:**

   - **Large:** That's the size of the Nav bar icons when you first install ACT!.

   - **Small:** If you're working on a small monitor — or just want to have a little more viewing room, you might want the Nav bar icons to be small so the rest of your screen can be larger.

   - **Standard:** The Nav bar shows you eight of the most common views.

   - **Expanded:** For those of you who live for detail, the Nav bar shows you 14 icons; you might want to set the size to small so that you don't have to scroll through all those options.

   - **Classic:** For those of you loyal ACT! fanACTics who want things, well, like you're used to seeing them, here's your chance to have the Nav bar look "just like it used to."

   - **Customize:** Just in case you're still not happy with the look and feel of the Nav bar, feel free to choose the Customize option. A little window magically opens that allows you to drag additional icons to the Nav bar — or get rid of the ones you don't want.

Modifying Menus and Toolbars

Customizing the various ACT! menus and toolbars to include functions that you use on a regular basis is a great way to improve your efficiency. Tweaking your toolbar literally allows you to perform various functions at the click of a button.

Tackling the toolbar

One thing you might find a little unique in ACT! is the variety of toolbars that you encounter along the way. You see one toolbar while working in the Contact Detail window, and an altogether different toolbar when you foray into the Group Detail window. That said, realize that an icon you add to one of your toolbars doesn't appear on another. That's okay because adding icons to any one of the ACT! toolbars is easy.

I encourage you to do a little homework before tackling the toolbar. Don't worry, the assignment is fairly simply; you need to decide in advance which icon you want to add, and know which menu it's located on. Although this step isn't critical, it saves you from floundering around later. Follow these steps to add an icon to any toolbar:

1. **From any of the ACT! screens, choose Tools⇨Customize⇨Menus and Toolbars.**

   For the right-clickers in the audience, you can also give the toolbar a click with the right button of your mouse and choose Customize.

2. **Click the Commands tab in the Customize Menus and Toolbars dialog box.**

   The Commands tab appears in the Customize Menus and Toolbars dialog box (see Figure 3-8).

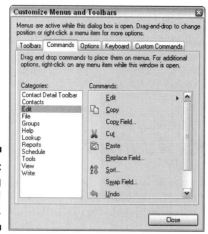

Figure 3-8:
Customizing the ACT! toolbar.

3. **Select the name of the menu that contains the command that you want to add to your toolbar.**

   If you did your homework, pat yourself on the back. If you didn't, have fun flipping through all the choices in the Categories list and scrolling through all the corresponding commands until you stumble upon the item that you want to add to the toolbar. I hate to be an "I told you so," but. . . .

4. **Drag the desired command up to the toolbar.**

   As you drag the command up to the toolbar, a black line materializes that indicates exactly where the icon is going to appear. If you want the new icon to be on the end of the toolbar, you need to drag it up so that it slightly overlaps the last item currently located on the toolbar.

5. **Click the Close button on the Customize Menus and Toolbars dialog box.**

Deleting toolbar icons

I'm almost embarrassed to tell you how easy you can remove icons from a toolbar. But, because you're such a good person I am going to tell you. You might store this information away for future reference and use it to impress your friends some time in the near future.

1. **Right-click the toolbar and choose Customize.**

   By the way, customize is not only the choice you want to choose — it's your *only* choice!

2. **Right-click the icon that you want to send packing.**

3. **Click Delete.**

4. **Click the Close button on the Customize Menus and Toolbars dialog box.**

Part II
Putting the ACT! Database to Work

The 5th Wave   By Rich Tennant

OK, one of you will stay in the field, but the other one will handle clients over the Internet.

But which one?! Brad or Igor?! Brad or Igor?!

In this part . . .

Okay, you've whipped ACT! into shape; now it's time to get your life back in order. ACT! is a contact manager, which, as the name implies, makes it a great place to manage your contacts. First you must add new contacts into your database, and then you need to know how to find them again. After you locate your contacts, you can schedule an activity with any one of them, set a reminder, and maybe add some notes for good measure. Sure beats the heck out of a yellow sticky note!

Chapter 4

Making Contact(s)

· ·

In This Chapter

▶ Adding new contacts

▶ Editing contact information

▶ Deleting contacts

▶ Updating contact information

· ·

A database is only as good as the contacts that it contains. In ACT!, adding, deleting, and editing the contacts in your database is easy to do. In this chapter, I show you how to do all three of these tasks to maintain an organized, working database. Adding new contacts is only half the fun; being able to find them again is the point of having the database in the first place. Inputting contacts in a consistent manner ensures that all your contacts are easy to find. After you add a new contact, you may need to change that contact's information or even delete the contact entirely. I demonstrate how to change contact information if necessary and even how to "unchange" changes that you might have made by mistake!

Adding New Contacts

On the very simplest level, the main purpose of ACT! is to serve as a place to store all the contacts that you interact with on a daily basis. You can add and edit your contacts from the Contact Detail window because it contains all the information that pertains to one particular record and allows you to see all your contact fields.

Every time that you add a new contact, ACT! automatically fills information in three fields: Record Creator, Record Manager, and Create Date. If you click the Contact Info tab of your layout, you'll notice these three fields. When you add a new contact, ACT! inserts your user name into the Record Creator and Record Manager fields and the current date into the Create Date field. This tab enables you to search for all the new contacts that you created within a given date range. The Record Creator and Create Date fields serve as a permanent record, and you cannot change them. Managers and Administrators can override the contents of the Record Manager field if they so desire.

You probably have lots of contacts that you're dying to enter into your database, so what are you waiting for? Jump right in and follow these steps:

1. **If you aren't already in the Contact Detail window, go there by clicking the Contacts icon on ACT!'s Nav bar.**

   Don't know about the Nav bar? Check out Chapter 2, where you find out all you need to know about the Nav bar and then some.

2. **In the Contact Detail window, choose from one of three ways to add a new contact to your database:**

   • Choose Contact⇨New Contact.

   • Click the New Contact icon on the toolbar.

   • Press the Insert key on the keyboard.

   Initiating any of the preceding commands results in a blank contact record. You're now ready to enter the new contact's information.

3. **Begin entering information by clicking in the Company field and typing the contact's company name.**

   ACT! doesn't distinguish between actual contacts and blank contacts. Failure to enter information or repeatedly pressing the Insert key results in numerous blank contact records, which are of no use and only serve to clog up the database. So, although you are free to leave any of the ACT! fields blank, you do have to enter something — at the very least, I recommend the key pieces of information — so you might as well begin with the company's name.

   You can always go back to a record later and add, change, or delete any information in any field. See the later sections "The Contacts, They Are A'Changin'" and "Deleting Contact Records."

4. **Click in the next field where you want to enter information and start typing.**

   You can also use the Tab key to advance to the next field. If, in your initial excitement to start entering all your existing contacts, you inadvertently press the Tab key once too often, you may find that you advanced one too many fields and ended up in the wrong field. But don't fret: Press and hold down the Shift key and then press Tab to move your cursor in the reverse direction.

5. **Continue filling in fields.**

   As I mention in Chapter 2, ACT! comes with approximately 50 preprogrammed fields that reflect the needs of most users. Many of the fields are fairly self-explanatory (and reflect the type of information that you probably expect to find in any address book): contact name, company name, phone, city, state, and zip code. These are conveniently located in the top half of the Contact Detail window; see Figure 4-1. A few of the fields are a little less obvious:

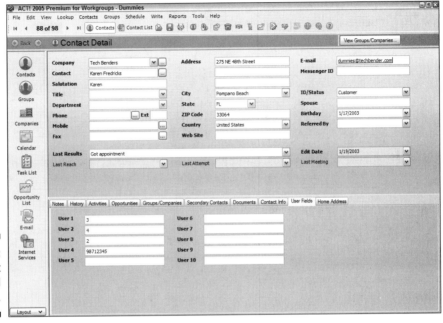

Figure 4-1:
The Contact
Detail
window.

- **Address:** If you assume that the three fields ACT! provides for the address is meant to store three *alternative* addresses, you're wrong! The second and third address fields are meant for really long addresses. This field is a good place to include a building name if it is an integral part of the address.

  5160-style labels, popularly used for mass mailings, generally print four lines of information: company, contact, street address, and city/state/zip code (all on the fourth line). If you need to use the second and third address fields, you need larger labels.

- **ID/Status:** The ID/Status field is essentially the category field, and it files each of your contacts into categories. By using the ID/Status field, you don't have to manually set up a variety of databases: one for your friends, one for your clients, one for your vendors, and so on. The ID/Status field comes preset with a couple dozen of the most commonly used categories, including friends, customers, vendors, and competitors, which makes searching for each of these categories in a flash easy.

- **Salutation:** This field refers to the name that comes after the word *Dear* in a letter, which is used in your letter templates. By default, ACT!, being the friendly type, uses the first name. Feel free to change the salutation to a more formal one.

If you prefer using the more formal salutation as the default setting, choose Tools⇨Preferences and click the Salutation Preferences button conveniently located on the General tab.

- **Referred By:** This field is one of the most commonly overlooked ones in the database. Information entered into this field is used in the Source of Referrals report; failure to enter Referred By information renders the report useless. So what's the big deal? Suppose you're paying for advertising in two newspapers — wouldn't knowing which one attracted the most prospects be nice? If you're attending trade shows or putting a lot of time and effort into your Web site, wouldn't you like to know if it has resulted in any new business? And, if an existing customer is sending you lots of new leads, wouldn't honoring him with a nice ham at Christmas rather than the customary fruitcake be nice?

- **User:** Notice that several User fields are in the bottom half of the Contact Detail window (refer to Figure 4-1). These fields hold information that's specific to your business. In Chapter 15, I explain how you can change these field names to better reflect their contents. For example, you might rename *User 1* to *Social Security number*.

  I recommend leaving these particular fields blank until you rename them. If you don't, you might end up with various kinds of data entered into one field.

  You can always go back and add, change, or delete field data at any time! (See the sections "Deleting Contact Records" and "The Contacts, They Are A'Changin'" later in this chapter.)

6. **Don't be alarmed when ACT! automatically formats some of your field data when you enter information.**

   See the later section, "Letting ACT! do the work for you: Automatic formatting," for the lowdown on what ACT! does and doesn't do for you.

7. **Add your data as uniformly as possible.**

   Check out the later section, "Getting the most out of ACT!: Using the drop-down lists," to find out how to easily keep your data uniform and yourself sane.

8. **If necessary, add multiple entries to a field.**

   Generally, limiting yourself to one item per field is the best practice. From time to time, however, you find a situation in which a contact falls into two categories. For example, JoAnne Chamar might be both a friend and a client. In this situation, you can use the drop-down list to enter more than one item into a field.

   To select several criteria to be included in a single field, follow these steps:

   a. Place your cursor in the field.

   b. Check off your desired selections.

      Figure 4-2 gives you an example of a drop-down list.

Figure 4-2:
An ACT!
drop-down
list.

c. Click the desired entries from the Edit List Values dialog box.

d. Click anywhere outside of the dialog box to close it.

The various entries appear in the field, separated by a comma.

9. **When you fill in the information for each new contact, don't forget to click the various tabs at the bottom of your layout.**

You find additional fields lurking on these tabs. The Home Address tab is the place you record personal information about a contact. You might have a few other tabs that you can also choose from (see Chapter 16).

Different layouts display different tabs. If you change your current layout, you're probably looking at a different set of tabs. Confused? Check out Chapter 2 for a quick refresher.

If you forget to click those tabs along the bottom of the Contact Detail window, you just might overlook some of the fields that you need to fill in important information. So be sure to click those tabs!

10. **Save the new contact information.**

Theoretically, you don't have to save new contact information; it's saved if you do any of the following:

- Execute any other ACT! command, which includes anything from adding a note or sales opportunity to scheduling an appointment.

- Move on to another record in the database.

- Click the Save button (represented by the small floppy disk icon on the toolbar).

- Press Ctrl+S.

Letting ACT! do the work for you: Automatic formatting

Entering a new contact into the ACT! database is so easy that you may over-look some of the magical things that happen when you begin to input contact information. ACT! is here to help by automatically formatting some of the contact information that you input, including

- ✔ **Automatic phone number formatting:** A great example of ACT!'s magic is found in the Phone field. When you type in a phone number, notice how ACT! automatically inserts the necessary hyphens. ACT! automatically inserts the dialing format for the United States each time that you enter a new phone number. Have relatives living in Turkmenistan? Have no fear: If you click the ellipsis button (the two little dots) to the right of the Telephone field, ACT! pops open the Enter Phone Number dialog box. By default, the country is listed as the United States, but you can scroll through the list of the countries for just about any country that you can think of, including Turkmenistan (see Figure 4-3). After you click OK, the correct telephone country code and format is applied to the telephone number.

- ✔ **Automatic name formatting:** Another field that ACT! automatically provides you with is the Salutation field. The Salutation field is the field that appears after the word *Dear* in a letter. If you enter Mary Ellen Van der Snob as the contact name, Mary Ellen magically appears as the salutation. Of course, if you prefer to address your contacts in a more formal manner, feel free to change Mary Ellen to Ms. Van der Snob. When you enter a contact name into the database, ACT! automatically divides it into a first, middle, and last name. Again, if you click the ellipsis button to the right of the Contact field, ACT! shows you how it plans to divide the contact's name. This allows you to sort your database alphabetically by last name or to look up a contact by first name. If you attempt to enter a rather large, unique name, ACT! automatically opens the Contact Name dialog box, as shown in Figure 4-4, and asks you how you want to divide the name.

- ✔ **History fields:** Any changes to a history field results in the information being preserved on the History tab. Say that you have six steps that you want your staff to perform when dealing with prospects. You might change the drop-down information for your history field to reflect those six steps. When you perform one of the steps and you enter the information into the field, the date and time of the change appears on the History tab so you know exactly when each step took place.

  Out of the box, only two fields — ID/Status and Last Results — are history fields. Theoretically, any field can be a history field, and Chapter 15 shows you how to do it.

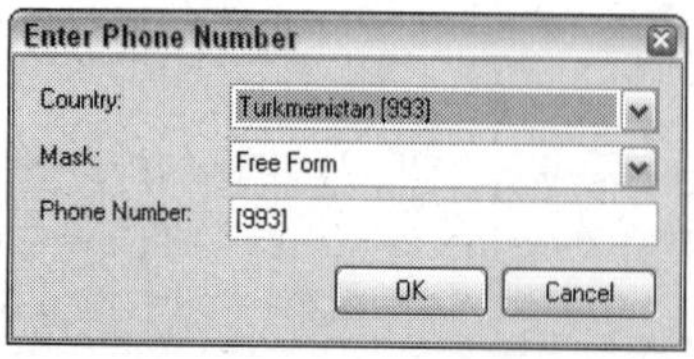

Figure 4-3:
Automatic
telephone
formatting.

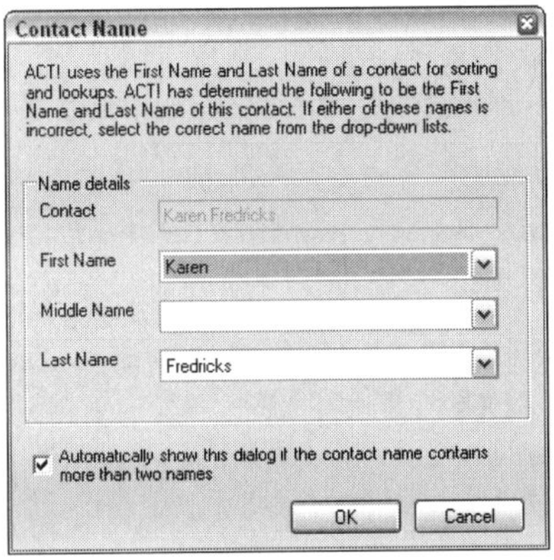

Figure 4-4:
The Contact
Name
dialog box.

✔ **Date fields:** If you don't want to forget one thing, it's the birthday of your significant other. However, as you discover in Chapter 7, entering data consistently is important if you have any hope of ever finding it again. What if an important birthday occurred in January — and you aren't sure whether the date had been entered as "January," "Jan," "01," or "1"? By now you've probably guessed that ACT! came up with a cure for the birthday blues with the addition of date fields. All date fields have a drop-down arrow; if you click the arrow you actually see a mini-calendar, as shown in Figure 4-5. Click the appropriate date, buy a card, and you're ready to roll. If you prefer, you can also manually enter the date as "01/17/04" or 1/17/04, and ACT! translates it to the calendar mode automatically.

Figure 4-5:
An ACT!
date field.

Getting the most out of ACT!: Using the drop-down lists

One sure-fire way to sabotage your database is to develop new and creative ways to say the same thing. In Florida, users often vacillate between *Fort, Ft,* and *Ft.* Lauderdale, resulting in a bad sunburn and the inability to correctly find all their contacts. You'll notice that several of the ACT! fields contain drop-down lists. In these fields, you can select an item in the list, or you can type the first few letters of an item, and the field automatically fills with the item that matches what you typed or clicked. When you type an entry that isn't in the drop-down list for the Title, Department, City, and Country fields, the item is automatically added to the list so that you can then select it for other contacts.

You have two ways of using the drop-down lists to enter information:

✔ Type the first few letters of an entry that already appears in the drop-down list, and ACT! completes the word for you. For example, if you type **Ch** in the City field, *Chicago* magically appears.

✔ Access the drop-down list by clicking its arrow and then choose the desired item(s) from the list.

Using these drop-down lists whenever possible helps ensure consistency throughout your database. In Chapter 15, I explain how to add additional drop-down fields to your database and control how you use them.

If you want to change the content of the drop-down lists that come with ACT!, follow these steps:

1. **Click in a field that has a drop-down list.**

2. **Click the drop-down arrow in the field.**

3. **When the drop-down list appears, click the Edit List Values button.**

   The Edit List Items dialog box appears, as shown in Figure 4-6.

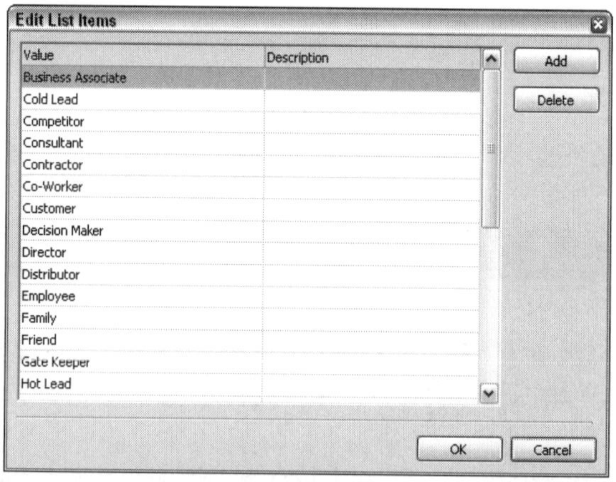

Figure 4-6:
Editing the drop-down list.

4. **In the Edit List Items dialog box, do one of the following:**

   • Click the Add button to add an item to the list. A new blank line appears at the bottom of the list. Enter the text that you want to appear in the list.

- Select an item and click the Delete button to remove it from the list. Click Yes when ACT! asks you to confirm the deletion.
- To modify an existing item, double-click it and edit it exactly like you would in a word processor.

5. Click OK when you finish editing your list.

That's all there is to it. A pretty easy way to ensure consistency, don't you think?

Duplicating Your Contacts

As you can see from the "Adding New Contacts" section, entering a new contact into ACT! involves quite a few things. Thankfully, ACT! makes duplicating a previously saved record easy.

Suppose that you just entered Jane Jones' contact information, and now you find yourself looking at a pile of business cards from Jane's co-workers. All of them have the same company name and address; the only variables are the contact name and phone number. ACT! gives you two options for duplicating contacts. You can either copy the *primary* information or *all* the information. Out of the box, the primary fields are Company, Address 1, Address 2, Address 3, City, State, Zip, Country, and Fax. When you copy all fields, *every* field copies into the new contact record except the Contact and E-Mail Address fields.

To duplicate contact information without extra typing, follow these steps:

1. Open the record that you want to duplicate.

2. Choose Contact⇨Duplicate Contact.

3. Select either the Duplicate Data from Primary Fields or Duplicate Data from All Fields radio button and then click OK.

A new contact record appears, filled in with the copied information from the original contact record.

4. Continue creating the contact record by filling in the variable information and proceeding as you would with an entirely new contact.

Deleting Contact Records

What do you do if you find that a contact is duplicated in your database? Or that you're no longer doing business with one of your contacts? For whatever reason that you decide that a name no longer needs to be a part of your database, you can just delete that contact record.

ACT! allows you to either delete one contact record or a lookup of contact records. (A *lookup* is the group of contacts that displays after a database search. Peruse Chapter 7 for more information about lookups.) Just realize that you are deleting either the current contact that you're viewing or the current group of contacts that you just created a query for. When you're on the contact that you want to delete, do one of the following:

 ✔ Choose Contact⇨Delete.

 ✔ Press Ctrl+Delete.

 ✔ Right-click the contact record and choose Delete Contact.

Any one of these choices brings up the warning shown in Figure 4-7.

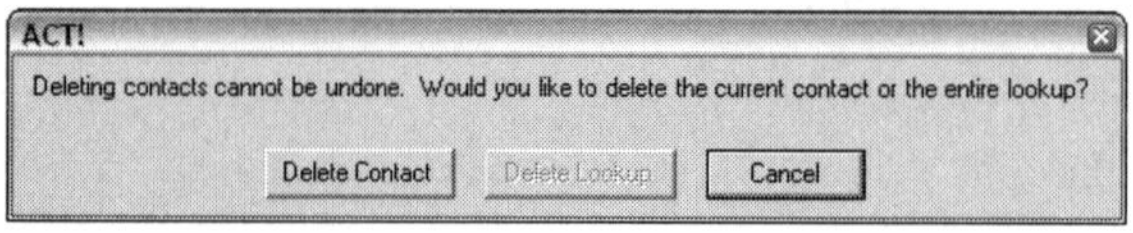

Figure 4-7:
An ominous
warning
when
deleting a
contact.

If you click the Delete Contact button, you delete the current contact that you're viewing. If you click the Delete Lookup button, you delete the current contact lookup.

Thinking before deleting a contact

Although the procedure is rather simple, you may want to rethink the issue of deleting contacts. When you delete a contact, you are also deleting all the associated notes and histories tied to that contact. For example, suppose that State College is using ACT! to keep track of all prospective students that it has contacted — or has been contacted by. State College admissions personnel may receive thousands of inquiries a month and fear that the database will become too large to manage . . . and subsequently think that deleting all prospects that they haven't had contact with in over a year is the best course of action. However, some of those prospects might be attending different schools that they aren't happy with and may want to enter State College as transfer students. Other prospects may transfer in after completing two years at a community college, and still others might consider attending State College as graduate students.

What to do in such a situation? I'd consider moving the contacts that you no longer need into another archival database. That way, should the need ever arise, you can still find all the original information on a contact without having to start again from scratch. How nice to be able to rekindle a relationship by asking, "So tell me, how did you find the accounting department at Podunk University?" Although the setup of an archival database is beyond the scope of this book, an ACT! Certified Consultant can assist you with this matter.

Three warnings before deleting a contact

Losing contacts in your database is a very scary thought. You undoubtedly rely very heavily on your ACT! database; losing that data can be potentially devastating to your business. Worst of all, if you realize that you have just accidentally removed several — or even hundreds of — contacts from the database, panic may set in!

Divert this panic by following these tips *before* you attempt to delete any of your contacts:

- ✔ Know the difference between deleting a *contact* and deleting a *lookup* so that you don't delete numerous contacts when you only wanted to delete a single record.

  The *current contact* is the single record that you view from the Contact Detail window. A *lookup* is the group of contacts that displays after a database search.

- ✔ Read the warning and make note of the number of contacts that you're about to delete. Don't be afraid to click Cancel if a large number of contacts start to disappear.

- ✔ Remember the three rules of computing: backup, backup, backup! Chapter 17 provides you with instructions on how to create a backup. A good backup provides the easiest method to restore all your information after you accidentally deleted it.

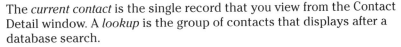

The Contacts, They Are A'Changin'

Companies relocate and change their names, people move, and your fingers sometimes slip on the keyboard. People change e-mail addresses. You might want to add additional contact information for one of your contacts. All these predicaments require the editing of contact fields. Not to worry; changing the information that you store in ACT! is as easy as entering it in the first place.

ACT! gives you two ways of replacing contact information:

- ✔ Click in the field that you want to change and then press the Delete or Backspace key to remove the existing field information. Then simply type in the new information.

- ✔ Highlight all the information in a field. By typing in the new information, the old information is automatically replaced.

If you accidentally overwrite information in a single ACT! field, press Ctrl+Z to undo the changes that you just made to that field — *before* you move your cursor to another ACT! field. For those who are keyboard challenged, an alternative is to choose Edit⇨Undo from the main menu. After you move on to another field, neither of these options is available to you.

To undo multiple changes that you've made to an ACT! record, choose Edit⇨Undo Changes to Contact *before* you move on to the next record.

After you execute another ACT! command or move on to another record, ACT! automatically saves the record. At that point you can't automatically undo any changes you've made to a contact record.

Chapter 5

A Few Good Tabs and Lists

In This Chapter

▶ Discovering the lists and tabs

▶ Customizing the lists and tabs

▶ Putting secondary contacts in the right place

▶ Linking documents to the Documents tab

*T*hroughout this book, you find all the neat ways in which you can customize ACT!. In this chapter, you discover how to change the appearance of the various ACT! tabs and lists. And, although you encounter numerous tabs and lists in your travels through ACT!, you'll soon discover that you can modify them in exactly the same way.

After you've seen one list or tab, you've seen them all! And, if you're a fanACTic, the lists and tabs work pretty much like they did in previous versions.

Meeting the Lists and Tabs

The bad news is that numerous lists and tabs are sprinkled through ACT! and new users may find themselves lost in a maze of windows. The good news is that lists and tabs all have pretty much the same look and feel to them, so if you master one, you master them all!

You can find all lists by clicking View on the menu bar and then selecting a list that sounds fun and exciting. Two of the lists are so much fun that they are included in the Nav bar running along the left side of ACT!. And, if you feel so inclined, you're welcome to flip back to Chapter 3 to find out how to add all the list items to the Nav bar.

TIP

Minding your filters!

When viewing the various system tabs, you must be aware of the effect that the filters have on what information you see — or don't see. In ACT!, you can choose to filter out information or to include it. Different tabs have different filters; however, all tabs include a date filter and a user filter. If the filter is set to show only items in the future, and you have an activity scheduled for today, you don't see today's activity. And, if you schedule an activity, but you set the filter to include only Alyssa's activities, you don't see your activity either.

When frustrated, check your filters! You might be puzzled at the fact that information you just *know* has been entered into the database has mysteriously disappeared. This becomes increasingly important on the Activities tab, which contains several options (including three buried away behind the Option button). The Task and Opportunity lists can be even more confusing; these lists contain a variety of options — all of which can be hidden away with one click of the Hide Filters button.

Here's a list of the lists you work with most often:

- ✔ **Contact:** Lists all your contacts; the list is filtered based on your current lookup.

- ✔ **Task:** Lists all the tasks and activities you scheduled for all your contacts; you can filter these by date, type, priority, user, public versus private, timeless, cleared status, and Outlook relationship.

- ✔ **Group:** Lists all groups and can optionally include subgroups.

- ✔ **Company:** Lists all companies and can optionally include divisions.

- ✔ **Opportunities:** Lists all the sales opportunities that you enter for all your contacts; you can filter opportunities by date, status, process, stage, probability, amount, and public versus private.

There are two types of tabs: *system* tabs, which are the same for any and all layouts you use; and *user* tabs, which you can rename and modify to best fit the way you work (see Chapter 16). The system tabs you use most often with ACT! are

- ✔ **Notes:** Lists all notes you record for the current contact, company, or group; you can filter the notes by date, private versus public, and user. See Chapter 8 for more on the Notes tab.

- ✔ **History:** Lists all correspondence, activities, and document information that was recorded automatically by ACT! for a contact, group, or company; you can filter the histories by date, private versus public, type of history, and user. Chapter 8 covers the History tab.

✔ **Activities:** Lists all activities for the contact, group, or company; you can filter the activities by date, private versus public, cleared, timeless, type of activity, priority, and user. I go in depth about the Activities tab in Chapter 9.

✔ **Opportunities:** Lists the financial lowdown on all the selling opportunities for the current contact, group, or company; you can filter the opportunities by date, status, private versus public, and user. Chapter 20 covers the Opportunities tab.

✔ **Documents:** Lists all files attached to the current contact, group, or company; you can't filter this tab. See the section, "Documenting Your Documents," later in this chapter for more about the Documents tab.

✔ **Secondary Contacts:** Lists the secondary contacts, for example, the butcher, the baker, and the candlestick maker, that are directly associated with the current contact; you can't filter this tab. Flip ahead a few pages to the "Corralling Your Secondary Contacts" section in this chapter where I discuss the Secondary Contacts tab.

✔ **Groups/Companies:** This tab has a dual-personality. You'll notice the addition of the Show Membership For drop-down list that lets you indicate whether you want to view the groups or the companies that the contact is associated with. This tab only appears in the Contact Detail window.

✔ **Contacts:** Lists all the contacts associated with the current group or company. You only see this tab in the Group Detail window or the Company Detail window.

You'll notice that the first five tabs appear on the Contacts, Groups, and Companies windows. That's because you can add a note, an activity, and so on to either an individual contact record, or to a company or group record.

Remodeling lists and tabs

One of the reasons that you might find the lists and tabs to be so useful is the ease in which you can customize them. You can change the order of the columns, widen the columns, add or remove columns, and then print out your final product. In this section, I cover a few ways in which you can change the look of your lists and tabs.

Adding or removing columns

Probably the first thing that you want to do to modify your lists and columns is to add or remove an additional column — or two or three! Follow these steps:

1. **Click the Options button (in the top-right corner) on any list or tab and choose Customize Columns from the menu that appears.**

   The Customize Columns dialog box appears (see Figure 5-1).

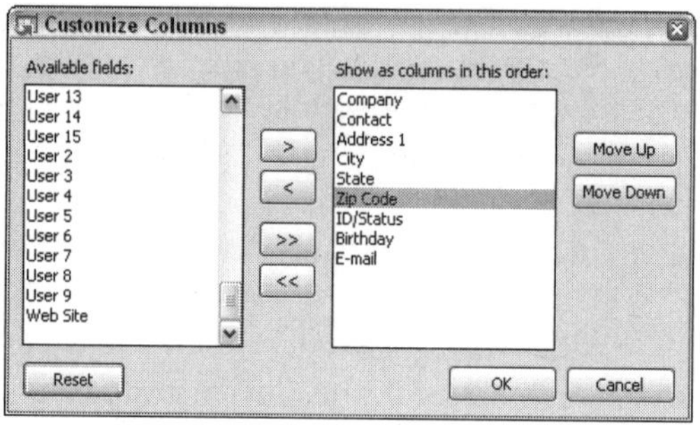

Figure 5-1:
Adding
columns to
the Contact
List.

2. **Select the field (column) that you want to add by clicking the appropriate choice in the Available Fields list.**

   Depending on the list or tab you're working with, you see various field choices. Feel free to include as many — or as few as your little heart desires.

3. **Click the single right-pointing arrow.**

   If you're really into seeing a lot of information, you can click the double right-pointing arrows; that adds all available fields to your list or tab.

4. **To remove an item, click the appropriate choice from the Show as Columns in This Order and then click the single left-pointing arrow.**

   If you really want to get rowdy, click the double left-pointing arrows to remove all the current fields. You might do this if you have an overwhelming desire to start from scratch.

5. **Click the Close button when you're done.**

Changing the order and width of columns

You can also change the order of the fields from the Customize Columns dialog box. Click the appropriate choice from the Show as Columns in This Order and click the Move Up or Move Down buttons.

The order that the items appear in the Customize Columns dialog box is exactly the way they appear in your final product. Knock yourself out, arrange and rearrange all you want, and sleep peacefully knowing that if you don't like the outcome you can always change it again. Now, if I could just do that with my living room!

You can also drag-and-drop the various column headings to change the order in which columns appear on the lists and tabs. For example, if you want the Date field to appear before the Time field, simply click the Time column heading and drag the heading over to the left of the Date column heading.

Changing the width of a column is almost as easy. If you move your mouse on the line between any two column headings, your cursor transforms into a double-headed arrow. When that arrow appears, hold down your left mouse button and drag to the left or right to narrow or widen a column. The column to the left of your mouse changes width.

Sorting your lists and tabs

In general I hate terms like "automatic" and "click of a button" because your vision of "automatic" might be quite different from that of a software engineer. That said, sorting the entries in any of your lists and tabs is, well, automatic and can be done with the click of a button: Just click the column heading that you want to use to sort the list. Want the contacts in your Contact list to be sorted alphabetically by city? Click the City column heading. Change your mind and want it sorted by zip code instead? Click the Zip Code column heading.

When you click a column heading, an up arrow appears indicating that the contacts are sorted in ascending order (in alphabetical, A-to-Z, or 1–10 order). To reverse the sort order, click the column heading again. If the list is sorted in ascending order, contacts that have no information in the selected column appear first in the list. In descending order, they appear last in the list.

Sorting your contacts is so simple that you may decide to get really adventurous and sort based on another criterion. Go ahead — I dare you! Click any column heading to re-sort the list by the field of your choice.

ACT! automatically separates the contact's name into a first and a last name. When you click the Contact column heading in any of the lists or tabs, you'll notice that your information is sorted by last name so that Lindsay Garrison appears alphabetically with the Gs rather than with the Ls.

Corralling Your Secondary Contacts

Does this scenario sound familiar? You have a main contact, but of course that person, being the big cheese, is rarely available so you often have to work with his assistant. But of course the assistant can't do any true decision making, so you might need to speak to Mr. Big's sales manager on occasion. And, when the sales manager goes on vacation, you need to call the assistant sales manager. Yikes! The Secondary Contacts tab, shown in Figure 5-2, allows you to store all the pertinent information about Mr. Big and his partners in crime in the same area so you don't have to go on a wild goose chase hunting down names, telephone numbers, and e-mail addresses. And, just like promotions that often happen, you can "promote" a secondary contact into a main contact.

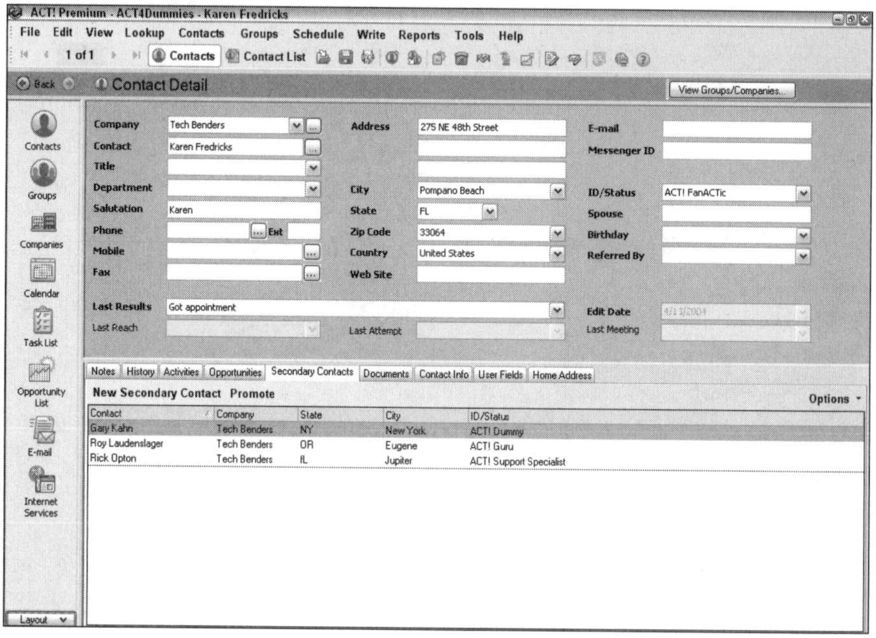

Figure 5-2:
The
Secondary
Contact tab.

Not sure whether to add a contact as a primary or a secondary contact? You might want to think of how you are going to use the secondary contact. If you just want to be able to access an assistant's phone number, then the assistant is a good candidate for entry as a secondary contact. However, if you want to be able to e-mail your monthly newsletter to the assistant or include her in some of your mail merges, you need to add the assistant as a primary contact record instead.

Adding a secondary contact

Of course, you can't add a secondary contact until you create a main contact (see Chapter 4 to do so). After you create the head honcho's contact record, here's what you do to create the secondary contact record(s):

1. **From the Contact Detail window, click the Secondary Contacts tab.**

2. **Click the New Secondary Contact button on the top of the Secondary Contact tab.**

   The Secondary Contact dialog box appears (see Figure 5-3).

3. **Fill in all the juicy details for the secondary contact.**

   Although you don't fill in quite as much information as you can for a main contact, you do have all the really pertinent fields. Don't forget to click the Business Address tab for even more fields.

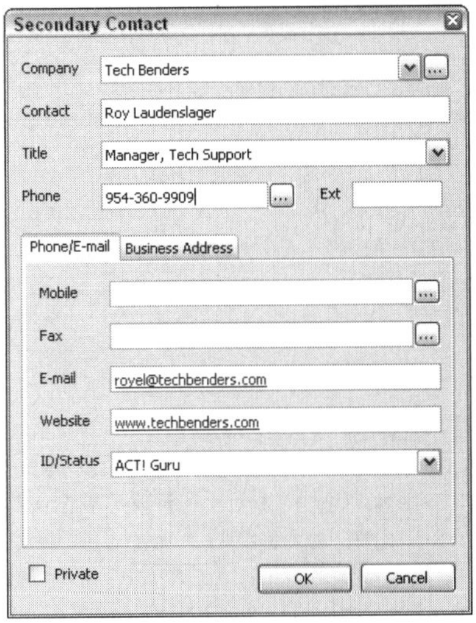

Figure 5-3:
Filling in the secondary contact information.

4. Click OK to create the secondary contact.

Congratulations! Your main contact has now given birth to a secondary contact. All the secondary contacts that you create appear on the Secondary Contacts tab of the primary contact.

If you need to go back and edit or add information for the secondary contact, just double click the name from the Secondary Contact list and *voilà,* you're back to the Secondary Contact dialog box.

Deleting a secondary contact

Sorry to say, but some of the secondary contacts may drift off into the sunset, leaving you with the need to remove them from your database. Not to worry; you can delete a secondary contact by following the bouncing ball through these steps:

1. Click the Secondary Contacts tab from the Contact Detail window.

2. Right-click the contact you want to delete and choose Delete.

You can never say that ACT! doesn't give you ample warning before deleting a contact. As usual, when you attempt to delete even a secondary contact ACT! shows you the scary warning seen in Figure 5-4.

3. Click Yes to delete the selected secondary contact.

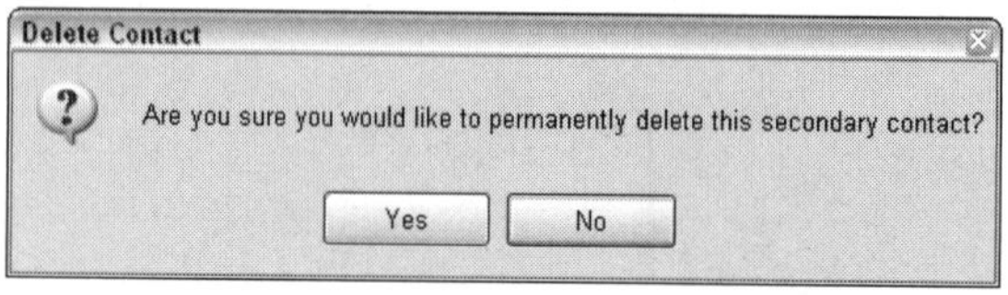

Figure 5-4:
The scary
warning you
get when
deleting a
secondary
contact.

Promoting a secondary contact

Promoting, promotion — it has a lovely ring to it, don't you think? That lowly assistant might be promoted through the ranks and some day become the "big guy" — or at the very least a more important contact than he/she is today. If you're worried that you have to reenter all that basic information in again, don't be. Just promote the contact by following these steps:

1. **Click the Secondary Contacts tab in the Contact Detail window.**

2. **Select the secondary contact that you want to promote.**

3. **Right-click and choose Promote from the menu.**

   The Promote Secondary Contact dialog box appears, as shown in Figure 5-5.

4. **Select whether to duplicate the main contact's primary fields.**

   With promotions come responsibilities and decisions. If the secondary contact is sliding into the role of the current primary contact, you want to copy all that information to the record of the newly promoted contact. If, however, the secondary contact doesn't have the same basic information as the primary contact, you can choose not to copy the primary fields.

5. **Click OK.**

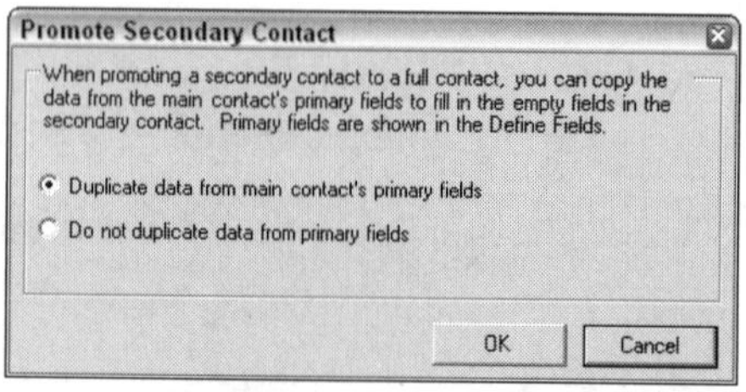

Figure 5-5:
Promoting a
secondary
contact.

Documenting Your Documents

No matter how organized you think your documents might be, you probably occasionally misplace one of them. Of course you can always have Windows search for it, but ACT! offers an easier — and faster solution. The Documents tab, which you can find on the Contacts, Groups, or Companies windows, allows you to attach any and all of your files related to the current contact, group, or company. You can add a proposal created in Excel, a contract created in Word, or even a PDF file that you scanned into your computer. By adding them to the Documents tab, which is shown in Figure 5-6, you are actually creating a shortcut to the document.

After you add a document to the Documents tab, you can open the file directly from ACT! to view, edit, or print. Or, if you prefer, you can still fish through your computer and open the document in your word processor as you're already used to doing. You can also link the same document to multiple records. Removing a file from the Documents tab does not remove it from your computer.

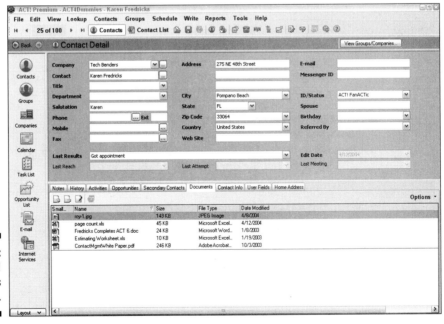

Figure 5-6:
The ACT!
Documents
tab.

Adding a document

Adding a file to the Documents tab is very easy, and considering the time you save down the road, well worth the effort. Just follow these steps:

1. **Display the contact, group, or company record to which you want to add a document.**

2. **Click the Documents tab.**

3. **Click the Add Document button on the Documents tab icon bar.**

   Alternatively, you can right-click in the file list area, and then choose Add Document from the menu.

   The Attach File dialog box opens.

4. **Browse to the document you want to add, select it, and then click Open.**

   ACT! adds the document to your ACT! database, creates a shortcut to the document, and displays the filename, size, type, and last modified date on the Documents tab. Because the document is now part of your database, remote synchronization users can now access the document as well.

You can drag and drop a file to the Documents tab from Windows Explorer or My Computer by dragging the document's icon to the Documents tab.

Opening a document

The true benefit of adding documents to the Documents tab is the speed in which you can open the documents that pertain to a specific contact, group, or company. Follow these steps:

1. **Click the Documents tab.**

2. **Select the document you want to open.**

3. **Click the Edit Document button on the Documents tab icon bar. Alternatively, you can right-click in the file list area and choose Edit Document from the menu.**

   Magically, the program associated with the document opens, revealing the document. You're on you own here — just remember that you can now edit, save, or print the document as you normally do. Any changes you make are reflected the next time you open the document again either through ACT! or the original program.

Removing a document

After you add a file to the Documents tab, you might change your mind and decide to make it go am-scray. Easy come, easy go. Follow these steps to rid yourself of the offending document:

1. **Display the contact, group, or company record that contains the document you want to eliminate.**

2. **Click the Documents tab.**

3. **In the Document List, select the document you want to remove.**

   You might have saved the same document to more than one contact record. Removing the association between a document and one contact record does not affect the link between that file and the other contact record. The document is still contained inside the database.

4. **Click the Remove Document button on the Documents tab icon bar.**

   Alternatively, you can right-click in the file list area, and choose Remove Document from the menu.

   ACT makes sure you want to remove the document by presenting a warning. Software programs very often present you with scary messages before deleting important information. This is a good thing. Heed the warnings!

   ACT! removes the link between the document and the current record. It also removes the document from within the database. And, because the document doesn't end up in the Recycle Bin, think very carefully *before* deleting the document.

5. **Click Yes to confirm that you really, truly want to remove the document.**

If you originally created the document somewhere in your computer, the document is still there. However, if you are a sync user who received the document as part of the synchronization process, you might want to first open the document and save it to your computer before removing it from the Documents tab — otherwise it's gone for good.

Chapter 6

Working with Your Data

In This Chapter

▶ Using the Contact List to display your contacts

▶ Changing the look of the Contact List

▶ Working with selected contacts

▶ Sorting your contacts

▶ Importing data

*T*he basic Contact Detail window shows you all the fields in your database as they pertain to a single contact. Conversely, the *Contact List* view allows you to see all your contacts together in one list. In the Contact List, you can find contacts, sort your list of contacts, and create lookups of contacts. Best of all, after you arrange the Contact List just the way you like it, you can print out the information exactly as it appears on-screen. ACT! automatically sorts all your contacts alphabetically by company; in this chapter you find out how to sort your contacts by up to three fields. After you get the hang of ACT!, you may want to import more contacts into your database — stay tuned!

Contacting the Contact List

The Contact List is a good way to view your contacts if you're working with large numbers of contacts at one time. Changing the columns that appear in the Contact List provides you with a way of comparing information between your various contacts. For example, you may want to see how many of your contacts purchased each of your products, and have the name of each product appear in the Contact List along with their telephone number.

Getting to the Contact List is half the fun

The road to the Contact List is simple to follow — just choose View⇨ Contact List. A list of your contacts displayed in columns appears, as shown in Figure 6-1.

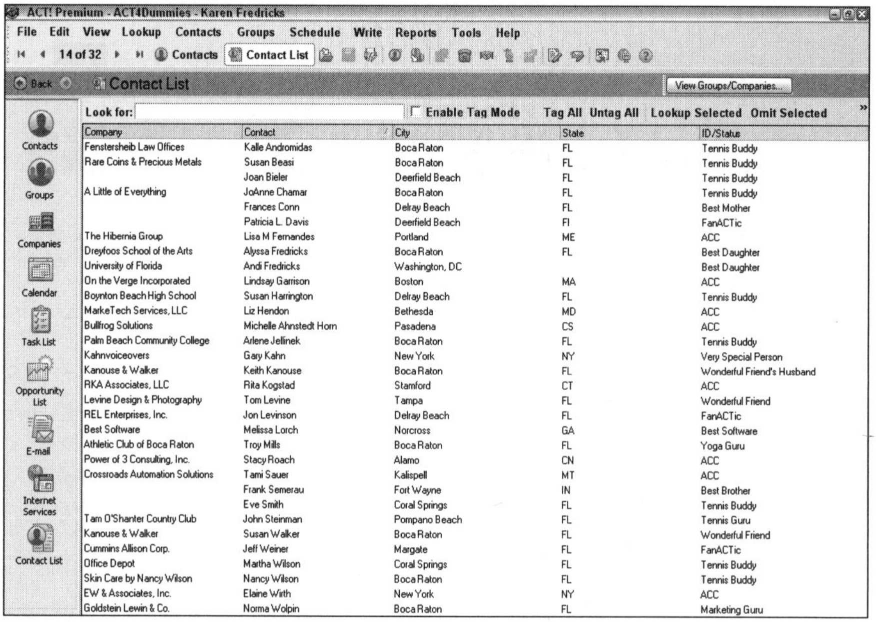

Figure 6-1:
The ACT!
Contact List.

When you come across a contact record in your list that requires a bit of tweaking you may want to flip to the Contact Detail window to make your changes. You can get to the Contact Detail window in a number of ways:

- Double-click a contact in the Contact List.
- Right-click the contact and choose Go To Contact.
- Click the Back button on the Back and Forward bar if you were just in the Contact Detail window.

The Contact Detail window appears with the selected contact's record. To return to the Contact List, choose View⇨Contact List or click the Back button on the Back and Forward bar.

Finding a contact in the Contact List

In Chapter 7, I show you how to create a lookup to find contacts that meet your specific criteria. The Contact List also allows you to go to a specific contact record in the blink of an eye. Here's what you need to do:

1. **Click the column heading to select that column.**

   For example, if you want to find a contact by last name, click the Contact column heading.

2. **Start typing the first few letters of the contact information that you want to find in the Look For text field.**

   If you click the Company Name column heading, type in the first few letters of the company that you're looking for. If you click the Contact column heading, start typing the first few letters of the contact's last name.

   ACT! scrolls down the Contact List to the closest match. For example, if you sorted the list by contact and typed the letter **s**, you might land on Colonel Sanders contact record. If you typed **sm**, you're probably looking at all your Smiths.

3. **Continue typing until you reach the contact for whom you are looking.**

Tagging contacts in the Contact List

Using the Contact List, you can easily select — or *tag* — contacts to manually create a lookup of your contacts. For example, say that you want to target some of your best clients for a special promotion; a general lookup probably doesn't produce a list of those contacts because you don't have a field that includes special promotions. Instead, you can tag those contacts based on your own instincts.

To switch to Tag mode, just make sure that a check mark is showing next to the Enable Tag Mode option, which is located at the top of the Contact List. You can do the following things in Tag mode:

✔ **Tag a contact:** Click anywhere in the contact; a gray bar appears across the contact record indicating that you tagged it. Figure 6-2 shows tagged contacts.

✔ **Untag a contact:** Click anywhere in a contact, and the gray bar disappears.

✔ **Tag a continuous list of names:** Click the first name in the list that you're selecting, and then press the Shift key while clicking the last name in the list that you're selecting.

Figure 6-2: Selected contacts in Tag mode.

Company	Contact	City	State	ID/Status
Fenstersheib Law Offices	Katie Andromidas	Boca Raton	FL	Tennis Buddy
Rare Coins & Precious Metals	Susan Beasi	Boca Raton	FL	Tennis Buddy
	Joan Bieler	Deerfield Beach	FL	Tennis Buddy
A Little of Everything	JoAnne Chamar	Boca Raton	FL	Tennis Buddy
	Frances Conn	Delray Beach	FL	Best Mother
	Patricia L. Davis	Deerfield Beach	Fl	FanACTic
The Hibernia Group	Lisa M Fernandes	Portland	ME	ACC
Dreyfoos School of the Arts	Alyssa Fredricks	Boca Raton	FL	Best Daughter
University of Florida	Andi Fredricks	Washington, DC		Best Daughter
On the Verge Incorporated	Lindsay Garrison	Boston	MA	ACC
Boynton Beach High School	Susan Harrington	Delray Beach	FL	Tennis Buddy
MarkeTech Services, LLC	Liz Hendon	Bethesda	MD	ACC
Bullfrog Solutions	Michelle Ahnstedt Horn	Pasadena	CS	ACC
Palm Beach Community College	Arlene Jelinek	Boca Raton	FL	Tennis Buddy
Kahnvoiceovers	Gary Kahn	New York	NY	Very Special Person
Kanouse & Walker	Keith Kanouse	Boca Raton	FL	Wonderful Friend's Husband
RKA Associates, LLC	Rita Kogstad	Stamford	CT	ACC

Playing tag with your contacts

One of things I like best about ACT!, and believe me there are a lot, is the ability to create custom lookups. Although Chapter 7 explains the most popular ways to create a lookup, sometimes you want to cut your database into "bite-sized" pieces — and none of the existing lookups help. For example, you may be planning a party and want to handpick all the invitees from your Contact List.

You can handpick items from a list or tab in two ways. Those of you who are familiar with Windows shortcuts probably already know them:

✔ If the items are all situated next to one another, click the first item in the list that you want to include, press the Shift key, and click the last desired item in your list.

✔ If the items appear rather randomly throughout your list, click the first item in the list, press the Ctrl key, and click the rest of the items to select them.

After you select all the items you want to include, right-click the selected area and choose Create Lookup.

Notice the four buttons to the right of the Enable Tag Mode option (refer to Figure 6-2). After you tag the contacts that you want to work with or those that you want to omit temporarily, choose one of the following four buttons:

✔ **Tag All:** Allows you to select all the contacts currently showing in the Contact List.

✔ **Untag All:** Allows you to deselect any contacts that you already selected.

✔ **Lookup Selected:** Allows you to create a lookup based on the contacts that you tag.

✔ **Omit Selected:** Allows you to remove the contacts that you select from the Contact List. Don't panic — it does not remove the contacts permanently from your database!

Flip to Chapter 11 if you need to print out any lists and tabs for the lowdown on Quick Reports.

Sorting your contacts

By default, your contacts are sorted alphabetically by the Company column. You can see this two different ways:

✔ A small triangle appears in the Company column heading in the Contact List.

✔ You remember your alphabet from grammar school, and you notice that companies starting with the letter *A* appear before those starting with the letter *B* as you scroll through your contacts.

Why aren't my contacts sorting correctly?

At times, your contacts may appear to not alphabetize correctly. Possible reasons for this include

✔ A stray mark or a blank space in front of the field name; *'Zinger & Co.* appears alphabetically in front of *Gadgets R Us.*

✔ Numbers appear alphabetically in front of letters. *1st Financial Savings & Loan* appears alphabetically in front of *AAA Best Bank.*

✔ ACT! may be a little confused about the first and last name of a contact; a quick trip to the Contact Detail window is worth your time. Click the ellipsis button next to the Contact's name and then double-check that the correct first and last names appear in the appropriate spots.

In Chapter 5, you discover that you can sort any list view by clicking the appropriate column heading that you want to use to sort the list. For example, to sort by the contact's last name, click the Contact column in the Contact List.

Although the Contact List provides you with a quick-as-a-bunny way to sort your contacts, it sorts the contacts based on the contents of a *single* field. If you want to sort your contacts based on multiple criteria, you have another way to do it:

1. **Choose Edit⇨Sort from either the Contact List or Contact Detail window.**

   The Sort dialog box appears (see Figure 6-3).

2. **Choose an option from the Sort By drop-down list to specify the first-level sort criterion.**

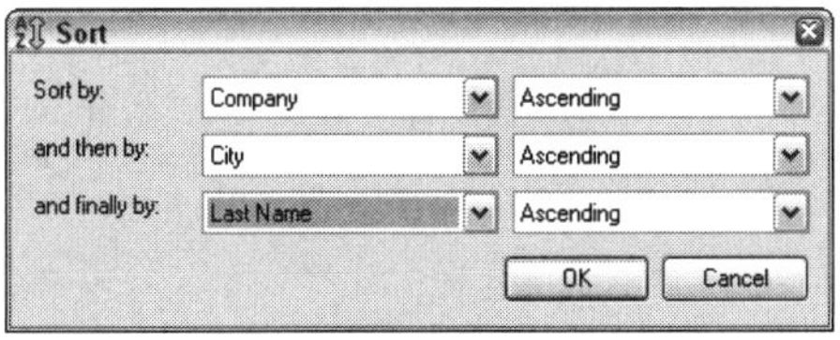

Figure 6-3:
The Sort
dialog box.

3. **Select the sorting order (Ascending or Descending).**

   Ascending sort order means from A–Z or from the smallest number to the largest number. Records with no information in the field used for the sort appear first. *Descending* means from Z–A or from the largest number to the smallest number. Records with no information in the field used for the sort appear last.

4. **Choose a second field option from the And Then By drop-down list and specify Ascending or Descending.**

5. **If you want a third level of sorting, choose a field from the And Finally By drop-down list and specify Ascending or Descending.**

6. **Click OK.**

Importing New Information into ACT!

You might have nothing but time on your hands and decide that the one thing you want to do with all that time is to sit down and enter in thousands of new contacts into your database. Or, you may have lots of excess cash in your drawer and decide to hire someone to enter in thousands of new contacts into your database. My hat is off to you, and all I can ask is that you send me a postcard in ten years when you finish.

If you're hoping that ACT! has an easier solution — it does! The question you need to ask yourself is where did that data come from? If your data came from any of the following sources I have great news for you:

- ✔ You purchased a list and received it as a download or on a disk.

- ✔ You downloaded a list from an Internet site.

- ✔ You received the list in conjunction with a trade show you attended on a disk.

- ✔ Someone in your organization has been keeping his or her contact information in another (gasp!) program besides ACT!.

- ✔ Another piece of software that you're using, for example QuickBooks, contains a good portion of the contact information you want to have in ACT!.

All these situations mean that your data is in electronic format, which you can easily import into ACT!. You get to head to the beach rather than head for your keyboard. ACT! can easily import your information if it is currently in one of the following formats:

- ✔ ACT! in either the current or prior versions
- ✔ Outlook

If you or someone in your organization is currently using Outlook for contact management, you need to check out Chapter 19 to find out how easily you can import that information into ACT!.

✔ dBase

✔ Palm Desktop

✔ Text-delimited

Most databases have an option to export the data. After you export the data, you need to save the data in text tab delimited format. You can easily save data in the correct format using Excel. If you are using a relatively old program that was written for DOS, you may not find an Export option. Not to worry — most DOS programs allow you to "print to file," which in essence is creating a text file.

To start importing information and stop spending countless hours hovering over your keyboard, follow these steps:

1. **Open the ACT! database you want to import your information into.**

   If you are importing another ACT! database, performing routine maintenance on that database and backing it up *before* attempting to bring in the new data is a good idea. Not sure how to perform these feats? Chapter 17 explains them in more detail.

   Only Administrators and Managers have permission to import data into the ACT! database.

   Before you start importing data, be sure to select the Duplicate Checking option. This option is particularly important if you suspect that your current database may include some of the same contacts as the imported information. Duplicate checking merges any duplicate records with existing ACT! records. If you don't have duplicate checking turned on, you might find yourself merging hundreds — or even thousands — of duplicate records *one pair at a time.* Check out Chapter 17 to discover the ins and outs of duplicate checking.

2. **Choose File⇨Import.**

   Holy guacamole! A wizard helps you out; if you follow the instructions, you have your data imported in a jiffy.

3. **Click Next to continue.**

   The Specify Source screen of the wizard appears (see Figure 6-4).

4. **Fill in the important information about your import.**

   • **What Type of File Do You Want to Import:** Choose the file type from the drop-down menu.

- **File Name and Location:** If you click the Browse button, you can navigate to the file that you're importing.

- **User Name and Password:** If you are importing an existing ACT! database into the current database, you need to supply this information for the old database. If you are importing data from another format, these options are grayed out.

Figure 6-4:
Specifying
the source
file for data
importing.

5. **Click Next to continue.**

6. **Specify the type of records you want to import and then click Next.**

   If you are importing an existing database, you can choose to import contact, group, or company records. If you are importing a text file, you can decide if you want the imported information to appear as contact, group, or company records.

   The Specify Import Options screen appears, as shown in Figure 6-5.

7. **Specify your import options if importing a text file and then click Next.**

   Here's where you can indicate whether your text file is in tab or comma format and whether you want to include the header row of your import file. The header row is the row that names each of the fields you are importing. If you include it, you end up with a contact record whose company name might be "company." Usually, you want to include the header row to make sure that all your fields map to the correct spot — and then delete it after you verify all your fields map correctly.

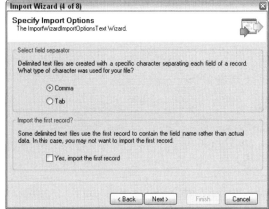

Figure 6-5:
Text file
import
options.

The Contact Map screen of the wizard appears, as shown in Figure 6-6.

8. **Map the fields from the new information to existing fields in the ACT! database and then click Next.**

Mapping fields allows you to associate field names from the import database to the corresponding fields in your current ACT! database. If the names of the fields in your import database exactly match the names of the fields in your current ACT! database, you're home free. You'll notice in Figure 6-6 that the left side of this screen indicates the field names of the *source* database you are importing; the right side indicates the field names of your current or *target* database.

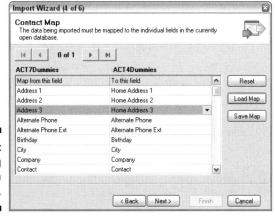

Figure 6-6:
Mapping
fields for a
data import.

Blank fields in the right column are indications that the field in the left column doesn't import. To remedy this situation, you need to click the drop-down arrows for all blank ACT! fields and indicate the name of the ACT! field you want to use to hold this new data. If your ACT! database is missing key fields, you need to add them to your database before you can import information; Chapter 15 tells you how to add fields to your database.

After you map the fields, you can save the mapping by clicking the Save Map icon. That way, you can click the Load Map button in the future if you ever import another similar database. It also comes in handy to save a map in case you have to stop the import in order to add in a few missing fields.

You'll notice a few arrow buttons along the top. If you click the right-pointing arrow, you're treated to a sneak preview of what your information is going to look like after the import completes.

To make life easier on yourself, you may consider renaming the fields in your import database to exactly match the names of your ACT! fields. For example, ACT!'s main address field is labeled *Address 1*. Renaming the address field in your import database to Address 1 causes the fields in both databases to map automatically.

 9. **Specify the merge options if importing another ACT! database into your current one.**

    ACT! is now asking for a bit of feedback concerning what happens if a contact record in the import database matches a contact record in your current ACT! database. Typically, you want to merge the information together so that the notes you entered for Nancy Wilson in your import database combine with the notes you added for Nancy in your current ACT! database. However, if you prefer, you can change the option so either

    • Duplicated information isn't imported.

    • Information from the import database overrides the information in your current ACT! database.

10. **Click Finish to start your merge.**

    You may want to take a quick break after completing the wizard. Depending on the number of contact you are importing, this step can take a while. Just make sure you keep an eye on your computer; ACT! may run into multiple duplicate contacts and ask you if you want to merge them together.

After importing your contacts, you may want to tweak them a bit. For example, you may want to change the ID/Status field to Prospect, or the Referred To field to Imported Database. Chapter 7 walks you through creating a lookup based on the contact's Create Date field, and Chapter 17 shows you how to perform a global search and replace.

ACT! version 2005 handles the set-up of custom and monthly recurring activities differently than in earlier versions of ACT!. If you import custom or monthly recurring activities from an earlier version, you'll notice a difference in the way the activities are set up for those scheduled to repeat on more than one day of each week in a month. To change how recurring activities display, see Chapter 9.

Corex CardScan

I discuss importing lists into ACT! in this chapter. However, you may be staring at a tower of business cards sitting on the corner of your desk, determined to start inputting all that information into ACT!. Ah, the best laid plans of mice and men! Do yourself a favor and buy the CardScan by Corex.

This cool little gizmo can easily fit on a corner of your desk. You simply feed in each business card, and the software translates the information from the business card into fields. Although the cards scan with better than 90 percent accuracy, you probably want to double-check the accuracy of each card. Then — and this part is my favorite — click the ACT! button in the card scanner software and watch as that mountain of cards you just scanned magically appears in ACT!. For more information, check my Web site at www.techbenders.com/ act4dummies.htm.

Chapter 7

The ACT! Lookup: Searching for Your Contacts

*I*f all roads lead to Rome, then surely all processes in ACT! lead to the lookup. A *lookup* is a way of looking at only a portion of the contacts in your database, depending on your specifications. A good practice in ACT! is to perform a lookup *first* and then perform an action *second*. For example, you might perform a lookup and then print some labels. Or you might do a lookup and then perform a mail merge. Need a report? Do a lookup first! In this chapter, I show you how to perform lookups based on contact information, on notes and history information, and on advanced query information.

ACT! Is Looking Up

The theory behind the lookup is that you don't always need to work with all your contacts at one time. Not only is working with only a portion of your database easier; at times, doing so is absolutely necessary. If you're changing your mailing address, you probably want to send a notification to everyone in your database. If you're running a special sales promotion, you probably only notify your prospects and customers. If you're sending out overpriced holiday gift baskets, however, you probably want the names of only your very best customers.

Don't create an extra database — use the ACT! lookup instead

Some ACT! users originally create several databases, not realizing that one database can be used to store information about various different types of contacts. Although you might want to create two separate databases — for instance, one for customers and one for vendors — a better alternative is to include both your customers and vendors together in one database. To this one database you can then add a few miscellaneous contacts, including prospects that aren't yet customers or referral sources that might lead to new customers. Just make sure that each contact is identified in some specific way; I recommend using the ID/Status field. Then when you want to see only vendors or only prospective customers, simply perform a lookup to work with just that particular group of contacts.

In ACT!, you can focus on a portion of your contacts by

- Creating basic lookups based on the information in one of the nine most-commonly used contact fields in ACT!. (See the later section, "Performing Basic Lookups.")

- Conducting a query based on information stored in your groups, companies, and opportunities. (See the later section, "Searching Your Groups, Companies, and Opportunities.")

- Creating lookups based on information from other areas in your database including notes, histories, activities, annual events, and contact activity. (See the later section, "Performing Special ACT! Lookups.")

- Creating your own, more advanced, queries based on the parameters of your own choosing by using logical operators. (See the later section, "Creating Advanced Queries.")

Performing Basic Lookups

The easiest way to pose a query is to choose one of your main contact fields from a menu and then fill in the search criteria. This way is easy because the menus guide you, but it's also the least flexible way. The Lookup menu that ACT! provides is probably the best — and simplest — place to start when creating a lookup; just follow these steps:

1. **Choose the Lookup menu from the Contact Detail window.**

   Figure 7-1 shows you the Lookup menu that drops down and the criteria that you can use to perform your lookup.

Figure 7-1:
The ACT!
Lookup
menu.

2. **Choose one of the criteria listed in Figure 7-1 to create a basic lookup.**

   The ACT! Lookup Contacts dialog box appears, as shown in Figure 7-2.

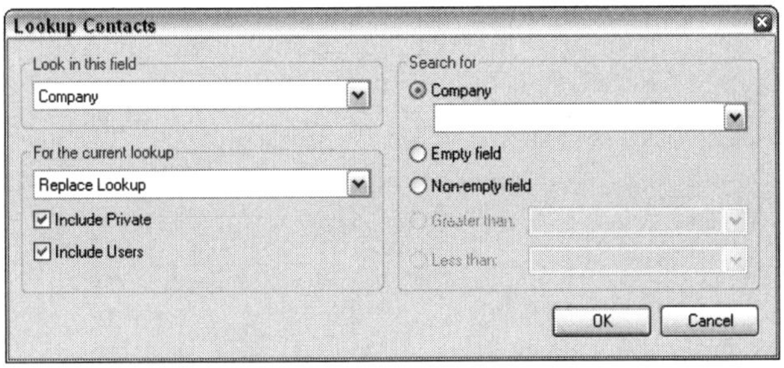

Figure 7-2:
The ACT!
Lookup
Contacts
dialog box.

3. **If you're searching based on an Other field, click the Look in This Field drop-down arrow and choose a field from the drop-down list.**

4. **In the For the Current Lookup area, select an option:**

   - **Replace Lookup:** Creates a brand-new lookup based on your criteria.

   - **Add to Lookup:** Adds the contacts based on your criteria to an existing lookup. For example, if you created a lookup for your contacts based in Chicago, select this option to add your New York clients to the set of Chicago clients.

Playing the wild card

Some of you old-timers may remember that the asterisk (*) was the DOS wild card. That same concept exists in SQL-based products like ACT! except that the percent sign (%) replaced the asterisk for some reason known only to the technical gods.

Say you're trying to find all companies that are carpet cleaners. If you created a lookup using the word **carpet**, you find *Carpet Cleaning by Joanne Chamar* but not *Joanne's Carpet Cleaning.* Enter the wild card. If you create your lookup using **%carpet%**, ACT! finds companies that both begin and end with *carpet.*

- **Narrow Lookup:** Refines a lookup based on a second criterion. For example, if you've created a lookup of all your customers, select this option to narrow the lookup to only customers based in Philadelphia.

5. **In the Search For area, select an option:**

- **Company:** Type the word to search for or select a word from the drop-down list if you're looking for contacts that match a specific criterion.

- **Empty Field:** If you're looking for contacts that don't have any data in the given field — for example, people who don't have an e-mail address — choose this option.

- **Non-Empty Field:** If you want to find only those contacts that have data in a given field — for example, everyone who has an e-mail address — choose this option.

When typing in the match criterion, remember that with ACT! less is more. ACT! automatically searches by the beginning of your string. If you type **Tech**, ACT! returns Tech Benders and Technology Consultants. However, if you type **Technology**, you only find Technology Consultants.

6. **Click OK.**

The record counter now reflects the number of contacts that match your search criteria.

7. **Choose Lookup⇨All Contacts when you're ready to once again view all the contacts in your database.**

Searching Your Groups, Companies, and Opportunities

Probably the most common lookups you create are based on your contact fields. However, you aren't limited to searching by just those fields. You can also query your groups, companies, and opportunities for key information. The best part is that all three queries work in pretty much the same way.

Grappling with your groups

To find the groups that match your search criteria, here's all you need to do:

1. **Choose Lookup⇨Groups.**

   The Lookup Groups dialog box opens, as shown in Figure 7-3.

2. **Choose from one of the following options in the Look in This Field area:**

   - **All Groups:** Opens the Group List showing you a list of all the groups in your database.

   - **Group Name:** Finds all groups that match the name you specify.

   - **Other Fields:** Allows you to search through any and all group fields for the groups that match your desired criterion. The list shows all group fields that you can search in the database.

   - **Save Lookup as Group:** Lets you create a group based on the currently displayed contacts.

   If you choose the All Groups or Save Lookup as Group options, you're finished. If you choose the Name or Other Fields option, you have to continue along your merry way following these remaining steps.

Figure 7-3:
The Lookup
Groups
dialog box.

3. **In the Search For area, type the word to search for, or select a word from the drop-down list.**

4. **In the For the Current Lookup area, select the Replace Lookup option.**

5. **Click OK.**

Like magic, the Group List pops open, displaying a list of all the groups that match your specifications.

Calling all companies

Hopefully, creating a lookup of companies seems vaguely familiar because it is so similar to creating a group lookup. To find the companies that match your search criteria, here's all you need to do:

1. **Choose Lookup⇨Companies.**

The Lookup Companies dialog box appears.

2. **Choose from one of the following options:**

- **All Companies:** Opens the Company List showing you a list of all the companies in your database.

- **Name**

- **Main Phone**

- **City**

- **State**

- **Zip Code**

- **ID/Status:** Just like you use the ID/Status field to classify each of your contacts into a separate category, assign your companies an ID/Status. For example, if one of your company ID/Status options is *wholesale,* it's a snap to find all your "wholesale" companies.

- **Other Fields:** Provides you with a drop-down list of all your company fields.

- **Save Lookup as Company:** Lets you create a company based on the currently displayed contacts.

Ogling your opportunities

To find the opportunities that match your search criteria, here's all you need to do:

1. **Choose Lookup⇨Opportunities.**

2. **Choose one of the following options:**

- **All Opportunities:** Opens the Opportunities List view, showing you a list of all the opportunities in your database.

- **Name:** Finds opportunities that match the name you specify. Typically, you want to use the quote number as the name of your quote so that you can lookup based on that criterion. Chapter 20 shows you how to name your quotes.

- **Stage:** Finds opportunities that match a specific sales stage.

- **Product:** Finds opportunities that pertain to a specific product.

- **Total:** Finds opportunities that match the total sale you specify. You can also search for opportunities that are larger or smaller than a specified dollar amount.

- **Status:** Finds opportunities that match a specific sales status.

- **Other Fields:** Finds all opportunities that match any other opportunity fields, including the eight opportunity fields you can customize.

If you chose the first option, you're rewarded with a list of all your opportunities. If you opt for one of the other options, the Lookup Opportunities dialog box, displayed in Figure 7-4, appears.

Figure 7-4:
The Lookup
Oppor-
tunities
dialog box.

3. **Select the field on which you wish to search in the Look in This Field drop-down list.**

   The list shows all opportunity fields that you can search.

4. **In the Search For area, type the word to search for or select a word from the drop-down list.**

   For example, if you're looking for all opportunities that are in the Negotiation stage, select Stage in the Look in This Field drop-down list and Negotiation in the Search For drop-down list.

5. **Select Replace Lookup in the For the Current Lookup drop-down list.**

6. **Click OK.**

Although you may be happy as a little clam creating and modifying your lookups, you can achieve the same results by filtering your Opportunity List. Filtering may even make you ecstatic because you'll probably find it a bit easier. Chapter 5 shows you how to filter your Opportunities List.

Performing Special ACT! Lookups

The ability to perform a simple lookup based on a single field criterion is an element common to most databases, but ACT! isn't your average database. All databases contain fields, but only special databases contain things such as notes and activities. And after creating a note to store a useful tidbit of information (which I show you how to do in Chapter 8), you'll want to find that information again. ACT! provides you with three special query options to find information that was entered into ACT! in a special way.

Searching by keyword

The *keyword search* can be an extremely useful way to find data about your contacts no matter where that information might be lurking. ACT!'s keyword search enables you to perform lookups for information in Contact, Notes/ Histories, Activities, Sales/Opportunities, and E-mail Addresses fields. For example, suppose that you're looking for someone to design a new logo for your business but you can't remember where you stored that information. Is *logo* part of the company's name, did you enter it into the ID/Status field, or did you stick it in a note somewhere? A keyword search searches throughout your database, checking all fields, until it finds the word *logo*.

Here's how to perform a keyword search:

1. **From the Contact Detail window, choose Lookup⇨Keyword Search.**

   The Keyword Search dialog box opens (see Figure 7-5).

2. **In the Search For area, enter the key piece of information you are searching for.**

   If you're entering criteria into a drop-down list, the word fills in automatically for you as you start to type.

3. **In the Record Type drop-down list, indicate whether you are looking for a Contact, Group or Company record.**

4. **In the Search These Records area, choose an option:**

   • **All Records:** ACT! sifts through all records in your database.

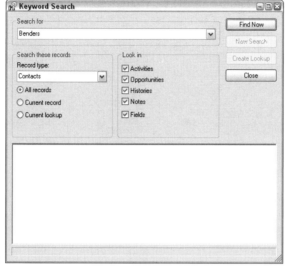

Figure 7-5:
The
Keyword
Search
dialog box.

• **Current Record:** ACT! searches only the record that was on-screen when you opened the dialog box. Use this option if you know that somewhere in the deep, dark past, you entered a specific tidbit of information as a note.

• **Current Lookup:** ACT! searches only the records that you selected in a previous lookup.

5. **In the Look In area, choose an option.**

The keyword search is a powerful searching tool, and it does take a bit longer to run than other searching methods. When you perform a key-word search, ACT! sifts through every last bit of information in your data-base, hoping to find a match that fits your specifications. To speed up the process, limit the amount of elements that you're searching through.

• **Activities:** Searches in your activities

• **Opportunities:** Searches the information on the Opportunities tab

• **Histories:** Searches through the histories that ACT! has created

• **Notes:** Searches in the notes you've created

• **Fields:** Searches through all your contact fields

6. **After making all your choices, click the Find Now button.**

ACT! responds with a list of records, similar to what's shown in Figure 7-6. The lookup results show the contact's name and company and the field in which ACT! finds the matching data, as well as the data that it finds. For example, if you searched for the word *ACT!,* your search includes such diverse words as *interactive* and *contractor* because the letters *act* appear in the middle of these words.

Figure 7-6:
Results of a
keyword
search.

7. **Decide what you want to do with the results.**

Like the old saying goes, be careful what you search for because you just might find it! Okay, the saying doesn't go exactly like that, but now that you've found a number of records using the keyword search, you must decide which one(s) to focus on. Here are some of your options:

- Click the Create Lookup button to see all the records in the Contact Detail window.

- Double-click any part of a single record, and you land on that contact record. To get back to your search, double-click the Keyword Search tab that now appears in the bottom-left corner of the Contact Detail window.

- Select multiple adjacent records by clicking the first record, pressing the Shift key, and then clicking the last record. Right-click one of your selections and choose Lookup Selected Records. You now have a lookup that consists of only the contacts that you selected.

- Select records that aren't adjacent by clicking the first record, pressing the Ctrl key, and then clicking the other records that you want. Right-click one of your selections and choose Lookup Selected Records. You now have a lookup that consists of only the contacts that you selected.

Annual event lookups

In Chapter 15, I show you how to create Annual Event fields. Annual events help automate the processes of tracking important dates, such as birthdays or anniversaries. When you enter a date in an Annual Event field, ACT! automatically tracks the event date from year to year. Because annual events don't appear on your calendar, you must perform an Annual Event lookup to display them. You can use the Annual Event lookup to generate a printed list to display events for the current week, the current month, or a specified date range.

Combining the power of an Annual Event lookup with an ACT! mail merge is a great way to save lots of time. Birthdays and anniversaries are good examples of annual events; like it or not, they happen once a year. The Annual Event lookup tracks them all down regardless of the event. After you create a lookup of these customers, you can then send them all a renewal letter by performing a mail merge. (I show you how to perform a mail merge in Chapter 13.)

Here's all you need to do to create an Annual Event lookup:

1. **From the Contact Detail window, choose Lookup⇨Annual Events.**

   The Annual Events Search dialog box opens, as shown in Figure 7-7.

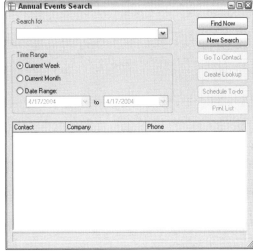

Figure 7-7:
The Annual
Events
Search
dialog box.

2. **Select an annual event from the Search For drop-down list.**

   If you've added more than one annual event field to your database, you can search for more than one of them at a time. For example, you might want to find everyone who has either a birthday or anniversary in the month of June.

  3. Choose a Time Range option in which you want to search.

    Your options are the current week or month, or a selected date range.

  4. Click the Find Now button.

    The results appear in the lower half of the Annual Events Search dialog box. Your results vary, depending on the number of contacts that meet your search criteria. If no contacts meet your search criteria, you receive a message nicely telling you so.

  5. Click one of the following option buttons:

    • **Go To Contact:** To go to the contact record of the selected contact.

    • **Create Lookup:** To create a lookup of all the contacts.

    • **Schedule To-Do:** To schedule an activity for the selected contacts. Unfortunately, you can schedule only one activity at a time.

    • **Print List:** To print a list of the contacts.

Searching by contact activity

I've often estimated that at least 20 percent of the average database consists of long-lost contact information. You can either ignore these forlorn contacts, or you might realize that there's gold in them there hills! What if you could find all the contacts that you haven't contacted in, say, the last two years? Chances are that many of those contacts will be glad to hear from you. Maybe they lost your contact information or chose a company other than yours that they weren't happy with. Suddenly those "lost" contacts have become a virtual treasure trove.

You can create a lookup of contacts based on the last time that you made any changes to their record or contacted them through a meeting, call, or to-do. You can look for the contacts that either have or have not been changed within a specified date range. You can also narrow the search according to activity or history type.

To create a lookup by contact activity, follow these steps:

  1. Choose Lookup⇨Contact Activity.

    The Contact Activity dialog box opens, as shown in Figure 7-8.

  2. Select either Not Changed or Changed from the Look for Contacts That Have area.

    The neat thing about using the Contact Activity lookup is that you can look for "touched" or "untouched" contacts. In other words, you're able to search for all the contacts that you *contacted* last month or for all the contacts that you *didn't contact* last month.

Figure 7-8:
The Contact
Activity
dialog box.

3. **Select a date.**

4. **Select options in the Search In area to narrow your search.**

   You can search in the following areas of ACT!:

   - Contact fields

   - Notes

   - Opportunities

   - History

   - Activities

   If you decide to search through your History and/or Activities tabs you can even indicate which specific types of histories or activities you want to include in your search.

5. **Click OK.**

   ACT! searches for the selected field or activity that was or was not modified within the specified date range. The Contact List appears and displays your selection.

   ACT! isn't searching just through all your contacts; it's also scouring all your notes, histories, and opportunities, so it may take a moment or two to create your search results. Relax and practice a few deep-breathing exercises while you wait.

Creating Advanced Queries

If you need to base your lookup on multiple criteria, you can perform a basic lookup and then use the Narrow Lookup option (refer to Figure 7-2) in the Lookup Contacts dialog box to create a more specific search. This option works fine if you're willing to create several lookups until you reach the desired results. A better alternative is to use a query to create a lookup. A *query* searches all the contacts in your database based on the multiple criteria that you specify and then creates a lookup of contacts that match those criteria.

ACT!'s other lookup functions require that you perform multiple lookups to add to or subtract from a set of contacts. By using an Advanced Query, you can find contacts based on criteria in multiple fields. You can enter values in any field on any tab in the Contact Detail window, except for the system tabs.

Looking up by example

When you create a Lookup by Example, ACT! responds by presenting you with a blank contact record and lets you specify the fields and values that define the query.

This is what you do:

1. **Choose Lookup⇨By Example.**

   The Lookup by Example window opens. The Lookup by Example window, as shown in Figure 7-9, looks just like any other contact record with one major difference — all the fields are blank!

2. **Click in the field that you want to query.**

   You can create a query on virtually any field in your database. Don't forget to check out some of those neat fields that might be located on your various layout tabs. For example, the Contact Info tab contains the Record Manager and Create Date fields, which are common things to query on.

3. **Fill in any criteria on which you want to search.**

   Fill in as many criteria as you need. The whole purpose of doing a Lookup by Example is that you're looking for contacts that fit more than one criterion. If you're looking for all customers who are located in San Diego, type **customer** in the ID/Status field and **San Diego** in the City field.

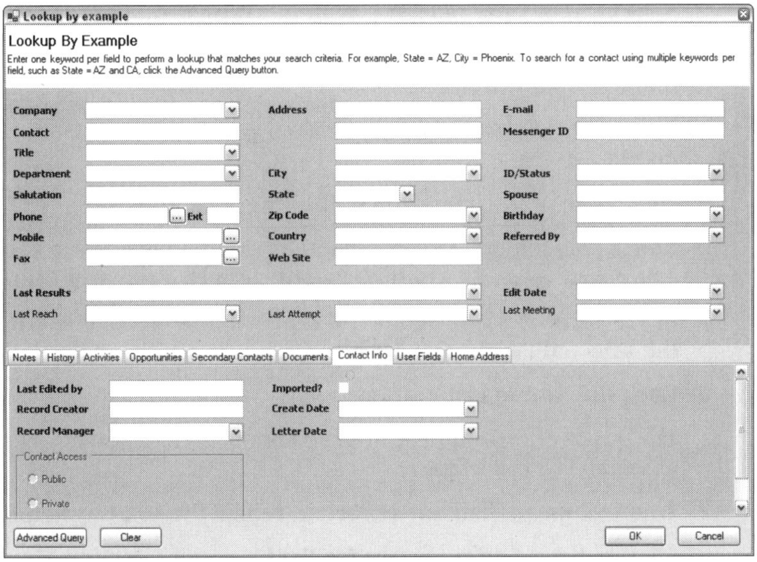

Figure 7-9:
The Lookup
by Example
window is
similar to
a contact
record, but
it's blank.

The Advanced Query

After you use your database for a while and it slowly but surely fills up with
more and more contacts, you may feel the need to add a little more power
into your lookups. In fact, you may even start using the term *query,* which is
computer-speak for "fancy lookup." Fortunately for you, although an Advanced
Query packs a lot of power, it's still a piece of cake to run. Just follow these
steps:

1. **Choose Lookup⇨Advanced⇨Advanced Query.**

   The Advanced Query window opens up, as shown in Figure 7-10.

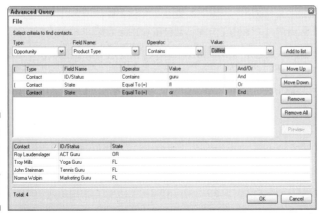

Figure 7-10:
The
Advanced
Query
window.

2. **Select Contact or Opportunity in the Type drop-down list.**

3. **Select one of the available contact or opportunity fields in the Field Name drop-down list.**

   To make life easy for you, you find all your fields listed in the Field Name drop-down list.

4. **Select one of the operators in the Operator field.**

   Knock yourself out! Indicate whether you're looking for a specific word, a field that contains a part of a word, or even a range of figures or dates.

5. **In the Value field, select one of the available items that correspond to the selected Field Name item.**

6. **Click the Add to List button.**

   The query criteria appear in the columns in the middle part of the Advanced Query window.

7. **To select more than one criterion, repeat Steps 2 through 6.**

8. **Click in the And/Or column for the item and select an option if necessary.**

   As you build the query you may want to make use of the And/Or column. This column helps you group your criteria in order to indicate the relationship between each set of criteria. In Figure 7-10, notice that the two state criteria are bracketed together and joined by the word *or,* indicating that you're looking for contacts from either Florida or Oregon.

9. **Use the parenthesis column if necessary.**

   The example in Figure 7-10 groups the two state criteria together with parentheses so that these queries are carried out together.

10. **Click Preview.**

    For those of you in need of instant gratification, you can see a list of all the contacts that match your specification. And, if you goofed and no contacts show up, you can quickly remove a few of your criteria and try again before anyone notices by clicking the Remove button.

11. **When you finish selecting criteria, click OK.**

12. **At the Run Query Options message, select the Replace Lookup option, and click OK.**

    The results of the query display in the Contact List or Opportunities List.

Chapter 8

Stamping Out the Sticky Note

· ·

· ·

*L*ook around your desk. If you have more than one sticky note attached to it, you need to use ACT! Look at your computer monitor; if it's decorated with sticky notes, you need to use ACT!. Does a wall of sticky notes obscure your file folders? Do you panic when you can't find your pad of sticky notes? Do you have small sticky notes clinging to larger sticky notes? You need to use ACT!!

In this chapter, I show you how to make a note in ACT!. I also tell you all about the notes or *histories* that ACT! creates for you automatically and give you a short course in reviewing your notes.

Getting to Know ACT! Notes

What if one of your best clients called requesting a price quote? You jot down some information on a piece of paper — only to have the paper disappear in the mountain of clutter that you call your desk.

Or imagine that one of your more high-maintenance customers calls you on March 1 in immediate need of an imported Italian widget. You check with your distributors and guarantee him one by March 15. On March 10, he calls you, totally irate that he hasn't yet received his widget.

Sound familiar? The ACT! note is one of the easiest features to master but one that too many users overlook. A simple note in ACT! provides you with several benefits:

- ✔ Your entire office can now be operating on the same page by having access to the same client data.

- ✔ You have a record, down to the date and time, of all communications that you have with each of your contacts.

- ✔ You won't forget what you said to your customer.

- ✔ You won't forget what your customer said to you.

Adding a note

Considering the importance of notes to the overall scheme of your business, they are amazing easy to add. Here's all you have to do to add a note to a contact record:

1. **Make sure that you're on the contact for which you're creating a note.**

2. **Click the Contacts icon on the Nav bar.**

3. **On the Notes tab (middle of the screen), click the Insert Note icon.**

   The Insert Note window appears, date- and time-stamped with the current date and time. Take a look at Figure 8-1.

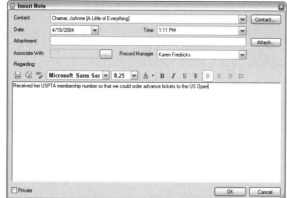

Figure 8-1:
Creating a
note in
ACT!.

4. **Start typing your note in the Regarding area.**

   Your note can be as long or short as you want. You can use the formatting options exactly as you do in any word processor to ***emphasize*** any portion of your note.

5. Click OK to record your note.

That was almost too easy for you; now you can move on to a few tricks that I have up my sleeve.

Working with notes

After you create a note (see the preceding section), you may need to change it. To edit a note, just double-click it to get back to the Insert Note window. After you open it, here are a few things you can change:

- ✔ **Change the note information:** Start typing in the Regarding area exactly as you do with any word processor.

- ✔ **Change the date on a note:** No matter how much you depend on your computer, sometimes you still rely on good old-fashioned paper. Maybe you've jotted down a note after you turned off your computer for the day or made notes — both mental and on paper — at a trade show. When you start to input those notes into ACT!, they all have the current date rather than the date when you actually created them. To change the date on a note, simply click the date and choose a new date from the drop-down menu that appears.

  Not all notes are created equally; some of your notes might be more important than others. As your list of notes becomes longer, various key notes may get lost in the shuffle. A real low-tech solution is to postdate the note by giving it a date several years into the future so that your note always appears at the top of the Notes tab.

- ✔ **Attach files to a contact record:** In Chapter 5, I talk about adding files to the Documents tab so that you can view and edit them right from the Contact Detail window. In addition, you can attach a file to a note in a contact record. To attach a file to a note, follow these steps:

  1. Click the Insert Note icon on the Notes tab.

  2. Click the Attach button in the Insert Note window.

  3. Navigate to the file that you want to attach and click Open.

  4. Click OK to record the note.

  To view the attached file, simply open the note and click the attached file.

- ✔ **Spell check a note:** If you're like me, you type notes while doing a hundred other things and end up with a lot of typos. Don't fret; just run a spell check by clicking the Spell Check icon in the Insert Note window. ACT! opens the spell checker and locates any misspellings. Unfortunately, you can check the spelling for only one note at a time.

Discovering ACT! Histories

If you insist on doing things the hard way, feel free to skip this section. If you love the thought of having someone else doing your work for you, read on!

Maybe you've noticed that the History tab is called, well, the History tab. In the earlier sections of this chapter, I show you how to add and modify notes. ACT!'s history entries are items that magically appear on the History tab after you

- Delete a contact (Chapter 4)
- Complete a scheduled meeting, call, or to-do (Chapter 9)
- Write a letter, fax, or mail merge (Chapter 13)
- Change information in a field designated to create history (Chapter 15)

When you clear an activity, a history of the activity is recorded in the contact record of the person with whom you scheduled the activity. You can also edit or add activity details to the history, such as adding information about the decisions made during the meeting. View these histories again later or create reports based on activities with your contacts.

Creating field histories

ACT! provides you with a very powerful tool when you combine the use of drop-down lists with the ability to create a history based on the changed information in the field. By default, ACT! automatically creates a history when you change the information in either the ID/Status or Last Results field. When you enter information into either of these fields, it's automatically saved on the contact's History tab.

Suppose that you've created ten steps to coincide with the average progression of one of your prospects into a customer. You need to create these steps by using ACT!'s Last Results field. As you progress through the sales cycle and change the content of the Last Results field, ACT! automatically creates a history indicating when the change took place. Figure 8-2 shows both the content of the Last Results field and the automatic histories that are created as the contact progresses through the sales stages.

By relying on the field's drop-down list to create new content information, you ensure that your information remains consistent. You can then create reports on the various sales stages by creating a lookup based on the notes and histories.

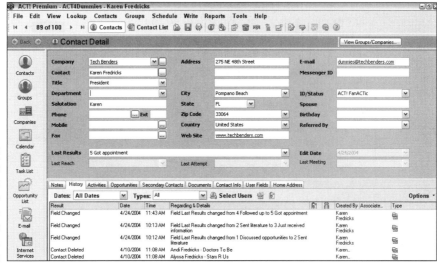

Figure 8-2:
Changing
the sales
step in the
Last Results
field.

In Chapter 7, I show you everything you need to know about creating
lookups — and then some! Chapter 11 explains the various ACT! reports
and shows you how to filter them by date range.

Recording activity histories

In Chapter 9, I explain how to use ACT! to plan your busy schedule. After you
hold or attend a meeting, place a call, or complete something on your to-do
list, clearing the activity is important. Figure 8-3 shows you the ACT! dialog box
that opens each time you clear an activity. Select the Add Details to History
check box, and ACT! automatically inserts a history on the History tab.

ACT! provides you with the same option when you get in touch with a contact
through a letter, e-mail, or fax. Figure 8-4 shows the Create History dialog box
that appears after you create a letter in ACT!. Of course, you can always
choose not to include a history, but you'll probably find recording one more
useful. You can even add more details in the Regarding area.

Manually recording a history

Situations arise when recording a history of an event just isn't possible. You
can create a history record for a contact without scheduling and clearing an
activity for that person. You can even add a history for someone who isn't
yet in your database. For example, you might have called a potential new
client from your car and found juggling the steering wheel, your phone, and

your lunch while typing on your laptop a bit too daunting a task. But when you return to the office, you still need to record the calls that you made and the tasks that you completed.

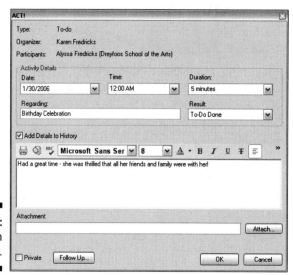

Figure 8-3:
Clearing an
activity.

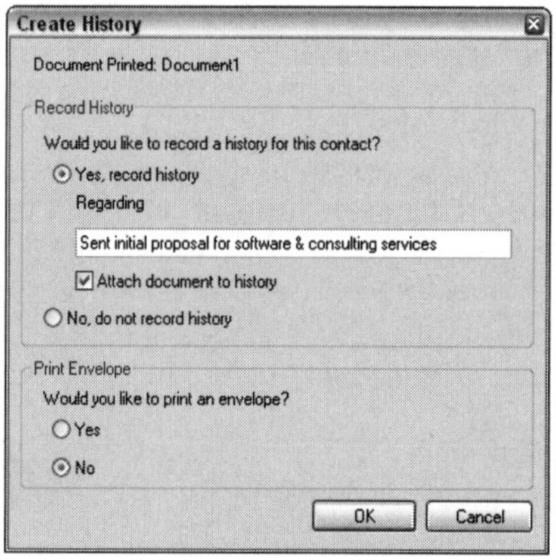

Figure 8-4:
Attaching
a history
to a letter.

You can also record one history for an entire group of people. For example, you might have attended a meeting at your local Chamber of Commerce and want to record a few details about the meeting for each of the attendees. Regardless of why you need to do it, here's how you create a history after the fact:

 1. **Find the contact for whom you want to record a history.**

    If you're creating a history for an entire group of people, create a lookup of the contacts for whom you want to add a note and then

a. Switch to the Contact List.

b. Click the Tag All button to select all the contacts. (See Chapter 6 for the details on tagging.)

2. **Choose Contacts⇨Record History.**

   The Record History window opens, as shown in Figure 8-5.

3. **Select an activity type from the Type list.**

   If you need more activity types, don't worry. Chapter 10 shows you how to increase your selection of activity types.

4. **Select a Result option.**

5. **Enter date, time, and duration information.**

6. **Enter activity information in the Regarding field or select a description from the drop-down list.**

7. **Add additional information in the Details area.**

   The information that you enter here is added to the Regarding field on the History tab.

8. **Click OK to record the history.**

   Your note is now recorded in the contact's record. If you created a history for an entire group of contacts, the note appears in the contact record of each individual in the group.

If you click the Follow Up button instead of OK, you can schedule a new, follow-up activity in the same way that you scheduled your original activity. Talk about one-stop shopping! The result of your phone call might be that you left a message or that you attempted to make the call but couldn't get through. By scheduling a follow-up activity, you have the results of your original phone call — and a reminder to try to make contact again in the future. You can also schedule follow-up activities for the next step in your sales process.

Figure 8-5:
The Record
History
window.

Working with Your Notes and Histories

The Notes and History tabs are very similar, and consequently, you can use them in similar ways. They are so similar in fact that in previous versions of ACT!, they were actually combined into one single tab. Here are a few things that you can do to make working with notes and histories even easier.

- **Delete a note or history.** To delete a note or history, you must first select it and then press the Delete key; the note is gone. You can also right-click the selected note and choose Delete Selected from the menu. Either way, ACT! presents you with a warning before you remove the note permanently.

- **Delete several notes and/or histories.** Eventually, you want to delete certain notes or even histories. To delete several notes in one fell swoop, just select the notes that you want to delete and then press the Delete key:

  - If you're selecting several continuous notes, click the first note, and then press the Shift key while clicking the last note that you want to delete.

  - If the entries aren't continuous, press the Ctrl key while clicking each note individually.

    Now that you know how easy changing a history is, you may want to prevent other users of your database from changing them. If you're the database administrator, choose Tools➪Preferences. Then, on the General tab, remove the check mark next to the Allow History Editing option.

- **Copy a note.** When you find duplicate contacts in your database, you probably want to delete them — but not any notes attached to them. Or, maybe you want a note from one contact record also attached to another record. Luckily, ACT! gives you the ability to copy notes from one contact to another contact with a simple copy-and-paste procedure:

  a. Highlight the notes or histories that you want to copy and then press Ctrl+C.

  b. Find the contact where you want to insert the copied notes and, on the Notes or History tab, press Ctrl+V.

If you're feeling somewhat artistic, in need of a change, or just plain having trouble with your forty-something eyesight, you may want to either add grid-lines around your notes or change the color and/or font style. Or, you might just decide to walk on the wild side and change the whole ball of wax. Take a stroll down preference lane to accomplish this:

1. **Choose Tools➪Preferences from any ACT! screen.**

   The Preferences dialog box opens.

2. **Click the Colors and Fonts tab.**

3. **Select the Notes tab.**

4. **Click the Font button to select a different font, style, or size.**

5. **Click OK to close the Font window.**

6. **Choose a text color and background color from the Appearance area.**

7. **Select the Show Grid Lines check box if you want gridlines to appear on the Notes tab.**

   The ACT! gridlines are just like the gridlines you see in Excel. If you change your preference to show gridlines, horizontal lines appear between each of your notes and vertical lines between columns.

8. **Repeat Steps 3 through 7 for the History tab.**

9. **Click OK.**

   Your Notes and History tabs are now modified according to the preference settings that you selected.

Chapter 9

Playing the Dating Game

*I*n this chapter, I show you how to schedule activities with your contacts, how to view those activities and modify them if necessary, and even how to find out whether you've completed a scheduled activity. You also discover the intricacies of navigating through the various ACT! calendars, how to use your Task List to keep you on top of your activities, and the joy of sharing a list of your scheduled activities with others.

Scheduling Your Activities

One of the most useful of ACT!'s features is its ability to tie an activity to a contact. More basic calendaring programs allow you to view your appointments and tasks on your calendar, but they don't offer a way of cross-referencing an appointment to a contact. For example, if you schedule an appointment with me and forget when that appointment is, you have to flip through your calendar until you see my name. Plus, you can't easily see a list of all appointments that you've ever scheduled with me. But ACT! offers these helpful features.

In ACT!, every activity is scheduled with a specific contact. If the contact doesn't exist in your database, add the person to your database — or schedule the appointment with yourself.

Here's what you do to add an activity to your busy schedule:

1. **Go to the contact with whom you're scheduling an activity.**

   Here's the drill. You create a lookup (I show you how in Chapter 7) to find a prospect's phone number. You call the guy, and afterward, you want to schedule a meeting. At this point, you're already on the contact record of the person with whom you're scheduling an activity.

2. Schedule a call, meeting, or to-do in one of three ways:

- Click the Call, Meeting, or To-Do icon on the toolbar in the Contact Detail window or the Contact List.

- Choose Call, Meeting or To-Do from the Schedule menu in just about any of the ACT! views.

- Double-click the appropriate time slot on any of the ACT! calendars.

Using different methods to schedule different activities is a smart plan of action. For example, I recommend scheduling meetings through the calendars to make sure that you don't have a conflict for a specific time slot. When you're scheduling calls and to-dos, however, which are generally "timeless" activities, you can simply click the corresponding icon on the toolbar.

In any case, all roads lead to the Schedule Activity dialog box, shown in Figure 9-1.

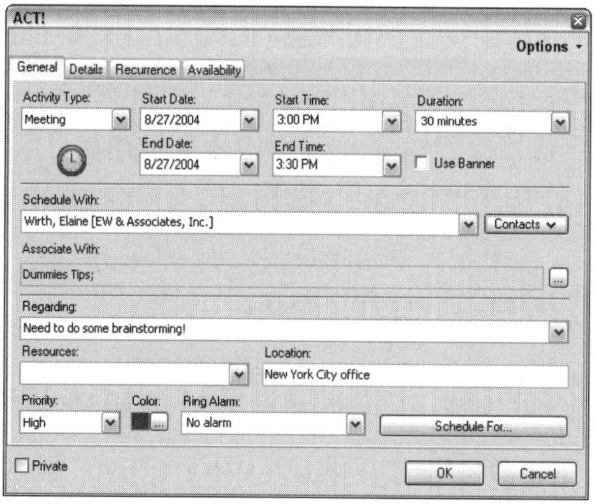

Figure 9-1:
Scheduling
an activity
in ACT!.

3. On the General tab, fill in the various options.

If Options is your name, ACT! is your game! The Schedule Activity dialog box offers a myriad of scheduling options from which to pick, and ACT! has thoughtfully filled in many of these options based on your default scheduling preferences. (Chapter 3 walks you through changing some of these preferences.) You can leave the information in the following fields as is or override the default preferences:

- **Activity Type:** Choose Call, Meeting, To-Do, Personal Activity, Support Ticket, or Vacation from the drop-down list.

- **Date:** Click the arrow to the right of the field to display the calendar and select a start and end date.

- **Time:** Enter a start and end time for the event. Choose Timeless for the Start Time if you're scheduling a call or to-do that doesn't need to occur at a specific time.

- **Duration:** Click the arrow to the right of the field to choose a duration for the activity. You can also manually specify a time range; an hour-and-a-half-long meeting can be entered as either **90 m** or **1.5 h**.

  The duration time is automatically set based on the starting and ending times you specify. If you change the duration, ACT! automatically adjusts the end time.

- **Schedule With:** The name of the current contact automatically appears here. Select a different contact by typing the first few letters of a contact's last name to locate the contact in the list.

- **Contacts:** Click the Contacts button and then choose Select Contacts to select more than one contact, New Contact to add a new contact, or My Record to schedule a personal appointment.

- **Priority:** Choose High, Medium-High, Medium, Medium-Low or Low.

- **Schedule For/By:** Click this button to assign a task to one of your co-workers. (As if ACT! hasn't made life easy enough for you already!)

You might want to use these optional fields as well:

- **Regarding:** If you want to give a brief description of the activity, type it here or choose an item from the drop-down list.

- **Color:** Click the arrow to the right of the field to display a color palette, and then choose the color that you want to assign to the activity. Feel free to design your own system of color-coding your calendar.

- **Ring Alarm:** Sets an alarm to remind you of a scheduled activity.

- **Use Banner:** Lets you display a banner on the monthly calendar if an activity involves one or more full days.

- **Options:** Allows you to confirm the activity with the contacts involved and then send the meeting as an attachment in an ACT! and/or Outlook format. You're also offered a second option to create a separate activity for each participant if you are scheduling your activity with more than one contact.

4. **On the Details tab, add additional details and print the details (if you want).**

These are two relatively important tasks:

- **Details:** Add additional information regarding an activity. For example, you may want to add special instructions about the items that you need to bring to a meeting.

- **Print:** This is where you can print the activity details.

5. **On the Recurrence tab, designate the activity as recurring if that's the case; otherwise, go to Step 6.**

   If the activity that you're scheduling repeats on a regular basis, you can designate it as a *recurring* activity rather than setting up several separate activities. For example, if you're taking a class that meets once a week for the next 12 weeks, you can designate the class as a meeting with a weekly recurrence. Be sure to specify the date on which the activity stops recurring.

   Here are the recurring option settings:

   • **Daily:** Select to schedule an activity that occurs daily and the date on which the activity stops.

   • **Weekly:** Select to schedule an activity that occurs weekly, on which day or days of the week the activity is scheduled, and the date on which the activity stops.

   • **Monthly:** Select to schedule an activity that occurs monthly, the weeks in the month when the activity is scheduled, the day of the week the activity is scheduled, and the date on which the activity stops.

   • **Yearly:** Select to schedule an activity that occurs every year, and the date on which the activity stops.

   The Annual Event field can eliminate the need to set reminders for activities, such as birthdays, anniversaries, and renewal dates. Find out how to set up an Annual Event field in Chapter 15.

6. **Click OK.**

   You now have a real, live scheduled activity!

After you create activities, ACT! is a worse nag than your mother! You can see your activities — and ACT! reminds you to complete them — in a number of ways:

   ✔ If you asked ACT! to ring the alarm when scheduling an activity, the ACT! Alarms window (see Figure 9-2) appears at the specified time before the activity is due. It also appears each time that you open ACT!.

   ✔ The Activities tab for a selected contact enables you to see what specific activities you've scheduled with that particular contact.

   ✔ The Task List shows a listing of everything you've scheduled for all your contacts during a specified time period.

   ✔ All ACT! calendars include a listing of the current day's events.

Later in this chapter, in the section "Exploring Activities," I show you how to view, edit, clear, and share your scheduled activities.

Figure 9-2:
The Alarms
window
reminds
you of
scheduled
activities.

Regardless of your method of viewing your activities, remember this tip: "When frustrated, check your filters." If you're just not seeing everything that you know is supposed to be showing in your calendar — check your filters! Not seeing anything scheduled for the future? Maybe your date range is set to show the activities for today only. Seeing too much? Perhaps your filters are set to show *everyone's* Task List or calendar. Not seeing *any* of your activities at all? Perhaps your filters are set to include everything *except* your own activities!

Working with the ACT! Calendar

The various ACT! calendars are great for viewing scheduled tasks. Here are a couple of ways to get to your calendars:

✔ Choose View and specify the type of calendar that you want to view.

✔ Click the calendar icon on the Nav bar.

You can view your calendar in any one of four different ways, depending on which way you feel the most comfortable:

- **Daily Calendar:** Shows you the time-specific activities of the selected day as well as a listing of the day's tasks (see Figure 9-3). The day is divided into half-hour intervals.

  Not happy with half-hour intervals? No problem; you can change that default setting in ACT!'s preference settings. Not sure how to do that? Take a peek at Chapter 3 to tweak your preferences.

- **Work Week:** Shows you the time-specific activities of the selected week as well as a listing of the day's tasks (see Figure 9-4). Each day is represented by a single column and divided into half-hour intervals.

- **Weekly Calendar:** Shows the entire week including Saturday and Sunday.

- **Monthly Calendar:** Shows you the time-specific activities of the selected month as well as a listing of the day's tasks (see Figure 9-5).

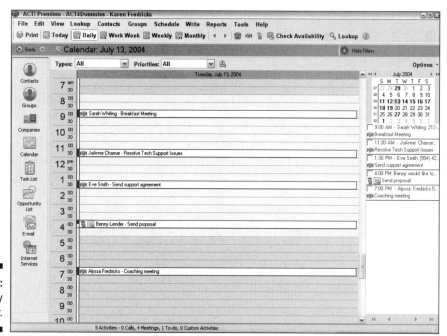

Figure 9-3:
The daily calendar.

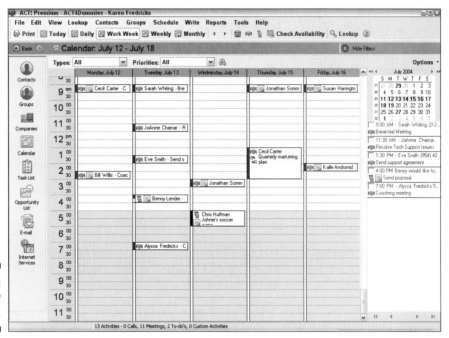

Figure 9-4:
A weekly
calendar.

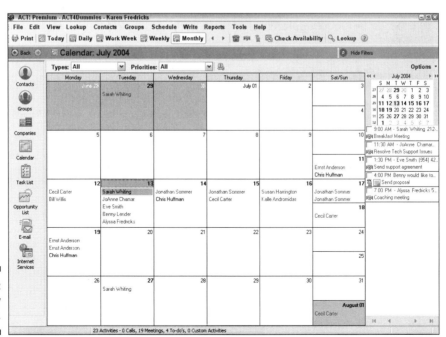

Figure 9-5:
The monthly
calendar.

The mini-calendar

The mini-calendar displays three months at one time (see Figure 9-6). The mini-calendar works a little differently from the daily, weekly, and monthly calendars. Press F4 to access the mini-calendar directly from the Contact Detail window. Right-click the day that you want to check, and a small window appears, displaying all activities scheduled for that day.

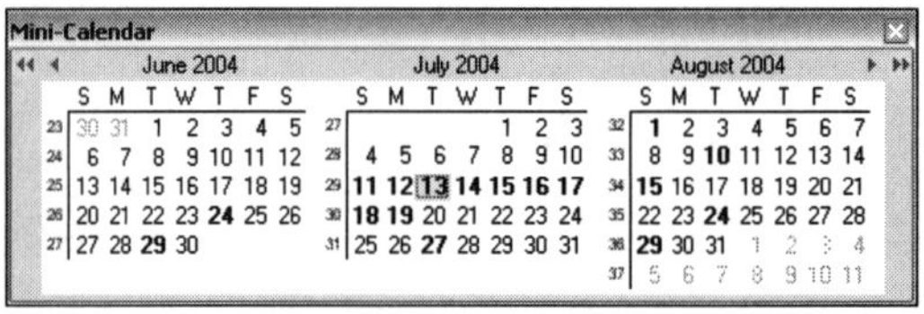

Figure 9-6:
A mini-
calendar.

After you access any of the ACT! calendars, you can navigate to a different date in one of the following ways:

- ✔ View today's activities by pressing Ctrl+Home.
- ✔ Get a daily synopsis by right-clicking any day on the mini-calendar.
- ✔ Go to a different year by clicking the double arrows.
- ✔ Go to a different month by clicking the single arrows.

The Recap List

If you take a peek at any of the calendars (except for the mini-calendar), you notice a little monthly calendar up at the top-right corner. This calendar provides you with a quick way to view a different calendar date by clicking it. A miniature to-do list appears right below the calendar. That's the Recap List. The Recap List lists all your scheduled activities on a specific day.

You can only view the Recap List of one user at a time, but you can have access to multiple users' Recap Lists. When you select multiple users, buttons with each user's name appear in the Recap List. Click the user's name to open or close his Recap List. If a selected user has no scheduled activities for the selected date, her name doesn't display in the Recap List. To view another user's Recap List, follow these steps:

1. **Click the Calendars icon on the Navigation bar.**

2. **Click the Select Users button.**

    The Select Users dialog box appears.

3. **Select the users whose Recap Lists you want to view, and then click OK.**

   I'm probably sounding like a broken record here, but remember that your friend, the Ctrl key, is conveniently located on both sides of your keyboard. If you press it, you can select more than one user by choosing the name in the dialog box.

4. **From the calendar, select the date for the Recap List you want to view.**

   The user's tasks display in the Recap List (see Figure 9-7). If you selected multiple users, you can click the button with the user's name to view that user's tasks.

Figure 9-7:
The Recap
List.

Using the Task List

Like the Honey Do list hanging from your husband's workbench, the ACT! Task List gives you a listing of *all* the activities for *all* your contacts.

The Task List is readily accessible by clicking the Task List icon on ACT!'s Nav bar. Figure 9-8 shows a sample Task List.

You can filter the Task List by using different criteria (see Figure 9-8):

- ✔ The date range of the activities
- ✔ The type of activity
- ✔ The priority of the activity
- ✔ The users whose activities you want to view
- ✔ The cleared status of the activities

Creating a lookup from the Task List

Here's the scenario. You wake up bright-eyed and bushy-tailed, ready to face another new day. You get to the office, view your Task List, and stop dead in your tracks: The length of your Task List is so long that you don't even know where to begin. Consider creating a lookup directly from the Task List. By spending the first hour of your day sending out all those faxes and brochures that you promised — and then the next hour returning your phone calls — you get everything done.

When you break down your tasks into manageable pieces — instead of having a breakdown yourself — the Task List becomes less intimidating.

Having said all that, I feel compelled to add that Rome wasn't built in a day, and you might not be able to complete *all* your tasks in a single day, either. ACT! has a preference that enables you to *roll over* your tasks to the next day if necessary. Check out Chapter 3 for a quick refresher on changing ACT! preferences.

1. **To open your Task List, click the Task List icon on ACT!'s Nav bar.**

2. **Select the date range of the activities for which you want to create a lookup.**

3. **Select the activity types in the Types area to indicate the activities that you want to work with.**

4. **Right-click the Task List and select Create Lookup.**

   ACT! creates a lookup of the selected activities. You can now scroll through your contacts and work on all similar tasks at the same time.

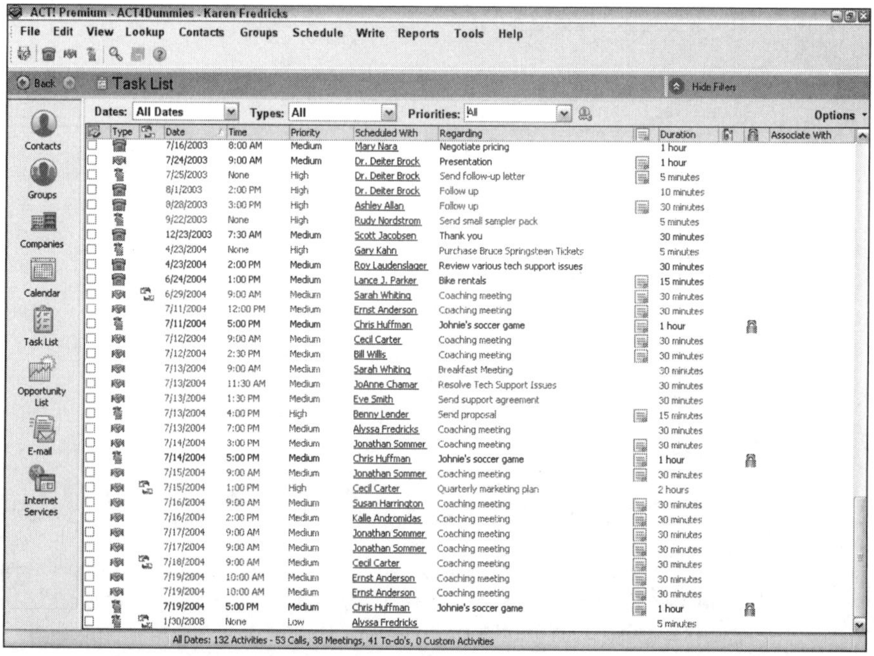

Figure 9-8:
The ACT!
Task List.

Printing the Task List

As great as ACT! is, it can be totally useless if you don't have access to a computer or hand-held device. Or maybe you work with a technically challenged co-worker (your boss?) who prefers to have a copy of his or her Task List printed on a daily basis. No need to fret; ACT! can easily perform this task for you:

1. **Click the Task List icon on the Nav bar.**
2. **Choose File⇨Quick Print Current Window.**

   The Quick Report dialog box opens.
3. **Click OK to print the Task List.**

Exploring Activities

In the first section of this chapter, "Scheduling Your Activities," I show you how to do exactly that. After scheduling an activity, you'll probably want to take a look at it. Or edit it. Or clear it. Or maybe even share it with others. So in this section, I show you how to do all these things.

Viewing the Activities tab

If you click the Activities tab at the bottom of the Contact Detail window, ACT! displays all the activities scheduled with the current contact. This is a great way to have a list of all the activities that you've scheduled with a contact.

You can see the Activities tab in Figure 9-9. You can filter your activities so that only certain activities show on the Activities tab. Your choices include

- ✔ Dates to show
- ✔ Types to show
- ✔ Priorities to show
- ✔ Users
- ✔ Private activities
- ✔ Timeless activities
- ✔ Cleared activities
- ✔ Outlook activities

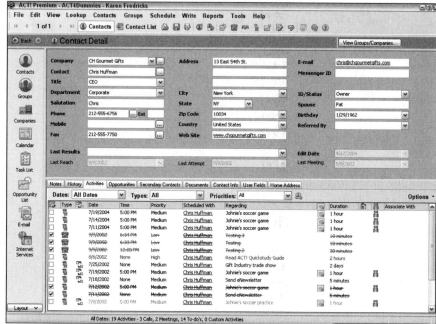

Figure 9-9:
The
Activities
tab.

TIP

Can't find the filter options for Private, Timeless, Cleared, and Outlook activities? Click the Options button, and you'll find them.

After you set your filters, you can also determine the columns that you want to appear on the Activities tab. These are the possibilities:

✔ The type, date, time, and duration of the activity

✔ The priority that you set for the activity

✔ The regarding information and any details that you entered for the activity

✔ The company and contact name

✔ The name of the group that the activity might be associated with

✔ The contact's phone number, extension, and e-mail address

✔ Additional activity details

✔ What ACT! user the activity was scheduled for and the ACT! user who scheduled the activity

✔ Any attachments associated with the big event

REMEMBER

After you determine the columns that you want to view on-screen, you can easily print a down-and-dirty report. In Chapter 5, I give you all the juicy details for rearranging the columns on the Activities tab — or on any other ACT! list for that matter — and turning it into a Quick Print report.

Editing your activities

Like all the best-laid plans of mice and men, your activities will change, and you need a way to make note of these changes in ACT!. Changing an activity is all in the click — or in this case, the *double-click* — of the mouse. If you can *see* an activity, you can *edit* it. That means you can edit your activities from the Activities tab, the Task List, or from any of the ACT! calendars. The only activities that you can't change are those that you've already cleared.

Clearing activities

After you complete a task, *clearing* the task is very important. When you clear a task, ACT! does several things:

✔ Stops reminding you about the activity

✔ Allows you to add some additional details about the activity

✔ Lets you schedule a follow-up activity if necessary

✔ Automatically updates the Last Reach, Last Meeting, or Last Attempt fields with the current date

✔ Creates an entry on the History tab of the contact with whom you had scheduled the activity

If you don't clear your activities, you're treated to a long list of alarms each and every time you open ACT!. Not only is this annoying, it can also be dangerous because you might also ignore *current* alarms!

To clear an activity, follow these steps:

1. **Select the activity that you want to clear by doing one of the following:**

   • In any Calendar view, select the check box next to the activity in the Recap List.

   • In the Task List or on the Activities tab, click the check mark column.

   • Right-click the activity and choose Clear Activity.

   Using any method, the Clear Activity dialog box appears (see Figure 9-10). The current date and time appear automatically. The Regarding information that you had originally entered for the activity appears as well. This information later appears in the Regarding column of the history that is automatically created when you clear an activity.

   The Clear Activity dialog box enables you to clear just one activity at a time. You can clear multiple activities from the Activities tab or the Task List:

   a. Hold down the Ctrl key while selecting additional activities to clear.

      b. Right-click the selected activities and then choose Clear Multiple Activities from the shortcut menu.

2. **Select a Result option.**

   The result determines the type of note that's added to the History tab as well as the system field that is affected. For example, if you indicate that a call was completed, two things happen:

   - A history is added to the History tab with Call Completed showing in the Type column.
   - The Last Reach field is changed to include today's date.

3. **Select the Add Details to History check box if you want to edit or add activity details.**

   Changes that you make to the Add Details area appear in the Regarding field on the History tab for the contact.

4. **Click the Follow Up Activity button to schedule a follow-up activity (if you want).**

   This is a very cool concept. When you clear an activity, ACT! gives you the option of scheduling a follow-up activity. Schedule a follow-up exactly like you schedule an original activity.

5. **Schedule the follow-up activity in the Schedule Activity dialog box and then click OK to return to the Clear Activity dialog box.**

6. **Click OK again, and you're done.**

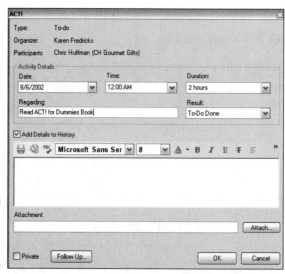

Figure 9-10:
Clearing an activity.

Part III
Sharing Your Information with Others

The 5th Wave   By Rich Tennant

"IT'S ANOTHER DEEP SPACE PROBE FROM EARTH, SEEKING CONTACT FROM EXTRATERRESTRIALS. I WISH THEY'D JUST INCLUDE AN E-MAIL ADDRESS."

In this part . . .

Entering contacts into ACT! is only half the fun. The other half consists of communicating with the outside world. So here you'll find out how to run and create reports for your internal purposes and also how to reach an audience of one or thousands through the use of snail mail or e-mail. You'll even find a large collection of commercial forms for printing (buried deep inside ACT!).

Chapter 10

Advanced Dating 101

. . . .

In This Chapter

▶ Scheduling an activity series

▶ Managing activity types

▶ Customizing results types and priorities

▶ Using annual events

. . . .

*O*ne common characteristic shared by most successful business people is their ability to verbalize the routine procedures that they do on a daily basis. In this chapter, you find out how to automate your procedures by creating an activity series. In Chapter 9, you discover how to create calendar activities; in this chapter, I show you how to modify the Activity and Result Type drop-down menus that you rely on when scheduling your activities. Finally, I cover Annual Events fields and how you use them to send out birthday and anniversary greetings.

Creating an Activity Series

Quite simply, an activity series is a series of steps that you may want to follow to achieve a specific goal. For example, you might have a six-step plan of action for every prospect that heads your way, or seven things you need to do during each of your customer related projects. Every time you meet a new prospect, you may want to lure him into using your services with a specific plan of action: send a brochure, follow it up with a phone call, send out a letter explaining some of the things you discussed in the phone call, and then finally send an e-mail further explaining your business. After the prospect becomes a customer, you may want to routinely send a welcoming letter, send out a proposal, wait for approval, and then wait for the deposit check to slide into your mailbox.

ACT! allows you to group these steps into one list in order for you to automate your process. By using an activity series, you can stick to your game plan. And, hopefully, some of those hot prospects turn into customers because you don't allow any of them to fall through the cracks. After this is created, you can schedule the series yourself or set a field trigger to automatically schedule the series.

Using the Activity Series Template Creation Wizard

Before you can schedule an activity series, you must create one using the Activity Series Template Creation Wizard. Here's where you develop the series by naming it, setting it as public or private, and adding activities. The wizard also allows you to edit or delete an existing activity series template. Follow these steps to start the wizard:

1. **Choose Schedule⇨Manage⇨Activity Series Templates from any ACT! screen.**

2. **In the Activity Series Template Creation Wizard, select the Create a New Activity Series radio button, and then click Next.**

    The wizard walks you through the next three steps.

3. **Fill in the name of your new activity series, indicate whether it's public or private, and then click Next.**

    Step 3 of the Activity Series Template Creation Wizard opens, as shown in Figure 10-1.

Figure 10-1: Creating an activity series.

4. **Click the Add button to add all the steps you want to include in your activity series.**

    The Add Activity dialog box opens; you can take a peek at it in Figure 10-2.

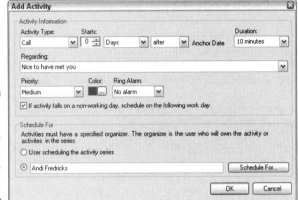

Figure 10-2:
Adding a
new activity
to an
activity
series.

5. Fill in the Add Activity dialog box and click OK.

Here's where you indicate all the pertinent details for each and every
step of your activity series. You have to enter several key pieces of information; don't worry if you make a mistake because you can always go
back and edit these steps if you don't get them right the first time.

- **Activity Type:** Indicate whether you're scheduling a call, meeting,
  to-do, or a custom activity (skip ahead to the "Adding custom
  activity types" section, later in this chapter, for more info about
  custom activities).

- **Starts:** Activity series are based on an *anchor date.* You can either
  schedule an activity that occurs *after* the anchor date, or activities
  that must be completed *before* the anchor date.

- **Regarding, Priority, Color, and Ring Alarm:** These fields are the
  exact same ones you encounter when scheduling a regular, run-of-
  the-mill activity.

- **If Activity Falls on a Non-Working Day, Schedule on the
  Following Work Day:** Select this check box to prevent an activity
  from being scheduled on a Saturday or Sunday.

- **Schedule For:** if you're like me, you like nothing better than dele-
  gating work on to another person. Here's where you can assign
  each Activity Series step to a poor, unsuspecting co-worker!

6. Repeat Step 5 as often as you need to and then click Next.

**7. Indicate whether you want to schedule the series now or later and
click Finish.**

Scheduling an activity series

After you create the template, you can schedule the series with one of your contacts and set the anchor date. All the activities link together so that if one activity changes to another date, you have the option to change only that activity to another date or to reschedule all the remaining activities.

1. **Create a lookup to find the contact or contacts with whom you want to schedule the activity series.**

   I've warned you repeatedly that ACT! saves you lots and lots of time. If scheduling an activity series with *one* person saves you time, just think of what scheduling one with a *bunch* of people does for you!

2. **Choose Schedule➪Activity Series.**

   The Schedule Activity Series dialog box appears, as shown in Figure 10-3.

Figure 10-3: Scheduling an activity series.

3. **Select the activity series template that you want to use, indicate the anchor date, and click OK.**

   The activities are now scheduled and appear on the appropriate spots on the contact's Activities tab, the Task List, and on the calendars. You might even notice that no time is associated with any of the activities; that's because activities scheduled as an activity series are automatically timeless.

   If you forgot to create a lookup or if you want to include a few more contacts, you can do it. Select one contact from the With drop-down menu, or select multiple contacts from the Contacts dialog box by clicking the Contacts button and selecting Select Contacts.

No conflict checking is performed when the activities are scheduled using an activity series. Your tasks are scheduled regardless if you are already scheduled to be on vacation or off attending a conference in Kalamazoo.

Before scheduling the series with a large number of contacts, test the series by scheduling it with just one contact. Then, take a gander at that contact's Activities tab to make sure that the activities appear in a logical sequence. If something appears amiss, delete all the scheduled activities from the contact's Activities tab and read on.

Modifying an activity series

Mistakes happen — and you may make one when initially setting up your activity series. Or you may wish to assign another employee to one of the steps in the series. Not to worry; here's all you need to do to modify the series:

1. **Choose Schedule⇨Manage⇨Activity Series Templates.**

2. **Select Edit an Existing Activity Series radio button in the first screen of the Activity Series Template Creation Wizard and then click Next.**

3. **Select the activity step that you wish to edit and click the Edit button.**

4. **Make the appropriate changes in the Add Activity dialog box and click OK.**

5. **Click OK in the Schedule Activity Series window when you finish modifying all the activities.**

Creating an Activity Series trigger

I have one other neat trick up my sleeve for you after you create an activity series. You can set a field trigger to automatically schedule the series when you leave, enter, or change a specific field.

1. **Choose Tools⇨Define Fields from any of the ACT! screens.**

2. **Select the field you want to add a trigger to and click Edit Field.**

3. **Click Next a few times until you arrive at the Select Trigger window.**

   The Select Trigger window appears, shown in Figure 10-4.

4. **Set one of the following trigger options:**

   • Select the Activity Series option from the When Changing a Field Launch drop-down menu to set a trigger when the value in a field changes.

- Select the Activity Series option from the When Entering a Field Launch drop-down menu to set a trigger when moving the cursor into the field.

- Select the Activity Series option from the When Leaving a Field Launch drop-down menu to set a trigger when moving the cursor out of the field.

5. **In the Activity Series Template field, select the activity series you want to launch, and then click OK.**

6. **Click Finish.**

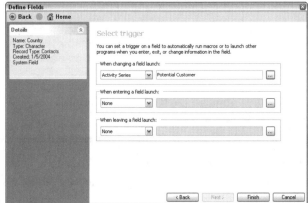

Figure 10-4:
Linking an
Activity
Series
template to
a field.

Adding custom activity types

Out of the box, ACT! gives you five activity types: call, meeting, to-do, personal activity, and vacation. You can modify this list of activity types by creating a custom activity type. To add a custom activity type, just follow the bouncing ball:

1. **Choose Schedule➪Manage➪Activity Types.**

   The Manage Activity Types dialog box appears, which bears a striking resemblance to Figure 10-5.

2. **Click Add.**

   The Add Activity Type dialog box appears, as seen in Figure 10-6.

   - Type the name for the activity type in the Name field.

   - Select the Active - Allow New Activities of This Type check box if you want to allow users to schedule activities of this type.

Figure 10-5:
Editing
existing
activity
types.

3. Create the result options to use when the task is completed.

When you create an activity type, two types of results are automatically assigned to it: *Completed* and *Not Completed.* You cannot delete these, but you can edit them. You can also add new result types. When you add a new result type, it's available as an option when you clear an activity.

- Click the Add button to add a new result type.

- Click the Edit button to edit a result type.

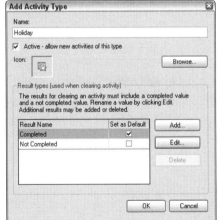

Figure 10-6:
Creating a
new activity
type.

4. Click OK in the Add Activity Type dialog box.

The activity type appears in the Activity Types list the very next time you schedule an activity.

Don't ask me why, but for some unknown reason, you can't delete an activity type after you create it. However, you can edit the activity and even change the name of the activity type. Go figure!

Editing priority types

If there is a square inch of ACT! that can't be customized, I haven't found it yet. Even the priorities you use can when scheduling activities can be tweaked. ACT! includes five basic priority types: High, Medium-High, Medium, Medium-Low, and Low. However, only three of the priority types (High, Medium and Low) are "active." A priority must have Active status in order for the Priority List to include it in the Schedule Activity Series dialog box. And, although you can't add a new priority type, you can rename an existing one if you so desire.

1. **Choose Schedule⇨Manage⇨Priorities from any of the ACT! screens.**

   The Manage Priorities dialog box opens, as seen in Figure 10-7.

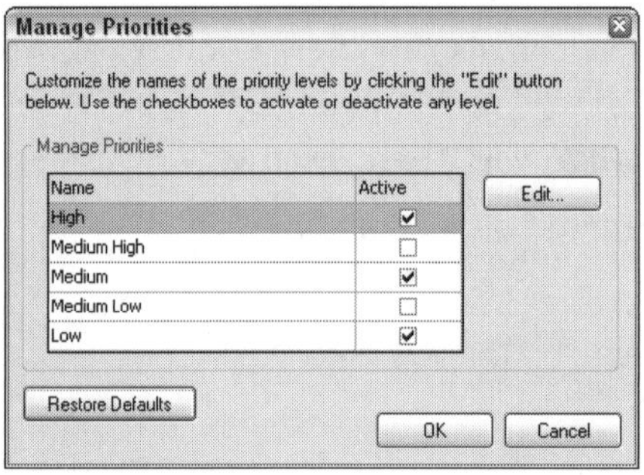

Figure 10-7:
The
Manage
Priorities
dialog box.

2. **Select the priorities you want to activate by selecting the check box in the Active column.**

3. **Highlight a priority and then click the Edit button to change the name of a priority.**

4. **Click OK when you finish editing the Priority List.**

Using Annual Events

You can create Annual Event fields that help you track events for important recurring dates such as birthdays, anniversaries, or annual policy renewals. The whole purpose of an annual event is that it happens once a year, like it or not. More importantly, you can query on an Annual Event field by day or month; for example, you could find all the January birthdays in your database without having to know the exact year of the birthday.

Annual Event fields are set up like other date fields in ACT! and, like other fields, can have specific options selected for them, such as whether the annual event is a required field, generates a history, or is protected.

Annual events do not display on calendars, but you can set a recurring to-do activity and an alarm to notify you of them. For example, you might create a to-do activity to remind you to create a lookup for all the birthdays occurring each month.

Creating an Annual Event field

Follow these steps to create an annual event:

1. **Choose Tools⇨Define Fields from any of the ACT! screens.**

2. **Select the field you want to turn into an Annual Event field and click Edit Field or click Create New Field and assign the field a name.**

3. **Select the Annual Event option from the Field Data Type drop-down menu and click Finish.**

    Your final product looks something like Figure 10-8.

Figure 10-8:
Creating an
Annual
Event field.

Creating a lookup of annual events

Follow these steps to create a lookup of your annual events:

1. **Choose Lookup⇨Annual Events.**

    As fast as you can say "abracadabra," the Annual Events Search dialog box, as shown in Figure 10-9, magically appears.

2. **Select an event or events from the Search For drop-down menu.**

    ACT! allows you to search on more than one field at a time. For example, you may wish to find everyone who has either a birthday or an anniversary in the month of January.

Figure 10-9:
Creating a
lookup of
Annual
Events.

3. Select a time range from the Current Week, Current Month, or date range options and then click the Find Now button.

After you find all the contacts that match your criteria, you have several options available to you. You can

- **View all contacts that match your criteria.** Click the Create Lookup button to look at your contacts on-screen or click the Print List button to print the lookup.

- **Display a specific contact record.** Select the contact from the list and then click the Go To Contact button.

- **Schedule a recurring to-do activity for the event.** Select a contact from the list and click the Schedule To-Do button.

Chapter 11

Using the Basic ACT! Reports

*A*fter you build your database, the fun part is sitting back and using it. If paper is your game, then ACT! is surely the name — at least of the software that you should be using for any type of reporting. In Chapter 12, I demonstrate how to design your very own reports. Here in this chapter, I discuss the various ACT! reports that are available.

In this chapter, I show you everything you always wanted to know about ACT! reports but were afraid to ask. After reading this chapter, you'll be familiar with the various reports, know how to run them, and also know techniques for sharing those reports with colleagues. You also find out about some of the "non-reports" that are buried away in some unexpected places.

Knowing the Basic ACT! Reports

ACT! comes with a menu of over 30 basic reports right out of the box. In Chapter 12, I show you how to customize existing reports or create new ones. Here I list the basic reports, briefly describing each. Chances are good that at least one of the basic ACT! reports gives you exactly the information that you're looking for.

If you really want to see first hand what each ACT! report looks like, consider opening up the Act7Demo database and printing out the first page of each report. Then, stick all the reports in a notebook. If you want to get really fancy, stick them in sheet protectors first. That way, if you ever need to run a report, you can go back to your printouts for a quick reference before you start running a lot of unnecessary reports.

The first three reports in the ACT! Reports menu are probably among the most useful because they supply you with information for each of your contacts. You can determine which one best suits your needs by deciding whether you want to view a page, a paragraph, or simply one line of information about your contact.

- ✓ **Contact Report:** A one-page report showing all the contact information for each contact, including the notes, history, and activities.

- ✓ **Contact Directory:** Prints the primary address and home address for each contact in paragraph form.

- ✓ **Phone List:** Prints the company name, company phone number, phone extension, and mobile phone number for each contact; the report displays one line of content for each contact.

The next several reports display information that's pertinent to you and your notes and activities:

- ✓ **Activities:** Shows you the scheduled and completed calls, meetings, and to-do's scheduled with each contact during a specified date range. The Task List is sorted by contact so that you can see a listing of all the time that you've spent — or are scheduled to spend — with any given contact.

- ✓ **History Summary:** Produces a list of every attempted call, completed call, meeting held, letter sent, and field changed for each contact during a specified date range sorted by contact. Figure 11-1 shows you the top part of an unfiltered History Summary report.

- ✓ **History Summary Classic:** Shows the numerical total of attempted calls, completed calls, meetings held, and letters sent for each contact during a specified date range sorted by contact.

The History Summary report displays only those contacts that you've contacted during a specific date range. The History Summary Classic report, however, displays a list of all your contacts, including contacts that you have contacted as well as those that you have not contacted. If you end up producing a 50-page report, I suggest creating a Contact Activity lookup before running the report. If you need help with creating a lookup, turn to Chapter 7.

- ✓ **History Time Spent:** Shows the date, time, duration, and information regarding activities scheduled with each contact during a specified date range. You get a subtotal of the time that you've spent with each contact as well as of the time that you're still scheduled to spend with them — if you assign a time duration to your meetings, calls, and to-do's.

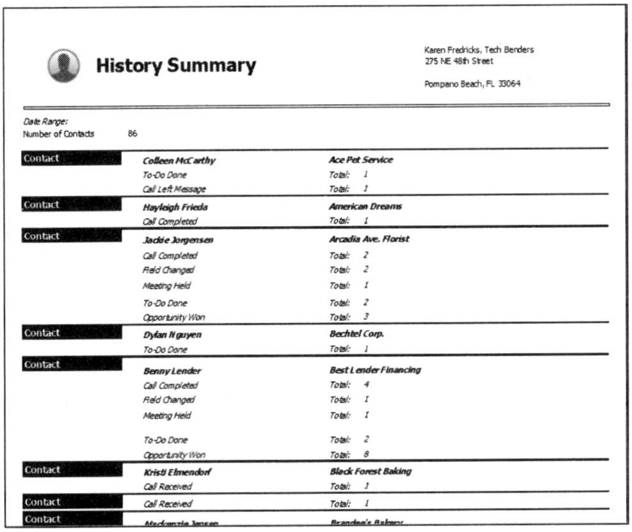

Figure 11-1:
The ACT!
History
Summary
report.

The next two reports are based on information in two of the key ACT! fields:

- ✔ **Contact Status:** Shows you the ID/Status, last reach, last meeting, and last results for each contact during a specified date range. You'll likely want to create a Contact Activity lookup before running this report to avoid having a lot of empty contact information in your final report.

- ✔ **Source of Referrals:** Changing certain default fields isn't a good idea. Here's one reason why: The Source of Referrals report relies on the information in the Referred By field. Figure 11-2 shows you an example of the Source of Referrals report and plainly shows what happens if you don't enter data consistently. *Dave* Davis and *David* Davis are probably the same person, yet they show up in two different spots in the report.

- ✔ **Other Contact Reports:** This is a good place to store other reports that you might have created. You also find two additional reports, E-Mail List and Fax List, stored here.

You can find the Group reports together in a subsection of the main Reports menu. These reports give you different ways to view the information in your groups. If you aren't using groups (which I explain fully in Chapter 21), these reports might not be of any benefit to you.

- ✔ **Group Membership:** Lists all groups and their members.

- ✔ **Group Summary:** Lists the notes, histories, and activities for all groups or for specific groups.

- ✔ **Group Comprehensive:** Lists all information (including notes, histories, and activities) for each group, subgroup, and their respective members.

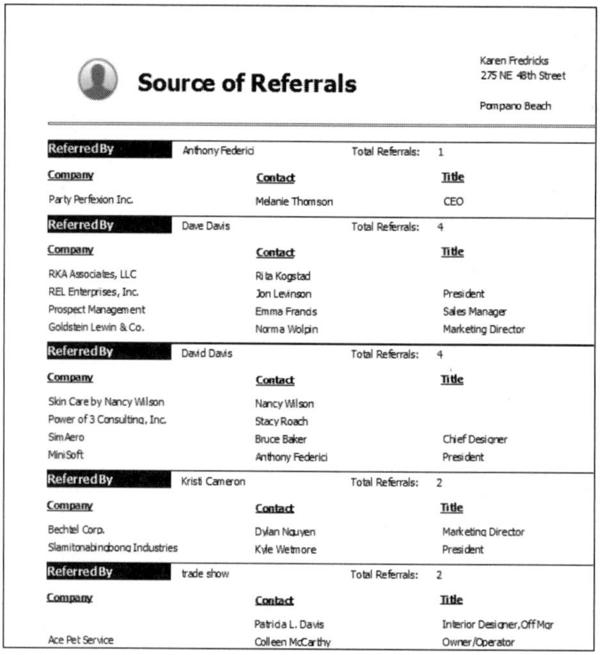

Source of Referrals

Karen Fredricks
275 NE 48th Street

Pompano Beach

Referred By	Anthony Federici	Total Referrals: 1
Company	**Contact**	**Title**
Party Perfexion Inc.	Melanie Thomson	CEO

Referred By	Dave Davis	Total Referrals: 4
Company	**Contact**	**Title**
RKA Associates, LLC	Rita Kogstad	
REL Enterprises, Inc.	Jon Levinson	President
Prospect Management	Emma Francis	Sales Manager
Goldstein Lewin & Co.	Norma Wolpin	Marketing Director

Referred By	David Davis	Total Referrals: 4
Company	**Contact**	**Title**
Skin Care by Nancy Wilson	Nancy Wilson	
Power of 3 Consulting, Inc.	Stacy Roach	
SimAero	Bruce Baker	Chief Designer
MiniSoft	Anthony Federici	President

Referred By	Kristi Cameron	Total Referrals: 2
Company	**Contact**	**Title**
Bechtel Corp.	Dylan Nguyen	Marketing Director
Slamitonabindbong Industries	Kyle Wetmore	President

Referred By	trade show	Total Referrals: 2
Company	**Contact**	**Title**
	Patricia L. Davis	Interior Designer,Off Mgr
Ace Pet Service	Colleen McCarthy	Owner/Operator

Figure 11-2: ACT!'s Source of Referrals report.

- **Group List:** Lists all groups and their description from the Group Description field.
- **Other Group Reports:** This is a great place to store your own customized group reports.

You find the Company reports together in a subsection of the main Reports menu. These reports give you different ways to view the information in your companies. If I sound like a broken record, it's because the five Group reports that I mentioned earlier all come in a "company version."

ACT! provides you with a variety of Opportunity reports, funnels, and graphs. The Opportunity reports use information inputted onto the Opportunities tab. If you aren't using the Opportunities feature (head to Chapter 20 for the lowdown), you can't use these reports. The Opportunity Reports are all housed in a separate Opportunity section in the Reports menu.

- **Totals by Status:** Garners totals of all sales opportunities and sorts them by Closed/Won Sales, and Lost Sales.
- **Adjusted for Probability:** Lists all sales opportunities by contact, with totals.
- **Pipeline Report:** Gives information about sales opportunities at each stage in the sales process.

- ✔ **Opportunities by Record Manager:** Lists sales opportunities, Closed/Won Sales, and Lost Sales sorted by Record Manager.

- ✔ **Opportunities by Contact:** Provides complete sales information for each contact with a sales opportunity or a closed sale.

- ✔ **Opportunities Graph:** Gives forecasted or closed sales, in a bar or line graph.

- ✔ **Opportunities Pipeline:** Gives the number of sales opportunities at each stage of the sales process, in a graphical form.

- ✔ **Other Opportunity Reports:** Check in this section for a number of additional opportunity reports including Gross Margin reports, opportunity reports by company and or group, and a Sales by Reason report.

Running an ACT! Report

The following steps apply to all ACT! reports. The dialog box is the same for all reports. Depending on the report that you're running, however, some of the options may be unavailable and thus appear grayed out.

To run an ACT! report, just follow these steps:

1. **Perform a lookup or display the contact record or records that you want to include in the report.**

   All roads in ACT! lead — or at least pass by — the lookup. Before running a report, decide which contact's or group's data you want to include in your report. For example, you may run a History Summary Report for a single contact or a Contact Report for all contacts in a state or region. You can include data from the current contact or group record, the current contact or group lookup, or from all contacts or groups.

2. **Sort the contacts before running the report if you want the contacts in the report to appear in a particular order.**

   Do you want the contacts to appear alphabetically by company name or by last name? If you have numerous contacts with the last name Smith, do you then want to sort them by company or state? You must make these decisions *before* running an ACT! report.

   Sort your contacts in one of two ways: Sort by up to three criteria by choosing Edit⇨Sort, or sort your contact by a criterion by clicking the appropriate contact heading in the Contact List.

3. **Choose the Reports menu and then select the name of the report that you want to run. To run a report that doesn't appear in the menu, choose Reports⇨Other Contact Reports and select the appropriate report.**

The Define Filters dialog box opens, as shown in Figure 11-3. The General tab is identical for any and all ACT! reports that you create.

4. **In the Send the Report Output To drop-down list, select an output for the report:**

   • **Preview:** Choose the Preview option if you're at all hesitant about your reporting capabilities. A preview of the report appears on-screen. After previewing the report, print it or run it again if it isn't looking exactly the way that you intended it to look.

   • **Rich-Text File:** Saves the report as an RTF file, which you can open in Word.

   • **HTML File:** Saves the report as an HTML file. Choose this option if you want to use the report on your Web site.

   • **PDF File:** Saves the report as a PDF file that can be read in Adobe reader.

   • **Text File:** Saves the report as a TXT file, which you can read with a wide variety of software, including Excel.

   • **Printer:** If you're fully confident that your report will print correctly the first time, go for it! This option sends the report directly to your default printer.

   • **E-mail:** Sends the saved report as an attachment to an e-mail message. The attachment has an `.rpt` extension and can be read only by recipients who have ACT! installed on their computers.

5. **In the Create Report For area, specify the contacts to include in the report.**

   The choices are self-explanatory. You're either going to run the report for the current contact, the current lookup, or all contacts.

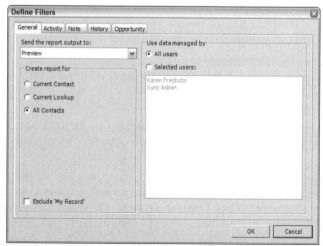

Figure 11-3:
The Define
Filters
dialog box.

If you sorted the contacts, select the Current Lookup radio button, even if you want to include all contacts in the database. If you don't select this option, the contacts in the report don't appear in the sort order that you specified.

6. **Select the Exclude 'My Record' check box to exclude information from your My Record in the report.**

   This option is not available for all reports.

7. **In the Use Data Managed By area, select the Record Manager of the contacts that you're including in your report.**

   • **All Users:** Includes contact records managed by all users of the database.

   • **Selected Users:** Includes contact records managed by selected users of the database. If you're the only user of the database, only your name appears in the list.

8. **On the Activities, Note, and/or History tabs, make the appropriate selections.**

   • On the Activities tab, select the type of activities and the corresponding date range of the activities to include in your report.

   • On the Note and History tab, select the type of histories and the corresponding date range that you're including in your report.

   • In the Use Data Managed By area, select the users whose information you want to include in the report.

9. **Click the Opportunity tab if you're running a Sales report.**

   Figure 11-4 shows the Opportunity tab that appears in the various sales report.

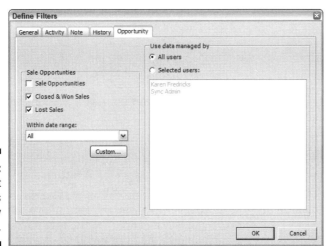

Figure 11-4:
The report
filter's
Opportunity
tab.

- In the Sale Opportunities area, select whether you want to include Sales Opportunities, Closed/Won Sales, and/or Lost Sales in your report.

- In the Within Date Range drop-down menu, specify the date range of the Sales Opportunities to include in the report.

- In the Use Data Managed By area, choose to include information from All Users or Selected Users of your database.

10. **Click OK.**

    ACT! runs the report. If you aren't happy with the results, run the same report a second time by using different criteria, or try running a different report. Better yet, read Chapter 12 to discover how to create your very own ACT! reports.

Printing Address Books

Printing an address book is probably one of the more common tasks used by ACT! users, and ACT! makes the chore an extremely simple one to perform. Creating a hard copy of your ACT! address book is basically a three-step process:

1. Add all your contact information into your ACT! database, making sure that your information is as complete as possible.

2. Create a lookup of the contacts that you want to include in your address book.

    Of course, you may want to include all your contacts in the print copy of your address book. You might even want to print separate address books for each of the different types of contacts in your database.

3. Choose the format for your address book.

Those are the basic steps. The following step includes all the down-and-dirty details for creating your own printed address book:

1. **Create a lookup if you intend on printing only a portion of your address book.**

    Refer to Chapter 7 if you need a refresher course in creating an ACT! lookup.

2. **From any of the ACT! windows, choose File⇨Print.**

    Okay, I know you're probably scratching your head wondering why I'm asking you to print when you haven't created anything yet. That's the concept with these non-reports: They aren't actually reports by definition, so ACT! just threw them into the Print menu. Go figure!

The Print dialog box opens, as shown in Figure 11-5.

3. **Choose Address Book from the Printout Type area.**

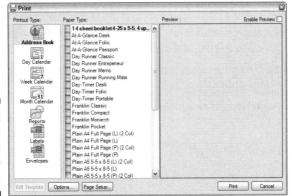

Figure 11-5:
Choosing
the form you
want to
print.

4. **Select the paper type for printing the address book.**

   ACT! enables you to print contact addresses and phone numbers in a variety of commonly used paper formats, including

   • At-A-Glance

   • Day Runner

   • Day Timer

   • Franklin

   You can print all your ACT! information onto preformatted addressing systems. ACT! provides you with the most popular, commercially available, addressing systems. The preprinted forms are available at any of the large office supply warehouse stores. If you are currently using an address system from one of these manufacturers, choose it from the Paper Type list.

   Figure 11-5 shows you some of your choices. You might notice that the Edit Template button is grayed out. That's because you can't make changes to the Address Book templates.

   Of course, if you don't want to spend the money on preprinted forms, or you just want a printout of your address book on a plain sheet of paper, you can always use my particular favorite form for printing an address book: plain paper.

   A preview of the selected printout appears in the Preview pane on the right.

5. **Click the Options button to specify the information to include in the address book.**

The Address Book Options dialog box opens, as shown in Figure 11-6.

6. **In the Print area, select the fields to include in your address book:**

 • **Primary Address:** Prints the contact's main address

 • **Secondary Address:** Prints the contact's home address

 • **Phone Numbers:** Prints all contact's phone numbers, including Work, Alt, Phone, Fax, Mobile Phone, Home Phone, and Pager

 • **Alternate Contacts:** Prints the second and third contacts' names and phone numbers

 • **E-mail Address:** Prints the contact's e-mail addresses

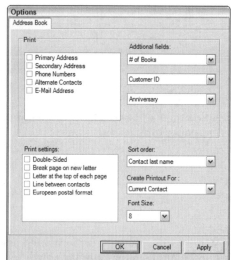

Figure 11-6:
The
Address
Book
Options
dialog box.

7. **In the Additional fields drop-down menus, add up to three additional fields.**

 The choices in Step 6 are based on the default fields that come with ACT!. If you've added several new phone number fields, they don't appear in the printout of your address book, but ACT! allows you to add up to three additional fields.

8. **In the Print Settings area, select your printing option.**

 Here's where you get to determine how your address book is going to print:

 • **Double Sided Printing:** Prints the address book on both sides of the page

 • **Break Page on New Letter:** Starts a new page for each letter of the alphabet

- **Letter at Top of Each Page:** Prints the current alphabetic letter at the top of each page

- **Lines Between Contacts:** Prints a line between contact entries

- **European Postal Format:** Prints the postal code before the city

9. **In the Sort Order drop-down menu, select the order in which you want entries to appear in your address book — alphabetically either by company name or contact last name.**

10. **In the Create Printout For drop-down menu, specify whether to include the Current Contact, the Current Lookup, or All Contacts.**

11. **If desired, change the Font Size option.**

12. **Click OK.**

    The Print dialog box re-appears.

13. **Click the Print button.**

14. **Click OK in the Windows Print dialog box.**

15. **Run to your printer and admire your newly printed address book.**

Creating Mailing Labels and Envelopes

All right. You've created a brochure that's guaranteed to knock the socks right off of your customers — and potential customers. Now all you have to do is send those puppies out in the mail. There is no easier method to do this than by creating mailing labels or envelopes using ACT!.

Some of you may be snickering about now because you're much too sophisticated to be using snail mail. You've probably already raced over to Chapter 13 to find out how to create e-mail blasts. You might still use the ACT! labels to create everything from file tabs to name badges.

You print out labels and envelopes in ACT! in exactly the same way. At first glance, printing envelopes in ACT! to match a customized letter template seems like a great idea. After all, they look a lot more personalized than an ordinary mailing label. However, if your mailing entails sending personalized letters to a large number of people, you may want to rethink your decision. Unless you have a specially designed envelope tray, you're probably going to have to print your envelopes in batches. But remember that 30 envelopes are much bulkier and harder to store than a page of 30 labels. While you print each batch of envelopes, you have to make sure that they remain in the exact same order as your letters, or matching them to the corresponding letter could become a nightmare.

If you're printing envelopes, I suggest limiting the number of envelopes that you print at any one time. If you're just printing a single envelope for one person to go with a letter that you just created using a document template, using your word processor to create the envelope is probably easier than using ACT!. ACT! automatically asks whether you want to print an envelope after you create a document using a document template. (See Chapter 13 for the details.)

To create labels or envelopes using ACT!, just follow these steps:

1. **Create a lookup of the contacts for whom you want to create labels or envelopes.**

   If you're creating a personalized mailing, I'd guess that you've already created a lookup of the contacts that get the mailing. By creating the corresponding labels using the existing lookup, you're guaranteed to have the same number of contacts and to have your labels print in the same sort order.

2. **Choose File⇨Print from any ACT! window.**

3. **Choose Labels or Envelopes from the Printout Type list.**

   From this point forward, I focus on creating labels, but these directions also work for envelopes. Just substitute the word *envelope* for the word *label* in any of the directions.

4. **Select a template from the list and click the Print button.**

   The available label templates are listed on the Paper Type area of the dialog box.

   Notice that all the labels are Avery labels. Chances are that even if you're using a generic label, you find the magic words "Same as Avery Label #XX" printed on the side of the box.

   The Define Filters dialog box appears, as shown in Figure 11-7.

5. **In the Send the Report Output To drop-down menu, select to immediately print or to first preview the labels.**

   Previewing the labels before printing them is always a good idea. You can print them directly from the Preview screen if everything looks hunky-dory.

6. **In the Create Report For area, specify whether you want to create labels for the Current Contact, the Current Lookup, or All Contacts.**

   If you've sorted your database, choose the Current Lookup option even if you are printing your entire database.

7. **Select All Users or Selected Users from the Use Data Managed By area.**

   This option refers to the Record Manager of each contact. You might want to print labels for just your own contacts.

8. **Click OK.**

   You're now the proud owner of a beautiful set of labels.

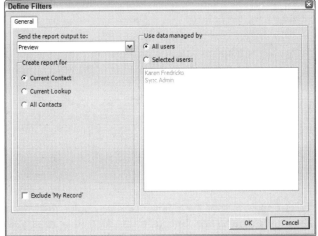

Modifying Labels and Envelopes

You may decide that your labels need a little extra pizzazz. Maybe you want to add another field or make a field longer. Maybe you think a font change is in order. All modifications that you may have in mind can be accomplished from the label template editor:

1. **Choose File⇨Print from any ACT! screen.**

2. **Choose Labels or Envelopes from the Printout Type list.**

3. **Click the Edit Template button to make modifications to an existing label template (if you want to make modifications).**

   The Label Designer dialog box opens, as shown in Figure 11-8. The Label Designer toolbox also opens; you recognize this toolbox if you design layouts or reports in ACT!.

4. **Before making adjustments to the existing label formats, save the template using another name by choosing File⇨Save As, typing the name of the template in the File Name field, and then clicking OK.**

   The next time that you run a set of labels, the template that you create appears as one of the label template choices.

5. **Modify the label formats to your heart's content:**

   • **To delete a field:** Click the Pointer tool in the toolbox, click a field, and then press Delete.

   • **To move a field:** Click the Pointer tool in the toolbox and drag a field to a new position.

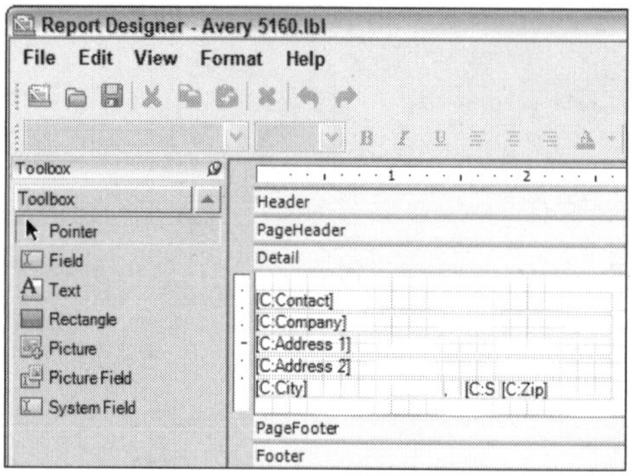

Figure 11-8:
The Label
Designer
dialog box.

- **To change the font for a field:** Double-click a field and then choose the Font menu to specify a different font, size, or attribute.

- **To add a field:** Click the Field tool and draw a rectangle to indicate where you want to place the field. You're then prompted to select the name of the field you wish to add.

- **To close the template:** Choose File➪Close and then click Yes to save.

6. **Click OK.**

If the label that you ordinarily use isn't listed, changing your labels to correspond to one of the labels listed in ACT! is probably your easiest choice. But if you rely on a special label, you can create a document template that corresponds with the dimensions of your labels. Check out Chapter 12 to find out how to create custom templates.

Working with Quick Report

I like to think the ability to print the various ACT! lists and tabs as somewhat of a secret weapon. By being able to print these lists, you can report quickly on just about anything that you can view throughout your database. This ability enables you to quickly create a report based on the specifications and criteria that you need immediately.

You're able to create a Quick Report for the following ACT! lists:

- ✔ Contact List
- ✔ Task List
- ✔ Group List
- ✔ Company List

You can also create a Quick Report for the following system tabs in the Contact, Group, or Company Detail windows:

- Notes
- History
- Activities
- Opportunities
- Groups/Companies
- Secondary Contacts
- Documents

Basically, if you're viewing a *list,* such as the Task List, ACT! can print the list. If you're viewing a *tab* that contains a list of items, such as the Notes, History, or Opportunities tab, ACT! can print those items.

Creating a Quick Report

Follow these steps to create a report:

1. **Display the list view or tab that you want to print.**

   - To display a tab, click the tab from the Contact, Group, or Company Detail window.
   - To display a list, such as the Task List or Contact List, choose View and then the appropriate list.

2. **Arrange the columns exactly as you want them to appear on your hard copy printout.**

   If you need help adding or removing columns, or changing the order or size of existing columns, check out Chapter 5.

   All lists that you see in ACT! work in exactly the same way.

3. **Choose File⇨Quick Print Current Window.**

   The Windows Print dialog box opens.

4. **Click OK.**

Setting the Quick Report preferences

Quick Print preferences allow you to modify the content of the headers and footers that appear on your Quick Reports.

1. **Choose Tools➪Preferences from any ACT! screen.**

2. **Click the Communication tab and then click the Quick Print Preferences button.**

   The Quick Print Preferences dialog box opens, as shown in Figure 11-9.

3. **Select a view from the When Printing This section.**

   You may want a Quick Report of your companies to look differently than the Quick Reports of your opportunities. Here's where you get to assign the various attributes for each view you plan to print.

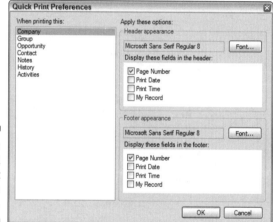

Figure 11-9:
The Quick
Print
Preferences
dialog box.

4. **Choose from the following options for both the header and footer for each view that you choose.**

   • Font

   • Page number

   • Print date

   • Print time

   • My Record

5. **Click OK.**

Chapter 12

Designing Your Own Reports

. . . .

In This Chapter

▶ Using the ACT! Report Designer

▶ Modifying an existing ACT! report

▶ Filtering report content

▶ Creating report sections

. . . .

ACT! comes with more than 30 reports right out of the box. Surely one of these reports can give you exactly the information that you need. Chapter 11 shows you how to run any of the existing ACT! reports. In this chapter, I show you how to create brand new reports or modify an existing one. If, after designing a report, you want to add it to the Reports menu, head to Chapter 3 where I show you how.

Understanding the Report Designer

Designing a database report can be a bit intimidating if you've never done it before. I like to think that you can tackle the chore of creating a report in one of two ways: the hard way or the easy way. The hard way consists of creating a brand new report entirely from scratch, which entails placing each and every element of your report onto a blank report template. The easy way consists of taking an existing report that is "kind of" what you're looking for and modifying it.

You might want to open the Act7demo database and print out a page of each of the existing ACT! reports for reference. Doing so helps you decide which report works as the best starting point for your modifications.

Being familiar with the structure of your existing database can prove helpful when you attempt to create a report. Thus, you need to know the field names that you're working with as well as their location in ACT!. For example, if you want to include the name of a company, you must know that the field is called Company and that you find the field in the Contact Detail window. If you want to include notes that you've added, you must know to include the Regarding field from the Notes tab.

Before starting to create or modify a report, create a lookup of the contacts that you're including in your report. This step is optional but can be timesaving. As you design your report, you'll notice that sometimes certain fields aren't large enough to contain their data or that columns don't line up correctly. By creating a lookup, you can check the progress of your report-designing efforts each time that you add a new element to your report.

Naming Your ACT! Report

After you pick the report you want to modify — or decided that you are a glutton for punishment, and start from scratch — you're ready to begin.

1. **Choose the Reports menu from any ACT! screen.**

   You have two choices here:

   - **New Template:** Even if you choose this option, ACT! shows you a list of all the report templates. The top choice, Empty Report, is the one you want to choose if you're adventurous enough to want to start working without a net.

     Yikes! The problem with designing an ACT! report from scratch is that you have to create the report from scratch. As shown in Figure 12-1, a blank template with Header, Contact, and Footer section titles appears on the left.

   - **Edit Template:** For me and most ACT! users, this choice is safer. You can now open the report that most closely matches your desired results. Compare Figures 12-1 and 12-2 to see the difference between a blank report and an existing one.

   Notice that there appears to be duplicate fields. The first field that you see is the Field label. You can edit any of these labels by clicking the Text icon on the toolbox, clicking the label, and then typing in any desired changes.

   You can distinguish the field itself by the colon that appears in each field. The actual data from your ACT! database appears in this area when you run the report. The letter in front of the colon indicates the Field type. For example, if you add your name in the Header section, the field appears as My:Contact. If you add a contact's company, it appears on the report template as C:Company.

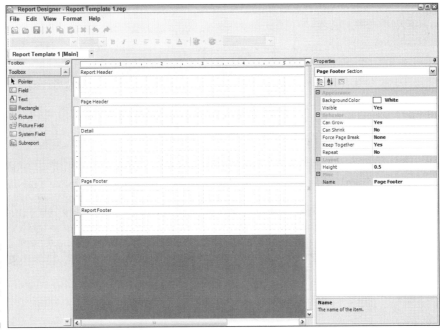

Figure 12-1:
Creating a
brand-new
ACT! report.

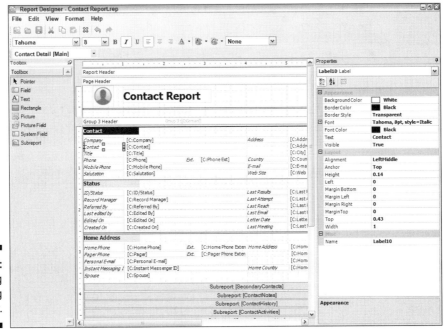

Figure 12-2:
Modifying
an existing
ACT! report.

2. **From the Report Designer, choose File⇨Save As.**

   I highly recommend giving your report a brand new name even if you're just tweaking an existing report. That way, you still have the original report to go back to, just in case.

3. **Fill in a name for your new report and then click Save.**

Saving early and often

Creating a report requires a great deal of patience. Even the most expert of report designers run into problems at times or (gasp) make a mistake. Imagine how you'd feel if after spending several hours working on a report, you made a huge mistake without realizing it until you ran your report for the first time. You would be heading back to the drawing board, and none too happily, I might add. For that reason, I suggest that you keep repeating the following procedure each and every time you make a change to the structure of your report.

From the Report Designer, choose File⇨Print Preview and give your report a good examination:

- ✔ If you like what you see, close Print Preview and choose File⇨Save. Your changes are now safe and sound.

- ✔ If something is wrong in Houston, or at least somewhere in the body of your report, close Print Preview and close the Report Designer without saving your changes. Cutting your losses is easier now rather than trying to untangle the mess you might inadvertently create later on.

Using the toolbox and properties

An ACT! report template consists of a number of elements. For example, you might have your company logo at the top of your report, and a series of column headings that appear at the top of each page in your report. ACT!'s Report Designer lets you modify those various elements using the toolbox and Properties features.

Tooling around in the toolbox

If you refer to Figure 12-2, you see the toolbox running along the left-hand side of the Report Designer. It consists of the following eight options:

- ✔ **Pointer:** You must click the Pointer in order to select any element in the Report Designer that you wish to modify.

- ✔ **Field:** Click this option if you want to add a new field to the body of your report.

- ✔ **Text:** This option allows you to create a descriptive text box.

- ✔ **Rectangle:** As its name implies, this option allow you to draw a box or rectangle in your report. Use this option to highlight a section of your report.

- ✔ **Picture:** This option allows you to add a graphic, such as your company logo, to your report.

- ✔ **Picture Field:** This allows you to add a contact's picture to your report.

- ✔ **System Field:** This allows you to add fields including date, time, and number of pages in your report.

- ✔ **Subreport:** This shows multiple objects for each contact in a report. For example, you may want to show the contact information for each contact listed on a sales report.

Using the properties properly

In addition to the toolbox, the Report Designer comes equipped with a Properties window guaranteed to give you more options than your local ice cream store. The Properties window runs along the right side of the Report Designer (refer to Figure 12-2). You can see what I mean by the options available to you. The purpose of the Properties window is to show you all the applied formatting to any given element.

Feel like the toolbox or Properties window is infringing on your territory? You can minimize them out of the way by clicking the thumbtack in the upper-right corner. Want to bring it back? Simply click the word *toolbox,* which now appears on the left side or "properties" that now appears on the right side of the Report Designer.

If you want to move the toolbox or Properties window out of the way, just double-click the window title bar. Each of these windows now detach themselves from the side of your screen. At this point, you can drag them to whatever area of the Report Designer that you are not using.

The left side of the Properties window lists all the aspects available for the element you selected. The right side shows you the currently selected choice. If you want to change any particular aspect, simply click the option on the right side and choose a different formatting option from the drop-down list that appears. For example, if I want to change a font color from black to red, I click the word *black* that appears to the right of the font color and choose red from the drop-down list.

You can also use the Properties window to change the attributes of several elements at the same time. You can click several elements at the same time by holding down the Shift key while clicking the elements you want to change. Once selected, you can change as many attributes as you want all in one fell swoop.

Changing the Report Content

I mention earlier that chances are that you began with a basic report and decided to modify it somewhat — or even give it a complete makeover. Probably the first thing you want to do is decide which fields will — or won't — appear in your report. After you make that momentous decision, you may decide that you want to tweak the order of the fields. Of course, then you're going to have to realign some of the fields that you moved so that they line up in an orderly fashion. You also have to decide how long a field should be — for example, the State field only needs to house two letters, but the City field may need to hold thirty. Whew! You have a lot of work to do, so read on!

Working with existing fields

Start by tweaking some of the fields already on your report template. Like anything else, it's simple if you know the trick.

1. **From the Report Designer, click the Pointer icon in the toolbox.**

2. **Select the fields you want to modify.**

   To select multiple fields hold down the Shift key while clicking any additional fields.

   You can identify selected fields by the handles that now appear along their edges and centers.

After you select the fields you want to work with, you can change a field in a number of ways:

- ✔ **To change field properties:** Select an item from the Report Designer Properties window and edit the properties. You can also select font attributes such as bolding, centering, and size from the Report Designer icon bar.

- ✔ **To delete a field or a field label:** Press the Delete key on your keyboard.

- ✔ **To resize a field:** Grab one of the selection handles on either side of field and drag to either the left or right depending on whether you want the field larger or smaller.

- ✔ **To move a field:** Place your cursor in the middle of a field or group of fields and drag them to the desired location.

- ✔ **To align fields:** First select the anchor field and then additional fields. The *anchor field* is the one that is correctly placed on the report template; all subsequent fields are the ones that you want align horizontally or vertically with the anchor field. Choose Format⇨Align from the Report Designer menu and indicate how to line up the fields.

You can distinguish between the anchor field and the other fields that you select by carefully examining the selection handles. If you look at Figure 12-3, the anchor field has filled-in handles whereas the secondary field has "open" handles.

Figure 12-3:
The anchor and sec-ondary selection handles.

Adding a field

If you want to add a field to a template, follow these steps:

1. **In the Report Designer, click the Field button in the toolbox.**

2. **Place your cursor on the template where you want to insert a field and drag down and to the right to define the field's length and position.**

   Most probably, you want to add the new field to the Detail section of your report. However, you can also add fields to any of the other sections as well.

   When you release the mouse button, the Select Field dialog box appears, as shown in Figure 12-4. You can now choose any of your existing ACT! fields to add to the report templates.

Figure 12-4:
The Select Field dialog box.

3. **Select the record type that you want to add from the Select a Record Type drop-down list.**

   Typically, you want to add a new Contact field to the body of your report. However, you may decide to add My Record fields to the header so that "your" name and other pertinent information appears at the top of the report. You may want to include Secondary Contact information. You can even choose to add Activity, History, Note, and Opportunity fields to your report.

   As you make a record type selection, notice that the list of fields changes. If you decide to add a Note field the choices include Date and Time whereas a selection of Contact Opportunity allows you to include any of your Opportunity fields.

4. **Indicate whether you want to include a field label.**

   If you don't want to include a field label for a field in the template, deselect the Include a Label check box.

5. **Click the Add button.**

   The Report Designer now contains the fields and field labels that you added. Refer to Figure 12-2 for an example of a report template that contains several sections, subsections, and fields.

6. **Continue adding additional fields if desired. Click the Close button when you finish adding new fields.**

Adding a summary field

After you add a field to a report template, you may want to make it a summary field. Examples of summary fields include having a count of all the contacts that appear in a report or a total for a column containing numeric data.

1. **Double-click the field in the Report Designer that you want to convert into a summary field.**

   The Field Properties dialog box appears.

2. **Click the Data tab and select the Summary option from the Field Type area.**

   You can check out the Data tab of the Field Properties dialog box in Figure 12-5.

After you create a summary field, you'll recognize it because ACT! inserts several letters in front of the field name. To make life easy for you, I include clues for you in the parentheses. The types of summary fields you can have are

✓ **Count (count):** This field counts the number of records for the selected field.

✓ **Total (sum):** This field calculates the total of all values in the selected field.

✓ **Average (avg):** This field calculates the average of all values in the selected field.

✓ **Minimum (min):** This field finds the lowest number or earliest date in the selected field.

✓ **Maximum (max):** This field finds the highest number or latest date in the selected field.

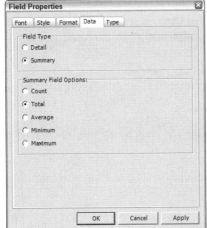

Figure 12-5:
Creating a
summary
field.

Filtering Data in a Report Template

Just like you can filter heaven knows what out of your water, you can filter data out of a report. You can change the filters each time that you run a report, or you can include filters in your report template to save you from having to do it later. Any filters that you set become defaults that you can change later when you actually run the report. Here's all you need to do to add that timesaving feature to your report templates.

1. **Choose Edit⇨Define Filters from the Report Designer.**

   The Define Filters dialog box appears. You can sneak a peek at it in Figure 12-6.

The Define Filters dialog box is divided into five tabs. Depending on the type of report you are creating, some of the tabs may not be available:

- **General:** Selects the default output for the report, the contacts to include, and the Record Manager of the contacts

- **Activity:** Lets you select whether you want to include calls, meetings, to-do's, and cleared activities within a given date range

- **Note:** Lets you specify the date range and creator of the notes to appear in a report

- **History:** Lets you determine whether you want to include histories, e-mails, and attachments within a given date range

- **Opportunity:** Lets you filter for Sales Opportunities, and Closed and Lost Sales within a given date range

2. **Select the data to include in the report from the Activity, Note, History, and Opportunity tabs, and then click OK.**

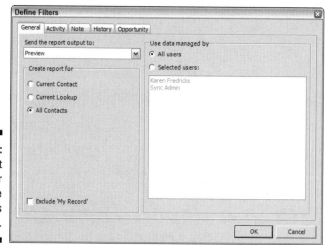

Figure 12-6:
The Report
Designer
Define
Filters
dialog box.

Sectioning Your ACT! Report

You create sections in a report template to help you organize the information that you want to include in your report. The fields that you include in each section vary based on the type of report you are creating. For example, in a Contact Report, you add Contact fields to the sections; and in an Opportunity Report, you add Opportunity fields.

Defining report sections

A report template is divided into *sections* of information. You can determine which fields you want to appear in each given section. A report template consists of five main sections; you can't delete or change the order of the sections, but you can hide a section if you don't want it to appear in your report:

- ✔ **Report Header:** Information that appears at the top of the report, such as the report's title and creator.

- ✔ **Page Header:** Information that appears at the top of each page, such as column headings.

- ✔ **Detail:** The area that contains one or more of your Contact or Group fields. The Detail section is the meat and potatoes of the report where you find pertinent information, such as the contact's name, address, and phone number.

- ✔ **Page Footer:** Information that appears at the bottom of each page in your report, such as the date and page number.

- ✔ **Footer:** Information that appears at the bottom of your report, such as a recap or a grand total.

Each section has a section title that appears in the report template but doesn't appear in the report itself. You can resize a section to make room for additional fields by dragging the horizontal gray line that appears at the bottom of the section lower on the template.

After you fiddle with your report template and have it exactly the way you want it, don't forget to resize each section back to the original size — or close it up as much as possible. Any blank areas in a section appear as blank areas in your report!

Modifying report sections

Most of you will be quite happy to rely on the five default report sections. However, from time to time, you may want to create subsection within your report. Not a problem; here's all you need to do:

1. **In the Report Designer, double-click any section header.**

   The Define Sections dialog box opens, as shown in Figure 12-7. You can choose a few other options as well:

- **Page Break:** Indicates whether you want to have each section appear on a new sheet of paper

- **Collapse if Blank:** Closes up a section if no information is contained in it

- **Allow Section to Break Across Multiple Pages:** Allows a long section to continue on to multiple pages

2. **Select the section to which you want to add a subsection.**

   In most cases, you want to add a subsection to the Details section of your report.

3. **Click the Add button to add a new section to the report.**

   The Select a Field to Group By dialog box opens.

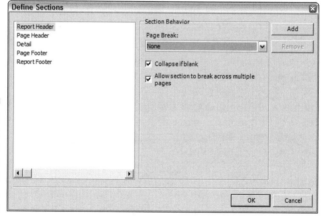

Figure 12-7:
The Report
Designer
Define
Sections
dialog box.

4. **Select the field you want to use to subtotal your report and click OK.**

   In Figure 12-8, you can see how I decided to subtotal my reports by city.

5. **Select an ascending order.**

   From the Define Sections dialog box, indicate whether the new section appears in alphabetical order.

After you create a new subsection, you can place as many fields on it as you want using the techniques in the "Adding a field" section.

Figure 12-8:
Determining
how
information
is grouped
in a report.

Hiding a report section

Although you can't remove any of the default report template sections, you can hide them, which gives you the same result. To hide a section:

1. **In the Report Designer, open the Properties window by choosing View⇨Properties Window.**

2. **Select the name of the section you wish to hide.**

3. **Click the Visible property in the Properties window and change it to No.**

Although you can still see the section in the Report Designer, it doesn't appear in your finished reports.

Chapter 13

Merging Your Information into a Document

A particularly useful ACT! feature enables you to create customized document templates. These templates are forms in which ACT! fills in your selected data fields. You can send these forms to a thousand people as easily as you can send them to just one person. You can send out routine documents one at a time on a continual basis, or you can send out the document one time to all or part of your database. After you create a form, you can send it out via snail mail, e-mail, fax, or Pony Express.

Mail Merge Isn't Just about Mailing

Poor mail merge! Folks often have two common misconceptions about mail merge. Some people think that the term *mail merge* is synonymous with *junk mail*. Also, the word *mail* makes some folks think that one requirement for a mail merge is a postage stamp. However, neither of these common misconceptions is true. A mail merge simply takes the content of one or more fields and puts that content into a template or form.

A good way to understand the concept of mail merge is to visualize this simple equation:

template + data field(s) = personalized document

Note the (s) at the end of data field, suggesting that you can use either one name or many names. Some of you may think that you will never perform a mail merge because you have no desire to send out a mass mailing. Others of you may have already perfected the art of mass mailing but never realized that a mail merge can be directed to one person or to thousands of people. I hate to be the one to break your bubble, but if you have any kind of routine documents that you're generating repetitively, you should be using ACT!'s mail merge to do it.

The three things necessary to create a mail merge are

- ✔ **A name or a list of names:** By now, you're the happy owner of a database and know how to create a lookup. (Don't know how to create a lookup? Better check out Chapter 7.) You can merge a document with your current contact, your current lookup, or the entire database.

- ✔ **A document template:** A *document template* is a letter or form that substitutes *field names* in place of names and addresses or whatever other information that will come directly from your database. ACT! comes with a number of document templates that you can either use as-is or modify. You can also create your own document templates by using a word processor.

- ✔ **A program that can combine the names into the template:** After you have a list of names and a document template, you need something to combine them. You could try to use your food processor, but I prefer to use the mail merge feature in ACT!.

Picking Your Word Processor

ACT! can use either its own word processor or Microsoft Word to create document templates. By default, ACT! is set to use its own word processor. Most ACT! users prefer using Word as their word processor, and I assume that you're no different. Although the ACT! word processor gets the job done, chances are you're already using Word — and using an application that you're already familiar with is preferable.

If your word processing preferences inside ACT! aren't set to use Microsoft Word as your default word processor, you can't use existing Word templates or any templates that you created by using Word. To change your word processor settings, follow these handy-dandy directions:

1. **Choose Tools⇨Preferences from the Contact Detail window.**

2. **On the Communication tab, select a word processor from the Word Processor list.**

   In this case, you're choosing Microsoft Word.

3. **Click OK.**

Using the "out of the box" templates

For those of you all set to write the Great American Novel, you may want to create all your own original documents. That's great, and I recommend that you skip to the section "Creating a Document Template." The rest of you may be interested in perusing some of the great templates that come pre-packaged in ACT!. Even if you decide that these templates aren't exactly what you're looking for, you can use them as a starting point for developing your own unique document templates.

The following figure shows you the Open Template dialog box that appears when you choose Write➪Other Document from any of the ACT! windows.

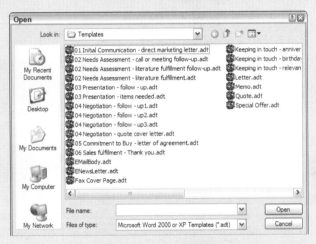

You may want to run each of the templates one time to determine which ones you think will be most useful to you. Later in this chapter, you find out how to modify them to your heart's content. Right now, I want to point out a few of my favorites that you might want to focus on.

These three document templates are listed for you right up there on ACT!'s Write menu. That's because you'll probably use these three templates the most often. The letter template is a great template to use when you need to create a letter on-the-fly to one of your contacts. It automatically dates a letter and addresses it to your current contact. It even includes your name, company, and title on the bottom. All you need to do is fill in the body of the letter, and you're good to go. Just don't forget to add the stamp!

✔ Letter

✔ Memo

✔ Fax Cover Page

These two templates contain graphics and are ready to send via e-mail:

✔ ENewsletter

✔ Special Offer

The Emailbody template pops up when you choose Write➪E-Mail Message from any of the ACT! windows.

You may want to hold off using the Quote template — it's designed for use with the opportunities you create. Flip to Chapter 20 for more details.

Converting Existing Document Templates

If you are a user of a previous version of ACT!, you may want to convert your document templates into the latest and greatest ACT! 2005 format. This is a fairly easy thing to accomplish.

1. **Choose Tools⇨Convert ACT! 3.0 – 6.0 Items from any ACT! window.**

2. **Select the type of document you want to convert.**

   - **ACT! WP Templates:** Converts documents that you created with the `.tpl` extension

   - **MS Word Templates:** Converts documents with the `.adt` extension

   - **E-Mail Templates:** Converts documents with the `.gmt` extension

3. **Browse to the folder that contains your "Oldie but Goldie" templates.**

   ACT!, being the smart program that it is, scrounges around and looks for a folder that contains document templates (see Figure 13-1).

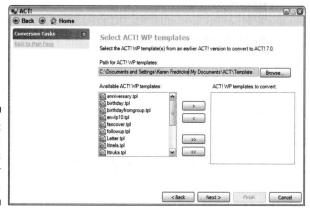

Figure 13-1: Selecting templates for conversion.

4. **Select the template(s) of your choice and click the right-pointing arrow.**

   Go ahead — convert as many templates as you want. There's no extra charge!

5. **Click Next and then click Finish.**

Reaching an Audience of One

Many of you might think creating a mail merge implies sending out a single message to thousands of people at one time. However, a mail merge can also be used to automate the most mundane and routine of tasks. You can use ACT!'s document templates to write a thank-you letter every time that you land a new client or to write an inquiry letter each time that you receive a new lead. After you discover this timesaver, I guarantee that you'll never go back to your old way of creating documents again!

To send a document to a single member of your database, follow these steps:

1. **Create a lookup to find the contact to whom you want to send a letter.**

   Feel free to turn to Chapter 7 if you need help creating a lookup.

   The current contact record that you have displayed is the one whose information fills in your template.

2. **Choose Write and then choose Letter, Memo, Fax Cover Page, or Other Document.**

   You can modify any of the ACT! menus. You might want to modify the Write menu to include some of your own templates. Flip over to Chapter 3 if you need a little refresher course in adding new items to an ACT! menu.

3. **Complete the body of the document.**

   Depending on the type of document that you choose to create and the modifications that you had previously made to the document template, you're looking at the start of a document. For example, by choosing to create a letter, the name, address, salutation, and closing are already provided. You just need to add the body of the letter to complete it. If you chose to create a fax cover sheet, you need merely to add the number of pages in the transmittal and an optional comment to proceed.

   If you choose Other Document, you're able to choose one of your own templates. These, of course, already include the body as well.

4. **(Optional) Save your document.**

   After you complete your document, you can save it to the location of your choice. If you don't think that it's necessary to save the document that you create from your own templates (because you can so easily recreate them), you aren't required to.

5. **Print, fax, or e-mail your document.**

   If you are using Word as the default word processor to create your ACT! documents, you can now print, fax, and e-mail exactly like you're already used to doing in Word.

If you chose to print, the Create History dialog box appears after printing is complete (see Figure 13-2). Now this is cool. I like to refer to this as the "Would you like fries with that?" step. After you create a document using a document template, ACT!, at your discretion, can create a record of the document on the History tab. You now have a history of the date on which you sent a document. Better yet, other people in your organization are also aware of your interactions with the contact.

Figure 13-2:
Creating a
history for a
written
document.

- If you do not want to create a history for the document, click the No, Do Not Record History option.

- If you want to attach the document to a note on the History tab, select the Attach Document to History check box. When you enable this option, a shortcut to the document is automatically added to the History tab; you can access the document by double-clicking the attachment.

- If you want to have additional information appear in the note that's added to the History tab, enter a description of the document in the Regarding field. This description appears on the History tab regardless of whether you saved the document.

- Specify whether to print an envelope for the contact. You have to hand it to ACT!: The program really tries to be as accommodating as possible. After you work your fingers to the bone creating your latest tome, ACT! gently asks you whether you want to print an envelope. If you click No, you're done with the letter-writing process.

After you complete the special order for your mail merge, all that's left to do is to click the OK button, close your word processor, and return to ACT!. If you selected Yes to print the envelope, the Print dialog box appears.

Creating a Document Template

Before you can win friends and influence prospects with your dazzling display of personalized documents, you need two basic elements: the data and the document template.

You're creating a template, not a document, to perform your mail merge. A *document* is a plain old file that you create and use in Word. You use it once, save it, and store it away for posterity, or delete it as soon as you're done with it. A *template* is a form that merges with your contact information. The convenience of templates is that you use them over and over again.

Because you already have your data tucked away nicely in your database, all you have left to do is to create the document template, which involves creating a form document. Your document template contains placeholders that are then filled in with information from your database after you perform a merge. Create a document template by following these steps:

1. **Choose Write⇨New Letter/E-Mail Template.**

   If you had previously chosen Word to be your word processor of choice, try not to look too surprised when Word opens. You've already demanded that ACT! use Word as your default word processor. Like an obedient contact manager, your wish is ACT!'s command.

2. **Resist the urge to close the Add Mail Merge Fields dialog box that's obscuring a portion of Word.**

   The Add Mail Merge Fields dialog box, as shown in Figure 13-3, is the main event of this little procedure. If you scroll through the Add Mail Merge Fields list, the various field names should ring a bell. After all — they're all of your database fields.

   You can drag those pesky fields out of your way by placing your mouse pointer on the Add Mail Merge Fields title bar and dragging it out of the way.

3. **Change all your page settings.**

   Go ahead and change your font, margins, and other formatting items exactly as if you're working in a regular ol' Word document.

4. **Create the body of your letter or form.**

   Nothing new under the sun here. You can backspace, delete, and type just like you do in a non-template document.

5. **Click the spot in your document where you want the field information to appear.**

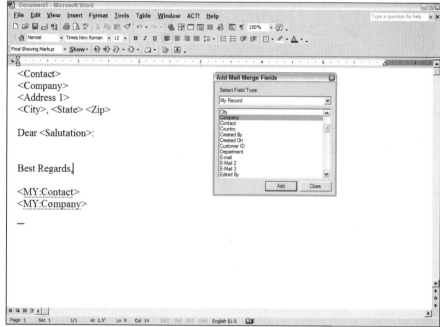

Figure 13-3:
The Add
Mail Merge
Fields dialog
box.

6. Determine what type of field you want to insert into your template.

The Add Mail Merge Fields dialog box allows you to insert three different types of field information:

- **Contact:** If you want your contacts' information to appear when you perform a mail merge, you need to insert a Contact field into your template. In a letter, the name at the top that you're sending the letter to is the Contact field.

  Whatever information you've entered into a field appears in the merged document. If any of the fields in the contact record are empty, ACT! skips that field; you don't see a blank line. In Figure 13-3, I've inserted the Company field; if your contact isn't associated with a company, that line is skipped.

- **Label:** Selecting the Field Label option inserts the name of the field, not the information contained in that field. You may wonder why you want to go through the effort of scrolling through the list of field names to insert a label when you could just as easily type in the field label. I am wondering the same thing!

- **My Record:** If you want your own contact information to appear, select the My Record Field option. If you're creating a letter document template, the name on the bottom is your name and is represented by the My Record field option.

Your My Record information resides on the first contact record that appears when you log on as yourself in the ACT! database.

7. **Insert fields where you want contact information to appear.**

Here's where the fun begins. Every time you get to a part that could be populated with ACT! information, you must scroll down that long list of fields, select the one to insert into your template, and click the Add button.

The field name appears in your document set off by a set of lovely brackets. Treat these field names exactly as you do any other words in your template. For example, if you want to see them set in bold, bold the field name. If the contact information appears at the end of a sentence, follow it by a period.

8. **Choose File⇨Save As.**

Okay, I know that you probably already know how to save a document in Word, but I want to draw your attention to an interesting phenomenon that occurs when saving an ACT! document template in Word. Your document is automatically saved with the .adt extension. And, unless you specify otherwise, your template is saved to your default template folder. In Chapter 3, I show you how to determine the location to save your templates, and also how to add a document template to the Write menu.

Document templates created with the ACT! word processor end in the extension .tpl.

9. **Check your document for accuracy and edit as necessary.**

After you create a template, you can change it whenever the need arises. You may need to go back and edit an ACT! template for a variety of reasons. After using it, you may discover a spelling mistake. The contact fields that you're using may not be working correctly or may lack the proper punctuation. You may even want to make changes to the wording in the template. The procedure for editing your document template varies only slightly from that of creating the document:

1. **Choose Write⇨Edit Template.**

2. **When the Open dialog box appears, select the document template that you want to open and then click Open.**

The template opens in Word, and the Add Mail Merge Fields dialog box automatically appears (refer to Figure 13-3).

When you're editing an existing template, you see your field names rather than your data. If you see actual data, you aren't editing the template, and the changes that you make affect only the current document that you're in; your document template remains unchanged.

3. **Make the appropriate changes to the template.**

4. **Click Save when you finish editing.**

Checking the spelling in a document template

Life is full of embarrassing moments. For many of you, the thought of sending a mailing out to several hundred of your closest friends with glaring spelling mistakes ranks right up there with the time you walked into that important meeting with a piece of toilet paper stuck to the bottom of your shoe. You'll want to proofread your templates carefully. You'll also want to use the spell checker to avoid embarrassment.

If you create your template using Word, you're on your own here — check your spelling as you normally do using Word.

To check spelling in the ACT! word processor, follow these steps:

1. **Open the template in the ACT! word processor.**

2. **Choose Spelling⇨Check Document.**

   If you really want to be precise, you can first select a section of your document and then chose Check Selection.

   The Spelling Check dialog box opens and points out your first boo-boo as illustrated

in the following figure. If your spelling is anything like mine, this one is the first in a long list of misspellings!

3. **Select one of the following options:**

✔ **Ignore:** Feel free to ignore the suggestion if you feel that the word is indeed correct.

✔ **Ignore All:** If you use a word several times throughout your template, you just may need to click the Ignore All button to avoid repetitious nagging.

✔ **Add:** You proba'' want to train your spell checker by adding things like your last name, city, or company name.

✔ **Change:** Like all good word processors, ACT! treats you to a list of suggestions. Choose the one you like from the list.

✔ **Change All:** If you misspelled a word once, there's a good chance that you misspelled it several times throughout your template. The Change All button fixes it once and for all!

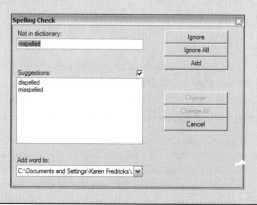

In general, using an existing template is easier than creating a new template from scratch. Basically, to create a new template, you simply open a similar template and follow the same procedure as if you're editing an existing template — but save the file with a *different name.* Or, if the document already exists in Word, you might want to first open the existing document in Word, highlight the information that you want to appear in your template, copy it to the Clipboard, and then paste it into the new template.

Initially, ACT! comes with a default letter, memo, and fax cover page template. You can access them by choosing Write from any ACT! screen and choosing letter, memo, or fax. You can easily modify these templates in the same way you modify any other template: Choose Write⇨Edit Template and choose `letter.adt`, `memo.adt`, or `fax cover page.adt`, respectively. Your personalized templates then appear as Letter, Memo, or Fax Cover Page in the ACT! Write menu.

We're Off to See the Mail Merge Wizard

When you create a mail merge to multiple contacts, follow these four basic steps:

1. Select the contacts to whom you're sending the letter.

2. Select the template that includes both the contact fields that you want to merge into the letter and the body of the letter itself.

3. Send the output to your word processor, printer, fax machine, or e-mail program.

4. Perform the mail merge.

Luckily, ACT! has taken the laborious task of mail merging and simplified it. Throughout the process, you encounter just four easy-to-navigate windows. Trust me — there's no chance of losing your way; ACT! holds your hand during the entire journey.

To perform a mail merge, follow these steps:

1. **Select the contacts to be the recipients of your mail merge.**

   To do so, either use a lookup to select certain contacts (such as all contacts in a specific state, city, or company) or select contacts from the Contact List.

   If you're creating one of those charming Christmas newsletters telling all about your two kids who just graduated from Harvard Medical School and your recent month-long excursion to purchase two Mercedes — leave me off the list!

2. **From any ACT! view, choose Write⇨Mail Merge.**

3. **Decide how you want to send the merge.**

   Decisions, decisions! The four choices on today's menu are

   - **Word Processor** saves all the merged documents into a single word processing document. This choice is good if you want to review your merged documents before printing them out.

   - **E-mail** sends all the merged documents as e-mail messages.

     If you choose to send out a mail merge via e-mail, each recipient receives an e-mail specifically addressed to that person. No one sees a list of the other recipients.

   - **Printer** is a good choice if you're sure that your contact information and that your template is perfect, as in *error-free*. This choice is also popular if you like to chop down trees in the Amazon. This option sends all the merged documents directly to the printer.

   - **Fax** sends all the merged documents as fax transmissions. If this option is grayed out, you don't have fax software installed on your computer.

     You cannot fax directly from your computer if you don't have access to a fax/modem.

4. **Pick your template and click Next.**

   You can now indicate the template to use in your mail merge by clicking the Browse button and selecting the name of the document template that you want to use.

   The Mail Merge Wizard continues and demands to know, in a loud booming voice, what contacts. All right, you caught me in one of my Judy Garland flashbacks. You can't actually hear the question, but it comes across loud and clear in Step 4 of the Mail Merge Wizard, shown in Figure 13-4.

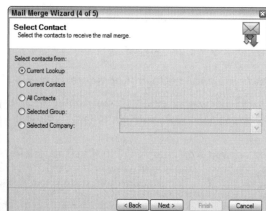

Figure 13-4:
Choosing the contacts to include in a mail merge.

5. **Choose to whom you want to send the mail merge to and then click Next:**

   - **Current Lookup** merges your document with the contact records that you chose in Step 1.

   - **Current Contact** sends the merge only to the contact currently showing in the Contact Detail window.

   - **All Contacts** goes to everyone in your database.

   - **Selected Group** enables you to merge your document with a specific contact group.

   - **Selected Company** enables you to merge your document with all the associates of a given company.

   Depending on the choice you picked in Step 3, you're pretty close to the finish line and you can just click Finish.

   - If you chose the printer option, you are hearing the happy sound of your printer spitting out 1,001 personalized letters to your dearest friends and relatives.

   - If you chose the word processor option, you can now spend the next two hours reviewing 1,001 personalized letters to your dearest friends and relatives, ensuring that all the information therein is accurate.

   - If you chose the fax option, your faxing software opened, and you're ready to fax.

6. **You have a little more work ahead of you if you chose the e-mail option.**

   Try not to be discouraged. Your e-mails are going to arrive at their intended destination long before those people choosing one of the other options even finishes stuffing envelopes or deciphers the new area code rules for a fax transmittal. Besides, you're treated to the options that you see in Figure 13-5.

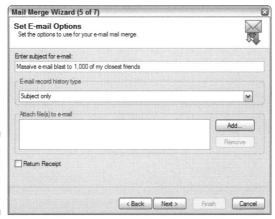

Figure 13-5:
E-mail
merge
options.

- Type the subject line of your e-mail.

- You can create a history of your e-mail by including the subject or the subject and message of your e-mail on the History tab. You also have the option of attaching the entire e-mail message to a history, or simply creating no history at all.

- If you like, you can send an attachment along with your e-mail blast.

- Specify that each recipient of your e-mail send you back a Return Receipt.

7. Set your options for the contacts who have missing e-mail addresses.

By now, I hope you are feeling appropriately ashamed by the fact that you've made ACT! work so hard while you simply sat back. ACT! now patiently asks you one final question regarding your e-mail addresses. As you can see in Figure 13-6, you have several choices as to how to handle the MIAs.

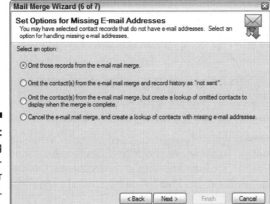

Figure 13-6:
Determining
the recip-
ients of your
mail merge.

8. After you choose all your options, click Finish.

Congratulations! You have now completed in a very short time what used to take hours and hours of work. Well-done!

Chapter 14

ACT! E-Mail

. . . .

. . . .

*I*n this chapter, I show you how to integrate ACT! with your existing e-mail client. ACT! enables you to send e-mail through it to contacts who are in your database, people who are not in your database, and to a selected group of contacts in your database. Finally, you discover the various preference settings that are crucial in order to e-mail successfully.

Getting Started with ACT! E-Mail

To fully understand the e-mail portion of ACT!, you must understand the concept of the e-mail client. An *e-mail client* is an application that runs on a personal computer or workstation and enables you to send, receive, and organize e-mail. A senior executive at Best, CRM once told me, "ACT! is not in the business of designing e-mail clients." What that means is that ACT! isn't built to replace your existing e-mail client; rather, ACT! works on top of it. It also means that if you really want to send out a lot of e-mail using ACT!, you probably want to investigate one of the add-on products I mention in Chapter 25.

As of this writing, ACT! 2005 supports the following e-mail clients:

✔ Internet Mail (an internal stand-alone e-mail client that supports the use of your SMTP and POP3 settings)

✔ Outlook Express

✔ Eudora

✔ Outlook

I didn't include America Online (AOL) in this list because ACT! doesn't support it. AOL utilizes its own proprietary e-mail client that does not use the SMTP and POP3 settings that are common to most other e-mail clients. For that reason, and for many other limitations of the AOL e-mail client, your needs are better served by using an alternative method of e-mail for your business purposes.

The two most commonly used e-mail clients are Outlook and Outlook Express in the Windows environment. For business purposes, Outlook is probably the e-mail client of choice. It has more features than Outlook Express and is more attuned to the business environment. Outlook comes bundled with most versions of Microsoft Office and is a common fixture on most office computers. Outlook Express comes as part of the Windows operating system. Because it is a much more basic program, Outlook Express isn't as often used for business e-mailing.

Setting your e-mail preferences

If you initially set up your database using the Getting Started Wizard (see Chapter 3, where I show you how to work your way through the wizard), you already specified your e-mail client. If you're working on an existing database, here's what you must do to configure ACT! for e-mail:

1. **Test to make sure that your e-mail is functioning correctly outside of ACT!.**

   Before you configure your e-mail preferences in ACT!, I recommend testing your e-mail to make sure that it's working correctly. Send a test e-mail to your significant other using Outlook or Outlook Express. Doing so helps eliminate possibilities if, for some reason, you have trouble e-mailing in ACT!.

2. **Choose Tools⇨Preferences⇨E-Mail.**

   The E-mail Preferences dialog box appears, as shown in Figure 14-1.

3. **On the E-Mail tab, click the Composing Options button.**

   The Composing Options dialog box opens, shown in Figure 14-2, where you set preferences for your ACT! e-mail.

4. **Choose from the following options:**
   - **Send E-Mails In:** Lets you select HyperText Markup Language (HTML) or plain text for the default format type of new messages.
   - **Default Priority:** Allows you to select either a low, normal, or high priority as the default preference for all your new e-mail.

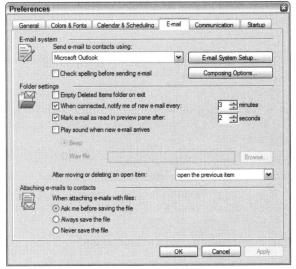

Figure 14-1:
The E-mail Preferences dialog box.

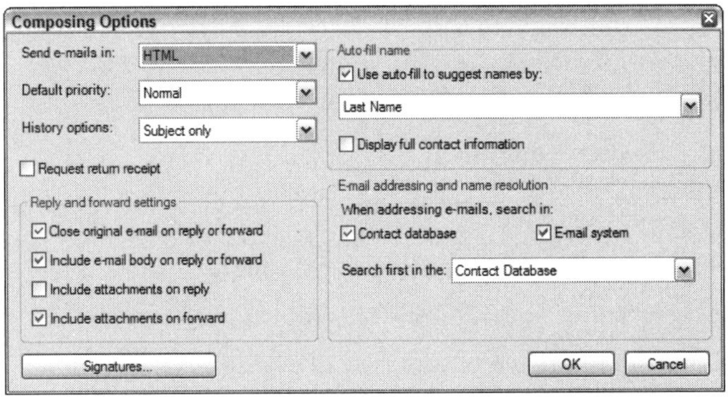

Figure 14-2:
E-mail composing options.

- **History Options:** Allows you to select the history type that is recorded after you send an e-mail. You can choose to have nothing, only the subject, the subject and full body, or an attached copy of your message recorded on the History tab.

- **Request Return Receipt:** Prompts the recipient of your message to automatically send a notification when he or she receives your e-mail.

- **Close Original E-Mail on Reply or Forward:** Closes the original message window when replying to or forwarding e-mail.

- **Include E-Mail Body on Reply or Forward:** Select this option so that ACT! includes the original message text when you reply to or forward a message.

- **Include Attachments on Reply:** Select this option so that an attachment is included when you reply to a message that includes an attachment.

- **Include Attachments on Forward:** Same as the preceding bullet, except that this option applies to messages with attachments that you forward.

- **Use Auto-Fill to Suggest Names By:** If you select this option, ACT! supplies the rest of a recipient's name after you type the first several letters of it.

- **E-Mail Addressing and Name Resolution:** This determines whether you want the auto-fill to search through the contact database (ACT!) and/or the e-mail system database (Outlook or Outlook Express) to find recipient names. You can also indicate which database you like to have ACT! search through first.

5. **Click the Signatures button.**

   The E-Mail signatures dialog box pops open. Here you type your signature and any other information that you want to appear in all new e-mail messages. If you want to include a hyperlink to your Web site, include the entire URL starting with `http://www`. For your e-mail address, you must insert **mailto:** before the e-mail address, like this:

   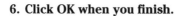
   ```
   mailto:karen@techbenders.com.
   ```

6. **Click OK when you finish.**

   The signature appears every time that you compose a brand-new e-mail in ACT! to a new contact or send an *e-mail blast* (a mass e-mailing that's sent to several recipients at once) without using a template.

7. **After you set all your Composing Option preferences, click OK.**

   The E-mail Preferences dialog box reappears.

8. **Click the E-mail System Setup button.**

   The E-mail Setup Wizard opens, as shown in Figure 14-3.

9. **Select your preferred e-mail client and then click Next.**

   - If you select Outlook, you're asked whether you want to use your default Outlook settings and to choose from the signatures that you composed earlier.

   - If you select Internet Mail, you have a bit of work to do as seen in Figure 14-4. You're prompted to enter the user name, e-mail address, and SMTP and POP3 assigned to you by your e-mail service provider. You might also be asked for your shoe size and blood type.

10. **On the final screen of the E-mail Setup Wizard, click the Finish button.**

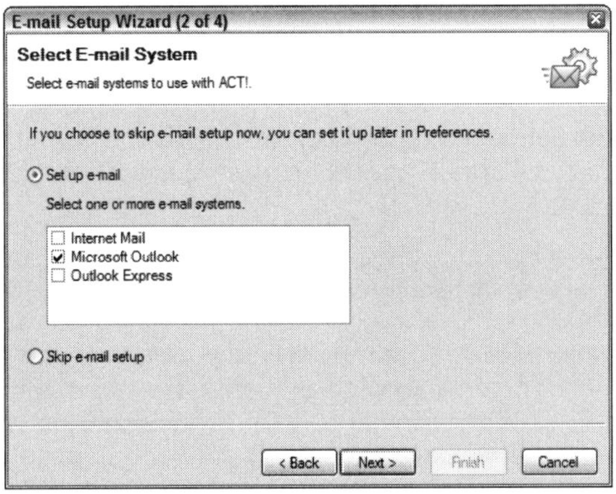

Figure 14-3:
The E-mail
Setup
Wizard.

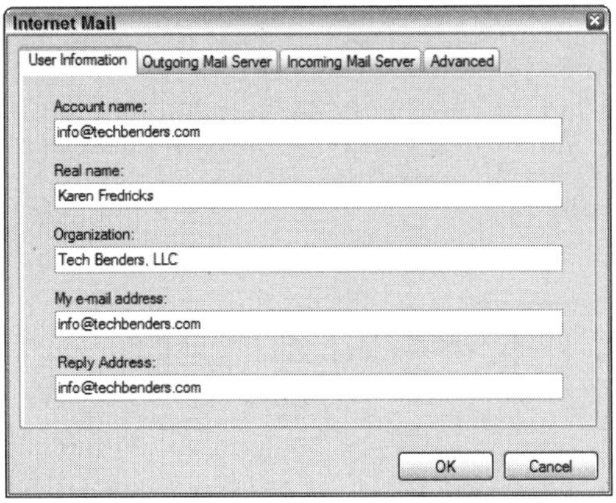

Figure 14-4:
Setting up
Internet
Mail.

Editing e-mail addresses

After you set your e-mail preferences in ACT!, you need e-mail addresses so that you can actually send some e-mails. No doubt that you've already added many e-mail addresses to your ACT! database, but I'm guessing that you haven't yet discovered a good way to correct or change existing e-mail addresses.

ACT! is designed to launch the e-mail window when you click the E-Mail field in the Contact Detail window. This feature allows you to easily send e-mail in ACT!, but makes editing existing addresses hard.

To edit the E-mail field, try one of these methods:

   ✔ Use the Tab key to move the cursor to the E-Mail field. After the cursor is in an E-Mail field, you can edit it by clicking the E-Mail field's drop-down arrow.

✔ Move the mouse pointer over the E-Mail field and right-click. You can now edit the E-Mail field.

✔ Hold the cursor over the E-mail field and wait a few seconds; the cursor changes from a hand to a vertical line.

E-Mailing Your Contacts

A benefit of sending e-mail from within ACT! is that a history of the event is added to your contact's History tab each and every time that you send an e-mail. E-mail is an increasingly popular form of communication, so having a history of all the e-mail that you sent to each of your contacts helps you keep track of it all. You can send e-mail messages to one or more contacts and attach contact records, group records, or files to your messages.

Depending on how you like to reach your contacts, you can send e-mail to them using ACT! in a variety of ways. You might be writing a one-time e-mail to an individual contact, or you might be sending a form e-mail to either an individual or a whole group of your contacts. You might also want to send a spur-of-the-moment message to one contact — or even thousands of your contacts. Explore the possibilities.

E-mailing an individual contact

To send an e-mail to the current contact, follow these steps:

1. **Create a new e-mail message with one of three methods.**

   Although the three methods all result in a new message (see Figure 14-5), they work in slightly different ways.

   - **Click in the contact's E-Mail field:** The contact's name appears in the To line, and the signature you created appears in the body.

   - **Choose Write⇨E-Mail Message:** The contact's name appears in the To line, and the wording of the E-mailbody template appears in the body of the e-mail.

     The E-mailbody template works exactly like all other ACT! templates. For a refresher course in template creation, check out Chapter 13.

   - **Click the E-Mail icon on the Nav bar and click New:** The To line is blank, and the signature you created appears in the body.

2. **In the Subject field, type a subject.**

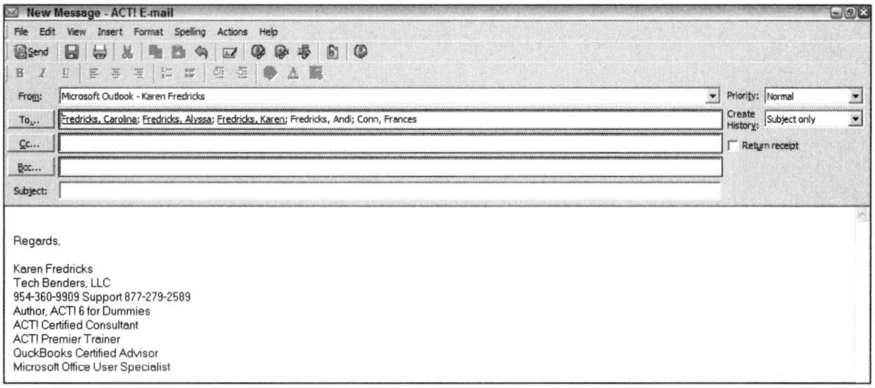

Figure 14-5:
Sending
an e-mail to
the current
contact.

3. **Edit or create the message in the text box.**

4. **Feel free to pick an option or two from the New Message toolbars, depending on how fancy you want to get with your e-mail.**

   When you create an e-mail in ACT!, two toolbars appear in the New Message window. If you hover your mouse over the various tools, a ToolTip appears, explaining the function of each button.

   - The top toolbar enables you to send attachments along with your e-mail. You're probably already familiar with the concept of file attachments. ACT! also allows you to send either a single contact record, a group of contact records, or a company to recipients (if they're using ACT!).

   - The bottom toolbar enables you to make changes to the text formatting exactly as you do in any word processor. Notice also two buttons (refer to Figure 14-5) that allow you to insert either a graphic or a hyperlink into your e-mail message.

   Is the bottom toolbar grayed out? You probably set your e-mail preference to plain text. Try switching it over to HTML if you want to add a splash of color to your e-mails — or at least if you want to be able to use the formatting toolbar!

5. **If you like, change the default options for Priority, Create History, and Return Receipt.**

   See Step 4 in the section "Setting your e-mail preferences," where I explain these options.

6. **Click Send.**

   Off your mail goes and, depending on the Create History option that you chose, a message appears on the contact's History tab.

Sending mass e-mails

ACT! makes a distinction between sending e-mail and sending *merged* e-mail. Merged e-mails all share the following characteristics:

- ✔ When you send a merged e-mail, ACT! relies on a template.

- ✔ When you send a merged e-mail, you must include at least one contact field in your template.

- ✔ E-mail merging in ACT! allows each individual contact name to appear in the To line rather than having to send the mail using the BCC (Blind Carbon Copy) field.

Important things to consider when sending a mass e-mail

Before jumping head first into the world of mass e-mailing, consider the following important points:

- ✔ **Test your e-mail preferences.** You should test your e-mail preferences before sending your missive out to thousands of people. If you don't, you might find yourself with a thousand e-mails in your outbox that can't be sent. Try sending a sample e-mail to a friend or colleague.

- ✔ **Test your e-mail template.** Again, testing your message before sending it across the universe is always a good idea. Try sending the message to a co-worker or colleague first. Having correct spelling and punctuation isn't a bad idea either.

- ✔ **Check with your ISP.** Many Internet Service Providers (ISPs) have implemented safeguards against *spam*. Before you send an e-mail to all the contacts in your database, call your ISP to find out how many e-mails you can send at a time. If your ISP limits the number of e-mails you can send at one time, you need to send your mailings in smaller groups or purchase an add-on product that sends your e-mail in batches. You can discover more about these products in Chapter 25.

Sending non-merged mass e-mails

If you're not entirely comfortable with the concepts of e-mail blasting, you might want to start out by sending an e-mail to your contacts rather than attempting an actual e-mail merge. This way is great for less computer-oriented ACT! users to reach a large number of contacts.

You can send non-merged e-mail at the spur of the moment, but it doesn't involve the creation of a template. However, you're not able to customize the To or Subject portions of the e-mail with any of your contact's specific information.

To send an e-mail to any number of your contacts, here's all you have to do:

1. **Create a lookup (Chapter 7 shows you how) to find the contacts to whom you want to send the e-mail.**

   For example, if you want to send an e-mail to all customers in the Southeastern Region, create the lookup and then narrow it to include only those contacts that have an e-mail address.

   Narrow your lookup by choosing Lookup⇨E-Mail Address; next select Narrow Lookup for the current lookup and finally click Non-empty Fields. *Voilà!* Your lookup is narrowed to include only those contacts having an e-mail address.

2. **Click the E-Mail icon on ACT!'s Nav bar.**

   The ACT! E-Mail dialog box opens.

   If you set your e-mail preferences to either Outlook or Outlook Express, you now see a mirror image of either your Outlook or Outlook Express folders.

3. **Click the New icon on the e-mail window's toolbar.**

   The New icon is easy to spot — it's the icon that says *New* on it!

4. **Click the To, Cc, or Bcc button.**

   The Select Recipients dialog box opens, as shown in Figure 14-6. Here's where you choose multiple contacts who all receive your e-mail blast.

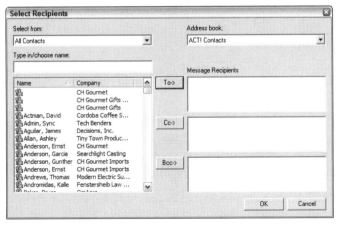

Figure 14-6: Selecting recipients for an e-mail blast.

5. In the Address Book drop-down list, select the address book that you want to use.

You can select to use either the currently opened ACT! database or your Outlook e-mail addresses.

6. In the Select From drop-down list, choose All Contacts, Current Lookup, Groups, or Companies.

- **Current Lookup:** Limits the list of recipients to contacts in your current lookup

- **Groups:** Displays a list of the groups in your current ACT! database

- **Companies:** Displays a list of the companies in your database

7. Select one or more names from the list on the left.

- To select a *single* name, click it.

- To select a *continuous list* of names, click the first name in the list, press the Shift key, and then click the last name in the list that you want to select.

- To select *multiple (non-continuous) names* in the list, click the first name that you want to select, and then press the Ctrl key while clicking any and all names that you want to select.

8. Click the To button.

The names that you select appear in the Message Recipients box.

Unless you want all the recipients of the message to know the names of everyone else who received your e-mail, click the Bcc button rather than the To or Cc buttons.

9. Click OK.

You return to the New Message window. Notice that the names of all your intended recipients now appear in the To (or Cc or Bcc) area of your e-mail message.

10. If you like, change any of the e-mail options.

Go for it! Insert a link to your Web site or attach a file. You find plenty of options in the New Message menu.

11. Verify that all your intended recipients have a valid e-mail address.

ACT! automatically checks to ensure that an e-mail address exists for each of your recipients. If you look at Figure 14-5, you'll notice that some of the names are underlined; those represent the contacts with valid e-mail addresses. If a name does not have a valid e-mail address, it is not underlined. When you send the message, you're prompted to add any e-mail addresses that ACT! doesn't find.

ACT! isn't perfect — although it comes pretty darned close! The e-mail checker finds contacts with blank e-mail addresses as well as those missing key pieces of information, such as the @ character. If you don't know someone's e-mail address, leaving it blank is better instead of inserting something cute like N/A that may serve to confuse — or at least slow down — the checker.

Don't know whether an e-mail address is correct? You can right-click any underlined name, and choose Properties to sneak a peek at the e-mail address you have on record for that contact.

12. **Click Send.**

You might want to pat yourself on the back, content with the knowledge that you have mastered the art of sending an e-mail blast.

Sending a templated e-mail

Using ACT! to create an e-mail merge enables you to send personalized templates for each recipient. The cool thing about ACT! templates is that you can use them for either mailing or e-mailing. In Chapter 13, I show you how to produce a mass mailing. The Mail Merge Wizard provides you with the option to e-mail as well as snail mail.

But how about if you want to send a thank you e-mail to just one of your contacts? You may not want to go through the entire wizard again, so here's a few shortcuts.

1. **From any ACT! screen, choose Write➪Other Document and chose the template that you want to use for the body of your e-mail.**

2. **Generate the e-mail message.**

   • In the ACT! word processor, choose File➪Send➪E-mail.

   • In Word, choose ACT➪Send E-mail. You have the choice of sending the template as an attachment or as the body of the e-mail. After you make your selection, select the name of your recipient and click OK.

Figure 14-7 shows how the message was personalized to include both the contact's name and pertinent information.

Mail merge must include at least one mail merge field. If you aren't personalizing your e-mails, you need to choose a different method of e-mailing. Also keep in mind that you'll probably want to create a lookup of the contacts you want to e-mail *before* starting the e-mail merge!

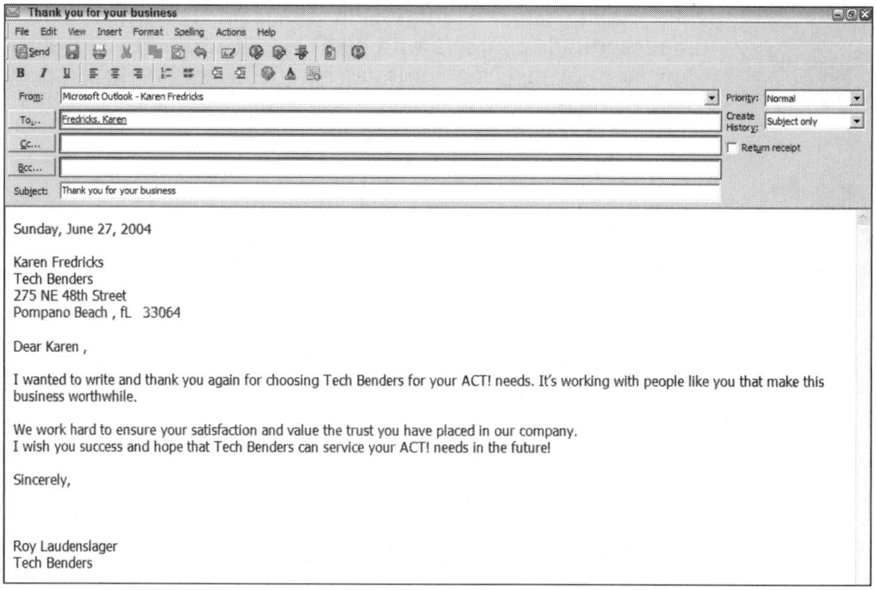

Figure 14-7:
Sending a
personalized
e-mail
template.

Working with Incoming E-Mail

When you're proficient in sending e-mail, you need to know how to read an
e-mail message. Although you can continue to view your mail using your
existing mail client, you'll want to familiarize yourself with the ACT! e-mail
client. After you open up ACT!'s e-mail by clicking the E-mail icon on the
Navigation bar, you may want to perform one of the following tasks:

- ✔ **Open a message.** Double-clicking the message does the trick.

- ✔ **Read messages in another folder.** Simply click the folder in the Folder
  List.

- ✔ **Sort your e-mail messages.** You can change the order by clicking any
  column header.

- ✔ **Create a new contact record from an incoming e-mail (if the contact
  isn't already in your database).** Right-click the message and choose
  Create Contact From Sender.

  This is a particularly timesaving feature of ACT! and ensures that potential contacts don't get lost in the shuffle.

- ✔ **Attach the e-mail to a contact's History tab.** Just like you can create an
  automatic history record each time that you *send* an e-mail to a contact,
  you can also create a history each time that you *receive* an e-mail from a
  contact.

1. Choose Actions⇨Attach⇨Attach to Contact.

2. On the Attach E-mail to Contact dialog box that appears, click the name of the contact(s) to associate with the e-mail message.

3. Click the To button and then click OK.

   ACT! places a note on the contact's History tab indicating that you received an e-mail from the contact.

✔ **Schedule a follow-up.** Right-click the message and choose Create Activity from Message.

You can now schedule a follow-up; the subject of the e-mail automatically appears in the Regarding area of your activity.

Part IV
Advanced ACT!ing

The 5th Wave   By Rich Tennant

"Your database is beyond repair, but before I tell you our backup recommendation, let me ask you a question. How many index cards do you think will fit on the walls of your computer room?"

In this part . . .

On the surface, ACT! is a deceptively easy program to master. However, those of you who are so inclined — or didn't run fast enough — might want to add ACT! Database Administrator to your current job description. The database administrator is the one in charge of adding new fields to the database and making sure that the database remains in perfect working condition. Best of all, when things go wrong, guess who everyone will turn to? Not to worry, though — just turn to this section for help.

Chapter 15

Creating Contact Fields

· ·

· ·

I am a firm believer that a little knowledge is a dangerous thing. Although adding a field to your ACT! database is not a hard thing to do, it is something that should be well thought out and planned in advance. This is particularly true if you plan on sharing your database with other users. Planning is important because you usually have a goal in mind for your database. If your goal is to create a report with three columns — one for the contact name, one for the birthday, and one for the Social Security number — you need to make sure that all those fields exist in your database. Planning also prevents you from adding thousands of contacts to your database, only to find you have to modify each record to include information that was omitted the first time around!

To add a field to your database, you must be a Database Manager or Administrator; the makers of ACT! made this a requirement so that you understand the importance of this responsibility. So unless you have administrative rights to the database, you don't even have to read this chapter! I suppose you still could, just for curiosity's sake, but it isn't necessary.

In this chapter, I show you (all of you who have Administrator or Manager level rights to your databases anyway) not only how to add new fields to an ACT! database, but also how to set the various field parameters to help users use the database more effectively and efficiently.

Before getting started, I want to briefly outline the three steps involved with adding fields to a database:

1. Understand why you want to add fields and what purpose these fields will serve.

2. Determine what fields you're going to add and what drop-down lists will be available in each.

   I can't stress enough the importance of this step. Plan ahead! Or you might end up with a big mess. . . .

3. Add the fields.

   And, *voilà!* You're done. (Okay, this one has a whole bunch of steps, but you get what I mean.)

Understanding the Concept of Fields

For most of you, adding a field to your database will be easy. After all, you're good at following directions. However, for some of you, knowing *why* to enter a field can prove to be more challenging.

To explore the question of why, I first want to reiterate the basic concept of fields. What the heck is a field? A *field* is a single piece of information. In general, a field contains just one piece of information. For example, you have only one business zip code; therefore, you have one business Zip Code field. Alternatively, you probably have at least eight phone numbers: home, business, toll-free, cellular, fax, beeper, and the list goes on. Each of these phone numbers requires a separate field.

A good field holds one fairly specific piece of information. A bad field contains too much information. For example, having a separate field for your street address, city, state, and zip code is a good thing. These separate fields allow you to perform a lookup based on any of the criteria: You could find clients by zip code, city, or state. An example of a bad field is lumping all the address information into a single field; you then lose your ability to perform a lookup by zip code, city, or state. (Need a refresher on performing lookups? Head to Chapter 7.)

You might want to consider the following basic rules when determining the criteria for adding a field to your database:

✔ A field contains an important tidbit of information.

✔ A field can be used to perform a query or sort. For example, you may want to send a mailing to all your customers in New York and sort your mailing by zip code. To do this sort, you need separate fields for contact type, state, *and* zip code.

✔ A field can be used to insert information into a report or template. If you want to create letters thanking one person for buying a purple polka-dotted vase and another for buying a leopard-print vase, you need a vase type field.

Do Your Homework!

Okay, I admit it — I'm a former secondary school teacher, and I guess that background just naturally spills over into my ACT! consulting. Well class, pretend you're back in school because you're now going to be assigned some homework. To be politically correct, I could have said you're now entering the *pre-planning stage of your ACT! implementation.* But I still consider it as important homework that you must complete *prior* to jumping in and adding new fields to your database, so your assignment is as follows:

1. **Jot down all the fields that you want to see in your database.**

2. **Scurry around the office and collect any documents that you want ACT! to create for you. This includes both forms and form letters.**

   You're going to have to get a little high tech here, but I think you can handle it. Get out your trusty highlighter and highlight any of the information in each document that is contact-specific. For example, each contact has its own unique address. Maybe you're thanking particular contacts for meeting to discuss purchasing widgets (as opposed to gadgets, which you also sell). This means that you need a Product field.

3. **Think of how to populate the fields with drop-down lists, and then on the list that you started in Step 1, jot them down to the side of each of the fields.**

   For example, if you run a modeling agency, you might need a field for hair color. The drop-down choices could contain red, blonde, black, and punk pink.

4. **Sketch out any reports that you want to create from ACT!, and add the column headings to the now rather-long list that you created in Step 1.**

   The idea here is to get your thoughts down on paper so that you can visualize what you want your ACT! report to look like. If you already have a sample of your report in Excel, you can use that. If not, get out your trusty pencil and outline what you like your report to actually look like on a piece of paper.

5. **Get out a red pen, and at the top of your paper, write 100%, Well Done, and draw a smiley face. Hang your list on your refrigerator.**

   Okay, that last step isn't really necessary, but now you're well on your way to having the database of your dreams!

Adding a New Field to Your Database

Believe it or not, after completing your homework (see the preceding section), you're done with the hard part of the task. The actual addition of fields is relatively easy; just follow the steps.

Only an ACT! user with Administrator or Manager privileges can add new fields to an ACT! database. If the Define Fields option is grayed out in Step 1, you aren't logged in as one.

1. **In any ACT! view, choose Tools⇨Define Fields.**

   The Contact Detail window is generally a good place to start for most of your customization projects. The Define Fields dialog box appears, as shown in Figure 15-1. The View Fields For drop-down list indicates that you're editing or adding new contact fields to the database. You can also add new group, company, and opportunity fields to your database by switching the View Fields For list to the appropriate choice.

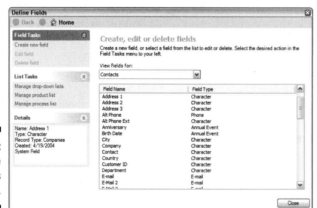

Figure 15-1:
The Define
Fields
dialog box.

ACT! does not allow you to add new fields or edit existing fields while other users are logged into the database. If you see the warning shown in Figure 15-2, you know that other users are indeed currently logged into the database. What to do? Storm over to their workstations in a huff and demand that they exit out of ACT! immediately. If that doesn't work, consider bribery. Conversely, as long as you are editing fields, other users are not able to access the database. If you look in ACT!'s title bar, you even notice that "*(Locked)*" now appears. To avoid frustration on everyone's part, you might want to explain this concept to the users of your database.

Figure 15-2:
Another
user is
using the
database.

2. **Start by renaming one of the 15 user fields. You find all your fields listed alphabetically by field name. Select one of them.**

   This is where you need to drag your homework off the refrigerator and type in one of the fields that you had planned to create in the Field Name box. ACT! supplies you with 15 user fields that you can customize to better serve the needs of your business. After all, *Social Security Number* is a lot more meaningful than *User 12*.

3. **Click the Edit Field option in the Field Tasks section.**

   You're rewarded with a friendly-looking dialog window that looks exactly like the one shown in Figure 15-3.

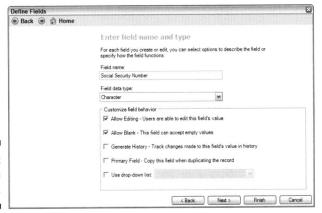

Figure 15-3:
Defining an
ACT! field.

When you run out of user fields to rename, feel free to click the New Field option in the Field Tasks section.

ACT! rewards you with a blank, new field in the Field Name box and assigns it the name *New Field* until you can think of something better to call it. At that point, the following steps are identical.

4. Type a field name.

Try not to get too fancy or long-winded when naming your fields. Using special characters such as <, >, $, or : can cause problems when creating queries and mail merges, so I recommend that you not use them. You can use spaces in the field name, but don't end a field name with a space. Long field names can be hard to place into mail merge templates and layouts, so you're better off keeping field names as short as possible.

5. From the Field Data Type drop-down menu (refer to Figure 15-3), choose a field type for the field that you're adding.

You can create a variety of different types of fields. Actually, there are eighteen different field types but who's counting? Among the choices are

- **Address:** Talk about a timesaver! When you designate a field as an address field, ACT! automatically creates seven fields: three for the street address, and another four for the city, state, zip, and country.

- **Annual Event:** Like it or not, some events take place once a year. Use this field to be reminded of birthdays, anniversaries, and yearly renewals regardless of the year.

- **Character:** This is probably the most common of the field type choices; a character field can contain both numbers and characters. It's a one-size-fits-all kind of field.

- **Currency:** As its name implies, this is for fields relating to cold, hard cash. The field comes equipped with a dollar sign, appropriate commas, optional decimal places, and a sunroof (optional).

- **Date:** A really cool thing happens when you make a field a Date field. When the time comes for you to enter information into a Date field, you see a tiny little calendar that enables you to select a date. The calendar is cute, but more importantly, it supplies a useful purpose. If you create a field for a birthday and make it a Character field, the other local yokels using the database might get creative and input anything from Jan 1 and January 1st to 01/01 and 1/1. Finding all birth dates in the month of January would become an exercise in futility.

- **Date/Time:** When you really want to be exacting, create a Date/Time field to record the exact date and time of an event.

- **Decimal:** This field only accepts numbers, a decimal point, and more numbers.

- **E-mail:** It used to be that everyone you know had several phone numbers. Now, the chances are pretty good that your contacts have numerous e-mail addresses. Here's your opportunity to include as many as you like.

- **Initial-Caps:** At first glance, this seems like a nifty option. The idea behind the Initial Capitals option is that you can turn *KAREN FREDRICKS* into *Karen Fredricks*. Seems like a great idea on paper. In reality, however, you end up with *Ibm Corporation* and *Marcus Welby Md.*

- **Lowercase:** i suppose you might want to type in all lowercase. i just can't imagine why.

- **Memo:** This is where you can store a large amount of information that you don't want to risk burying away amidst your other notes. For example, you might want to include your driving directions in this area.

- **Number:** This option enables you to enter only numbers into a field. Say you want to find all your customers that have more than 30 employees. You can easily search for a number greater than *30,* but you can't possibly search for a number greater than *thirty.*

- **Phone:** In Chapter 4, I show you all those nifty things that ACT! does to speed up the data input process. If you designate a field to be a Phone field, you automatically get a year's supply of dashes.

- **Picture:** A picture is worth 1,000 words, and here's where you can stick a picture of each client or a picture of each product that they bought.

- **Time:** If time is of the essence, this is where you can input a time.

- **Upper Case:** I NEVER TYPE IN ALL UPPERCASE BECAUSE I FEEL LIKE I'M SCREAMING. BESIDES, I'M AFRAID I MIGHT DEVELOP POLYPS ON MY FINGER TIPS.

- **URL Address:** Use this field type if you need to associate another Web address with your contacts.

ACT! already comes equipped with e-mail and Web site fields for your viewing pleasure. And, you can add several additional e-mail addresses to the existing ACT! E-mail field. Add a new URL field with caution!

- **Yes/No:** This actually creates a check box field that you can click. Call me old-fashioned, but I think *check box* would have been a more appropriate name. To further confuse the issue, a query on this field looks for "true" or "false" values.

6. **Assign any of the five optional attributes and click Next:**

- **Allow Editing:** Enables any of your users to add new data to a field.

- **Allow Blank:** If you want to require that a field must be filled in you need to remove the check mark from this field. Use this option if you want to require a user to enter information into a certain field.

- **Generate History:** This neat little feature generates a history on the History tab when you change the contents of the field.

- **Primary Field:** When you duplicate a contact record, the primary fields are the fields that are duplicated.

- **Use Drop-Down List:** When you choose this feature, you can either pick an existing drop-down list or create a new, unique drop-down list later. I cover creating drop-down lists later in this chapter in the "Creating a drop-down list field" section.

7. **Customize your field further by choosing from the following optional selections and then click Next.**

   The next Define Fields screen opens, offering you a few more choices for your editing pleasure.

   - **Default Value:** If 80 percent of your database consists of customers, you might assign *Customer* as the default value of the ID/Status field.

   - **Field Format:** If you want dashes to appear automatically in a field, here's the place to do it by inserting the # symbol where you want data to go. For example, a Social Security number looks like ###-##-####.

   - **Field Length:** You might want to limit the number of characters that a user can enter into a given field; for example, you can limit a field looking for values of "yes" or "no" to three characters.

8. **Set optional triggers and click Finish.**

   Adding a trigger to a field causes something magical to happen when entering data into a field. For example, you might want an Excel spreadsheet to open when you move your cursor into the field, and an activity series to start when you leave the field. In Figure 15-4, you see three ways to start a trigger: when changing a field, when entering a field, and when leaving a field.

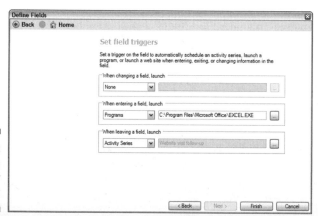

Figure 15-4:
Attaching
a trigger
to a field.

For each type of trigger you can assign one of three possibilities:

- **None:** If you want nothing to occur, choose this option.

- **Program:** Clicking the Browse button allows you to navigate to virtually any file in your computer. You can browse to a program, a URL, or even to a specific file.

- **Activity Series:** Clicking the Browse button takes you to a list of the activity series that you've created. If you haven't created any activity series, you may want to pay a visit to Chapter 10 to find out how.

Many of the neat add-on products that complement ACT! are designed as field triggers; when you purchase the add-on you might need to link the product to a specific field. Check my Web site at `www.techbenders.com/act4dummies.htm` to find out more about some of these special trigger products.

Working with Lists

The sure-fire way to destroy a database is by adding information in an inconsistent manner. Drop-down lists help ensure that users input data in a uniform manner. As an extra, added bonus, drop-down lists also save you time; when you type in the first several letters of an item in your drop-down list, ACT! responds by completing the word for you.

In ACT!, you find three major list types. Two of them, the Product List and the Process List, are associated with your opportunities. The other list type, drop-down, is associated with your contact, group, company, and opportunity fields. Although you can add new items to a list as you are using it, managing your lists in one central location is easier.

Creating a drop-down list field

Associating a drop-down list with a field requires two things:

- ✔ Specifying that the field is to contain a drop-down list.
- ✔ Adding items to the drop-down list.

Although which one comes first doesn't matter — the field or the drop-down list — I start by creating a field with a drop-down list:

1. **From any ACT! window, choose Tools➪Define Fields.**

   The Define Fields dialog box opens in all its glory (refer to Figure 15-1). You might even notice those three items in the List Tasks area. Hold that thought — I discuss those in the next section.

2. **Click the field name that you want to contain a drop-down list and then click the Edit Field option in the Field Tasks area.**

3. **Select the Use Drop-Down List check box.**

   If you want to use an existing drop-down list, here's your golden opportunity. For example, the last time I checked, there were 50 US states; those states are the same for my mailing, business, and home addresses. You could have one State drop-down list and associate it with the mailing, business, and home state fields.

4. **Click Finish.**

Whew! That was pretty easy, and if you're using an existing drop-down list, you're finished. However, if you need to build a drop-down list from scratch, you have more work. Fortunately, ACT! returns you to the Define Fields dialog box, which is right where you need to be to create or edit a drop-down list.

Creating a drop-down list

This might seem like a case of "which came first, the chicken or the egg?" In the previous section, I tell you how to associate a field with an already created drop-down list. For example, if you create a mailing list address, you can use the existing State drop-down list to avoid having to type in all the states into a new drop-down list. In other cases, you need to go back and create the drop-down list. Here's what you need to do:

1. **From any ACT! screen, choose Tools➪Define Fields.**

   If you just created the drop-down field, you can skip this step because you're already there!

2. **Select the Manage Drop-Down Lists from the List Tasks area.**

   The Create, Edit, or Delete Drop-Down Lists window appears.

   - **To create a drop-down list:** Click Create Drop-Down List from the Drop-Down List Tasks area.

   - **To edit a drop-down list:** Select the drop-down list and then click Edit Drop-Down List from the Drop-Down List Tasks area.

   The Enter Drop-Down List Name and Type window opens, as shown in Figure 15-5.

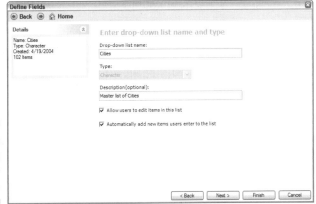

3. **Configure the following drop-down list options and click Next:**

- **Drop-Down List Name:** To make things less complicated for your-self, use a name that very closely resembles the name of the field that will be associated with the drop-down list.

- **Type:** Choose what type of field goes in the list — for example, character.

- **Description:** If you have a lot of drop-down lists, you might need to give your list a bit of further explanation.

- **Allow Users to Edit Items in This List:** Users have the ability to edit the drop-down list as they are entering in contact information.

- **Automatically Add New Items Users Enter to the List:** Lets your users define the items that will be used in a drop-down list by auto-matically adding each item they enter into the drop-down list.

If you decide to allow users to automatically add new items to a drop-down list, you might want to do so only temporarily. Although this option is a great way to build a drop-down list from scratch, you run the chance of creating a mess. Make sure that all users have a good idea of the kind of items that should — and shouldn't — be added to the drop-down lists. And, more impor-tantly, make sure they peruse the existing entries in the drop-down list before adding new items to avoid duplication.

4. **From the Enter Drop-Down List Values window, choose one of the fol-lowing options:**

- **Add:** When you click the Add button, your cursor jumps down to the bottom of your list of drop-down items. Type in the new drop-down item and an optional description, and you're all set.

- **Delete:** This permanently removes the selected item from the drop-down list. However, previously entered information based on the removed drop-down item still remains in your database.

5. **Type in the drop-down list item and an optional description.**

   Chances are that you don't need to include descriptions in your drop-down list. Once in a while, though, they can prove to be priceless. The State drop-down list consists of the two letter state abbreviations; the description includes the full name of the state for those of us who can never remember whether MA stands for Maine, Maryland, or Massachusetts! You can see what I mean in Figure 15-6.

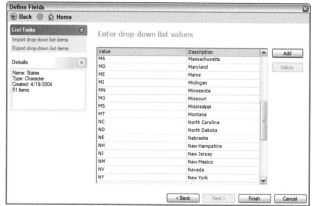

Figure 15-6:
Adding items to a drop-down list.

6. **Click Finish when you finish adding all the items you want to your drop-down list.**

Managing the Product List

In Chapter 20, you can find most everything you need to know about the exiting world of Opportunities — and believe me, there are a bunch of cool things. However, in this chapter, you discover how to modify your fields — and the drop-down lists associated with them.

Don't think that because your company doesn't sell widgets — or some similar item — that you can't use the Product List. Perhaps a better name for this field would have been Products/Services. At any rate, if you are gaining financially from your customers, use the Product List to help you analyze your profit centers.

To modify your Product List, follow these steps:

1. **From any ACT! screen, choose Tools⇨Define Fields.**

   The Define Fields window opens.

2. **Click Manage Product List.**

   The Manage Product List dialog box opens, as shown in Figure 15-7.

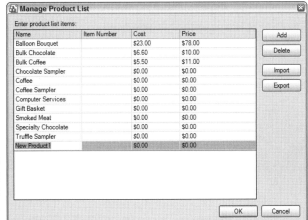

Figure 15-7:
Editing the
Product List.

3. **Click the Add button.**

   A New Product item appears at the bottom of the list of your product names.

4. **Fill in the appropriate fields.**

   You can move on to the various fields by pressing Tab.

   a. Assign a name to your product.

   b. Enter an item number if you use them.

   c. Add the cost that you pay for the item.

   d. Include the price you're going to charge your customers for the item.

   If your costs and prices fluctuate, feel free to leave those fields blank. You can always change them each time you enter a new sales opportunity.

5. **Click OK to close the Product List and then click Close to close the Define Fields window.**

Managing the Process List

The ACT! program was originally developed as a sales tool for busy sales people. Today, the product has evolved to the point that just about any industry and individual can benefit by using ACT!. However, the tradition of sales tracking remains, and the Process List is just one of those examples. ACT!'s Process List allows you to set up the steps that everyone in your organization follows when trying to close a sale. You can even associate a probability with each step. It is rumored that you need to contact someone 12 times before you convert them from a prospect to a customer; here's where you can be reminded of where you are in that process.

To edit or create a Process List, follow these steps:

1. **From any ACT! screen, choose Tools⇨Define Fields⇨Manage Process List.**

   The Create, Edit, or Delete Opportunity Processes dialog box, as shown in Figure 15-8, appears. If you have already set up a Process List, you see it listed by name, description, and number of stage in the Process List.

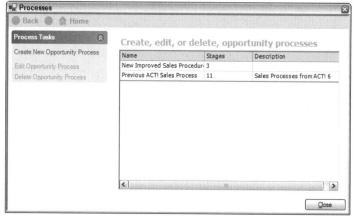

Figure 15-8: Creating or editing a sales process.

2. **Select one of the following three options and click Next:**

   • **Create New Opportunity Process:** Creates a brand spanking new Process List.

   • **Edit Opportunity Process:** Allows you to edit an existing Process List.

   • **Delete Opportunity Process:** Deletes an existing Process List. Rather than deleting an existing list, you might decide to make it inactive. You see that option on the next screen.

3. Double-click a name, description, or probability to change it.

If you are editing an existing Process List, modifying an entry by double-clicking is easy. The steps from the previously created Process List appear, as shown in Figure 15-9. If you are creating a new Process List, your processes are empty. Don't worry though — you can fill them up easily enough.

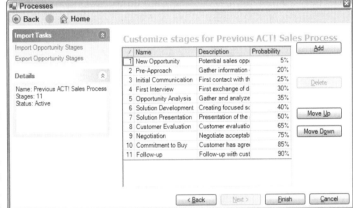

Figure 15-9:
Customizing the stages in a sales process list.

4. Click the Add or Delete button to further configure your Process List.

The steps are numbered. ACT! automatically numbers the steps in a Process List, saving you the effort. If you want, you can change the order by choosing one of the options to either move an option up or down on the list. When you move an option, all subsequent steps automatically renumber.

5. Click Finish when you are done.

In ACT!, you can often skin a cat or solve a problem in more than one way. You can access the Product and Process lists from two other areas of ACT!:

✔ From any ACT! screen, choose Contacts⇨Opportunities⇨Manage Product (or Process) List.

✔ Scroll down to the bottom of the Product or Process List when creating a new, or editing an existing, opportunity. From there, you can select Edit List.

Chapter 16

Customizing Layouts

. . . .

. . . .

Many ACT! users are confused about the concept of the layout. In fact, some of you might have ended up renaming a layout label when you wanted to rename fields. ***Remember:*** A *field* is a place to store information. A *layout* refers to how you actually see those fields. Your layout determines both the order of the fields and the format of each field. A layout is the name for a file that determines which fields you see and in what order those fields appear. After you add new fields to your ACT! database, the next step is to stick them into an existing layout (or design a new one).

The layout confusion is further compounded by users who share their database across a network. Problems occur if the users are accessing different layouts. Depending on the layout that they are using, some users may not be able to see all the fields of the database.

In this chapter, I show you how to use the Layout Designer to modify an existing layout. Here you master adding or replacing tabs on your layout, reordering all the fields when you finish, and finally, adding a few artistic touches to your masterpiece.

Only database users with the Administrator or Manager level of security have access to the Layout Designer. If you are a Standard, Restricted, or Browse level user you get to sit back, put your feet on the desk, and direct the Administrator or Manager as to how you want to have the layout designed. Be careful what you wish for, however; if you are an Administrator or Manager, you get to do all the dirty work, so keep reading!

Modifying an Existing ACT! Layout

Before you begin modifying an existing layout, think about how you want your fields arranged on your layout. Why not try out all the layouts that come with ACT!? This way, you get a feeling for the one that's most comfortable to you. Don't worry about colors or the names on the tabs — you can change all that.

Designing a new layout completely from scratch is possible, although more trouble, than modifying an existing one. If you feel the urge to design a new layout from scratch, you need to know that you'll start with an entirely blank canvas. If you like to have a go at it, choose File➪New from the Layout Designer, and a brand-new — absolutely blank — layout appears. You have a lot of work ahead of you. And I'm guessing a lot of headaches, too. So why bother with creating a new layout from scratch? I can't think of a good reason. I recommend just making changes to an existing layout — you save yourself a lot of time and grief and will probably be very happy with the results.

When you save a contact layout, ACT! automatically assigns it the extension .cly. When you save a group layout, ACT! gives it the .gly extension. And when you create a company layout, the file is given the .aly moniker.

Arranging fields the way you want them

Ah, the age-old question of form versus function. This hint may sound like a no-brainer, but many ACT! users never realize the importance of changing the field locations in their layout. For example, you might choose a layout that has the main business phone number on the top portion of your layout, the home phone number on a different tab along the bottom, and the mobile phone number in a third location. If you're constantly flipping between tabs to find phone numbers, move them together into one strategic place on your layout. This organization might not make your layout *look* better, but you'll certainly *feel* better! The point is to design your layout in such a way that data input becomes easy — and possibly even fun!

Here's what you do to modify an existing layout:

1. **Choose the layout that's closest to the one that you want to have.**

   If you need help with switching layouts, take a peek at Chapter 2.

2. **Choose Tools➪Design Layout➪Contact.**

   You'll notice that you're also given a choice of group and company. That's because you can also design — or redesign — your group and company layouts in exactly the same way as you do for your contact layout.

The Layout Designer opens. Each field consists of two elements (see Figure 16-1):

- The *field label* is an optional element but usually appears immediately to the left of a field.

- The *field* itself is identified by the down arrow that appears at the field's right edge.

3. Maximize the Layout Designer.

Okay, this step isn't a necessity, but it sure makes your design chores a whole lot easier! I'm always amazed when I see someone struggling with layout on a small portion of the monitor.

4. Make sure the toolbox and Properties window are both open.

These are two important windows that you need to have open in order to create or modify a layout. The toolbox sits on the left side of the Layout Designer, and the Properties window sits on the right side. Feel free to move them out of your way if you like, but trust me — you're going to need them momentarily!

If the toolbox and/or the Properties window are nowhere to be seen, try giving the View menu a click to open them. You see both of them listed right there; a check mark next to either Toolbox or Properties Window means they are alive and well — and living on the Layout Designer.

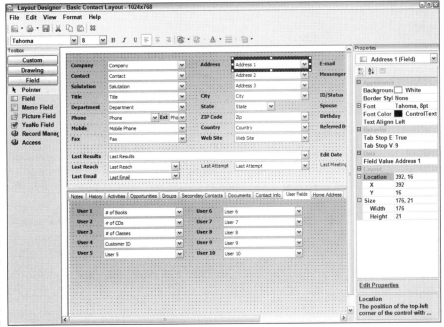

Figure 16-1:
The ACT!
Layout
Designer.

5. Choose File⇨Save As and give your layout a new name.

I recommend renaming your layout so that you can later go back to your original layout (if you totally annihilate this one) and easily identify your layout (if you choose a recognizable name).

The name of your layout appears in the Layout Designer title bar (refer to Figure 16-1).

As you make changes to your layout, the Save icon on the Layout Designer toolbar comes to life. Click it to save your work. Relying on the old undo standby (Edit⇨Undo) is an option, but saving your layout early and often is always a good idea!

6. Select the Pointer tool in the toolbox.

The *Pointer tool,* the tool that you'll probably use most often, enables you to select fields so that you can move, change, or remove them.

7. With the Pointer tool, select the fields and field labels that you want to move — or remove — from the layout.

Removing unused fields can simplify a layout and make room for other fields that you want to add. I recommend removing what's unwanted before moving on to other aspects of the layout design process.

Make your selections by any of these methods:

- Click any field or field label to select it.

- Click any field and then press Shift or Ctrl while clicking additional fields to select multiple fields and labels.

- Create a box around the desired labels and fields by holding down the left mouse button and then dragging to create a selection box.

When you select a field, a border of small boxes appears around the field indicating that it is selected. In Figure 16-1, the Address field is selected.

8. Press the Delete key.

The unwanted fields go away.

In Chapter 15, you find out how to create and edit fields. One of the field options is the ability to allow users to edit the contents of a field. If you remove that option, users can view the contents of a field, but they can't change it.

Removing a field from the layout does not remove the actual field from the database. The field remains in your database but isn't visible in the layout. See the "Using layouts to restrict access to key fields" sidebar for more details.

9. **To move fields around, select them with the Pointer and then drag them to a new location on your layout.**

   If only rearranging the living room is this easy! The idea is to *drag* the selected fields and their corresponding labels to the place on your layout that seems the most logical to you. When you hold your mouse over selected fields, your cursor transforms into a plus sign, indicating that you're ready to move the field.

   If you only need to make a minor adjustment to the field location, you might try using your keyboard's arrow keys for really fine-tuning your layout.

You can cut a group of fields by selecting them and then pressing Ctrl+X. Move your cursor to the new spot on your layout where you want to place the cells and press Ctrl+V. *Voilà* — you've moved the group of fields *en masse*.

Adding new fields to the layout

In Chapter 15, you find out how to modify existing fields or to create new ones from scratch. When you rename an existing field in ACT! that is already present on your layout, the new name is magically reflected on the layout. Typically, you start by renaming the 15 user fields; after you do, your work is over because that new name is now included in your layout.

Adding a new field to your ACT! database is a bit more complicated because after you create the new field (see Chapter 15), you now need to find a place for it on your layout. But, if you follow the upcoming steps, you'll find that adding the new field to your layout is certainly not an insurmountable task:

1. **Click the Field button in the Layout Designer's toolbox and then hold down the left mouse button and drag the cursor to the right to define the field's size and position on your layout.**

   The Select Field dialog box opens, presenting a list of all the fields that do not currently appear on your existing layout. The fields are listed alphabetically. If you added an address block, all the related fields appear together, which allows you to easily add them all to your layout in one fell swoop. You'll notice in Figure 16-2, for example, that all the credit card address fields are lined up together.

   Clicking the Field button allows you to add the vast majority of new fields that you've added to your database. However, you'll notice a few other field types lurking in the field section of the toolbox. These include

   • Memo

   • Picture

   • YesNo

Figure 16-2:
Adding a
new field to
an ACT!
layout.

The Memo and Picture fields are super-sized fields that need to be made larger than your other fields. The YesNo fields are tiny little ones that are only large enough to hold a check mark. Don't worry if you're having trouble "guesstimating" the size of those fields; ACT! automatically resizes them for you.

Even though the field is called a YesNo field, it is actually a check box field that you click to indicate yes or no.

2. **Select the field that you want to add to the layout, deselect the Include a Label check box (if you don't want the field to have a label), and then click the Add button.**

   The field is added to your layout. You can add as many fields to your layout as you like, but you're allowed to use each field only once.

3. **When you're done adding fields, click the Close button in the Select Field dialog box.**

Using layouts to restrict access to key fields

If you have certain fields in your database that you don't want other database users to have access to — for example, a record of your customers' credit card information — you can't restrict your users from viewing selected fields because ACT! doesn't have field-level security. You can create specific layouts, however, that don't include the fields that you're concerned about.

What you do is create a custom layout based on your current one, *remove* the fields that you

don't want other users accessing, and then distribute the new layout to your staff. As long as your users don't have access to other layouts that include these fields, these fields remain invisible to them.

Although this method of securing your database isn't foolproof, creative use of your layouts can help you add more security to your database.

Changing the tabs

Just like you can add, move, or remove the individual fields of your database on your layout, you can also add, move, or remove the tabs that are on your layout. Using tabs is a great way to organize the fields in your database. You might have a Products tab that, ironically, lists the various products that you are tracking. You may even have a Personal tab that includes all the personal information about a contact: their birthday, anniversary, blood type, IQ, and shoe size. The whole point of being able to customize your layout is to make it comfortable for you. If you find yourself constantly hunting for a field, chances are that your fields are not arranged in a logical fashion. If that's the case, consider editing the tabs on your layout:

1. **From the Layout Designer, choose Edit⇨Tabs.**

   The Edit Tabs dialog box appears (see Figure 16-3), where ACT! gives you several tab customization options.

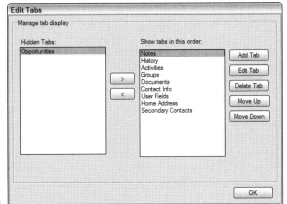

Figure 16-3: Editing tabs in an ACT! layout.

2. **Hide any tabs you no longer want to display in your layout.**

   You'll notice the single left- and right-pointing arrows in the Edit Tabs dialog box. These arrows allow you to hide a tab. Although the system tabs — Notes, History, Activities, Groups, Opportunities, and Documents — can't be deleted, you can hide them by moving them into the Hidden Tabs area on the left side of the Edit Tabs dialog box.

   Hiding a tab on a layout is a great way to hide certain key pieces of information from the lesser beings around your office. You might prefer that the temporary help doesn't have access to the credit card information of your customers or that your staff doesn't have access to employment information that you might be storing on your database. Then, when no one's looking, you can always unhide the tab to access that top-secret information.

Unless you want to drive yourself nuts, you might want to be very careful about hiding tabs. You can place a field only on one layout. Be careful that you don't place a field on a tab and then hide the entire tab or you might drive yourself nuts looking for the field that appears to be MIA.

3. **Customize your tab according to your own sense of design and order.**

   • **Add Tab:** Add an additional tab to your layout. Enter a name for the new tab in the Add Tab Layout dialog box and then click OK. You now need to go back and add some fields to that shiny new tab.

   • **Edit Tab:** Give the tab a new name.

   • **Delete Tab:** Remove a tab from your layout.

   When you remove a tab from a layout, all the fields located on that tab are removed as well. Consider moving — or removing — all the fields from a tab *before* you delete the tab itself!

   • **Move Up:** Move a tab so that it appears *before* another tab.

   • **Move Down:** Arrange a particular tab so that it appears *after* another.

4. **Click OK when you're happy with the name and order of your tabs.**

Changing the order of things

You can — and should — use the Tab key to progress through your fields as you input contact information into your database. When you start with an ACT! layout "right out of the box," you can tab through the fields in a logical order — that is, from top to bottom. However, you may prefer to move horizontally across the layout rather than vertically from top to bottom. Or, you might find that after adding a few fields you can no longer tab through your fields with the greatest of ease. Modifying layouts generally renders the field entry order non-sequential.

Although having out-of-sequence field ordering doesn't damage your database, it does make inputting data difficult. Each time that you press the Tab key, your cursor skips to the next *numbered* field instead of to the next field that you see on your layout. This could be a real bummer if not for the fact that you can reorder your fields when necessary. A *tab stop* is associated with every field on your layout; the Tab Stop number determines the order of the fields.

Although an important step, you might want to hold off on changing the field order until you are absolutely, positively, 100 percent certain that you are happy with the way you've placed the fields on your layout. There is no magic way to simply number the fields consecutively from one to one hundred; unless you want to waste a lot of your time by redoing your work, you might save this step until after you live with your layout for a while.

1. **Choose View⇨Tab Stops⇨Show Tab Stops in ACT!'s Layout Designer.**

   The tab stop appear in the Layout Designer, as shown in Figure 16-4.

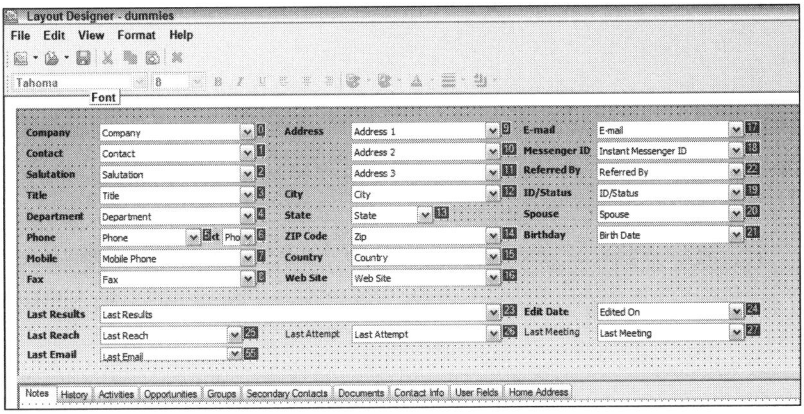

Figure 16-4:
Changing
the order of
the tab
stops.

When you enter the land of Tab Stops, you'll probably notice two things: Little red numbers now appear to the right of each field, and you no longer have the toolbox and Properties window to play with.

When you add a new field to your layout, ACT! automatically assigns the field the next available field number. When changing the field number order, focus on those fields because that's where the numbering is out of whack. If you previously removed a field number and not assigned it to another field, ACT! automatically assigns that number to the next field that you add to your layout.

2. **Select any fields for which you want to change the field order.**

   If you select the fields whose field entry order you want to change (refer to Figure 16-4, where the fields are not numbered sequentially), the number disappears.

3. **Select the fields a second time to reassign the field the next available number.**

   When you select the field again, the next available number is assigned to the field. Feel free to select the fields in any order you want. After all, this is your layout!

4. **Right-click a field, choose Set Index, and type in a field number to "advance" several fields at a time.**

   This is a great party trick in the event that you need to squeeze a field or two in among all your existing fields and don't want to have to "click" and "re-click" each and every field in your layout. Say, for example, that your fields are numbered sequentially from 1 to 61, and you want to stick a new field smack under field 1. Whew! You're looking at a lot of click time. But wait! If you right-click field 2, choose Set Index, and change the field number to 3, you see all the fields from 2–61 magically increase by one digit.

   I wish I had a great tip for decreasing the field numbers in the event that you remove a field. Unfortunately, I don't. And, I wish I could undo the field numbers if I increased them by accident. I can't. All I can tell you is to be careful when setting the field index because it can't easily be reversed.

5. **Choose View⇨Tab Stops⇨Show Tab Stops to leave the tab stop area.**

6. **Click View⇨Enter Stops⇨Show Enter Stops to begin editing the enter stops.**

   Just like the tab stops control the order that your cursor follows as you tab through your layout, the *enter stop* controls the path your cursor takes as you press Enter. Think of the enter stop as a bypass, allowing you to skip merrily from one area of your layout to the next.

   The enter stop looks and feels pretty much like the tab stop with two major differences: The Enter Stop dialog box is tastefully decorated in green instead of red, and you use a whole lot fewer of them. In general, you want to place an enter stop at the beginning of each group of fields. You may want to have one at the beginning of the address, one at the start of the phone numbers, and a third one conveniently located on the first of the personal fields.

7. **Choose View⇨Enter Stops⇨Show Enter Stops to return to the Layout Designer.**

Beautifying Your Layout

I'll admit that I count myself among the artistically challenged of this world. If you read and assimilated everything in the beginning of this chapter, you're now pretty much equipped to go forth and design a nifty new layout. But before tackling that new design project, you might first want to give some thought to some of the things that can make your layout a bit more artistically pleasing.

Doing minor touch-up work

At this juncture, you have left the area of function behind you and have moved on to some of the more aesthetically pleasing aspects of layout design. You can also decide whether your layout needs a major or minor makeover. The Edit Properties dialog box allows you to make changes to the font, font size, and other attributes, and to the basic border style. This is great for simple touch-up work but is rather limiting if your layout needs an extreme makeover. You can change the font and border attributes in the Edit Properties dialog box (see Figure 16-5). Right-click the label or field you want to change and choose Edit Properties.

Figure 16-5:
The Layout
Designer
Edit
Properties
dialog box.

Creating an extreme makeover

Use the Properties window if you want to create some major changes. There are two great advantages of using the Properties window over the Edit Properties dialog box. First, you can edit more than one field at a time. Secondly, you have a whole lot more choice about which elements you can edit.

If you click around in the Layout Designer, the choices in the Properties window change accordingly. If you click in a field, you can change the various color and font attributes; if you click in a label, you can edit the text of the label.

If you're having trouble reading the various options on the Properties window, you may want to resize it so that you can read it better. Simply place your cursor over the left edge of the window; when your cursor changes to a double pointing horizontal line, drag to the left to expand the window.

Changing a field label

In most cases, the field name and the field label are exactly the same. Having a field label differ too radically from the name of the actual field proves to be quite confusing when you wander into the area of template and report creation. However, sometimes you might want to tweak the field label so that it fits on your layout better. For example, the Cellular Telephone Number field might be represented by the Cell label.

You can change a field label with two different methods:

- ✔ **Double-click the label.**

  The label turns into a text box with a blinking cursor. Delete any unnecessary letters and type the new label.

- ✔ **Type the new field label in the Text section of the Properties window.**

Adding color to your drab life

ACT! comes with close to a zillion colors that you can add to your layouts. Okay, you caught me; there might be a few less than a zillion, but I think just about every color of the rainbow is represented. To use one of those nifty colors, follow these steps:

1. **Click in the background of your layout in the Layout Designer.**

2. **Select a background color from the Properties window.**

   You can now change the background color by clicking the Background Color drop-down arrow and selecting a color that matches your mood — or the décor of your office. Like magic, your background color changes. If it doesn't, it's probably because a graphic is hiding that beautiful background color. If that's the case, go on to the next section.

You'll notice that the background colors are further divided into three tabs: Custom, Web, and System. By default, you're on the Web tab; that's where you find the largest selection of colors to work with. The System tab is for the drab members of the audience who prefer to work in the more refined shades of gray.

Some of you may be a little hard to please and find that the colors provided in ACT! just don't match the décor of your home or office. If you want to add your own custom-blended color to your layout, you can easily do so by mixing your very own custom color on the Custom Color tab. When you create a custom color, the Properties window displays the RGB (red, green, and blue) number associated with the custom color. Feel free to change those numbers if you've worked with graphic programs in the past and want to match your layout to a specific color.

Changing the colors of your fields and labels is just as easy. Just select the fields or labels and change the color option in the Properties window exactly like you do for the layout background.

You can select as many fields and/or labels if you like and then change the color for your entire selection at the same time.

Got a few fields that you want to make sure are used by your users whenever possible? Make a field mandatory by turning off the Allow Blank option in the Define Fields dialog box. This option can be an annoying one if you just don't have the information needed to fill in the field at the time of your data input; ACT! demands that you supply the missing information before you leave the record. An alternative might be to highlight the critically important fields in a stunning shade of yellow so that users recognize their importance without be asked to supply information that they might not have.

Adding the Finishing Touches

Whew! After you add, delete, move, and color your fields, you're ready to sally forth into the world and start using your new layout. But wait! If you look carefully at your layout, things might look a bit, well, *cock-eyed*. That's an official computer term to indicate that your fields seem out of whack because they consist of various sizes and aren't aligned properly. If I didn't like you so well, I'd tell you to grab your mouse and start adjusting those whacko fields by dragging them into submission. Several hours later, after much dragging, resizing, and probably quite a bit of cursing, you'd probably end up in pretty much the same place as you started. But because the point of this whole book is to show you how to do things the easy way, you might want to read the following sections instead.

Lining up fields and labels

One way to give your layout a truly polished look is by aligning all fields and labels. When you move a field to a new location on your layout, you have a strong possibility that the field is slightly out of line, both vertically and horizontally, with the other fields. Of course you can always try to "eyeball it" by dragging the field around trying to get it into just the perfect spot. This method can be very time-consuming, aggravating, and hard on your carpal tunnel. I have a much easier — and precise — way to accomplish your goal:

1. **Select the errant field that is out of alignment.**

2. **Click the anchor field (the field that is properly aligned).**

   If you look closely, the selection boxes around the errant field are white, and the selection boxes around the anchor field are black. This is your indication that the anchor field stays in place and the other field lines up with it.

   You can align several fields at a time by selecting them and right-clicking the anchor field. The field you right-clicked now becomes the anchor, and all the other selected fields line up with it.

3. **Right-click any of the selected fields and choose an alignment option.**

   As you can see in Figure 16-6, you're given a whole bunch of options from which to choose. Here are the two you'll probably use the most often:

   • **Align Lefts:** Typically your fields look the best if they are lined up along the left edges looking vertically down the layout. To do this, you want to select your fields from top to bottom before aligning.

   • **Align Tops:** If you have two or three columns in your layout, you want your fields to align along the top edges as well. Select your fields horizontally, from left to right, before choosing this option.

   If you choose the incorrect alignment option you might end up with a mess in which all your fields are now on top of one another. Quick! Reach for the Undo button. Don't see it? Choose Edit➪Undo.

4. **Click anywhere in your layout to remove the selection boxes.**

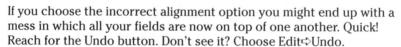

Figure 16-6:
Aligning fields and labels.

Bring to Front
Bring Forward
Send to Back
Send Backward

Cut
Copy
Paste
Delete

Align Lefts
Align Center
Align Rights
Align Tops
Align Middles
Align Bottoms
Align to Grid

Select All

Resizing fields

You'll probably find yourself in a number of situations in which you need to resize one or more fields. Typically, you want to make several fields smaller so that you can squeeze more fields into your layout. You might want to make several fields larger so that you can add more data into those fields. Or, you might find that a new field you just placed on your layout isn't the same exact size as the other fields. Again, you can manually resize your fields one at a time. You can also knock your head firmly against the wall several times, but I don't recommend either activity.

✔ **To resize several fields at a time:** Select all the fields that you want to resize *en masse*. Then place your cursor on one of the selection boxes on either the left or right edge of the selected fields. When your cursor turns into a single horizontal arrow, drag the selection box to the left or right, depending on whether you are making the fields larger or smaller.

✔ **To resize against the anchor:** Select all the fields that you want to be the same exact size as an anchor field. Press the Ctrl key, click the anchor field once, pause, and then click it a second time so that the selection boxes are now black. Choose Format⇨Make Same Size⇨Width.

Adding a logo or a graphic

Perhaps the best way to truly personalize your layout is by adding your very own logo to it. Adding a graphic to the layout means that the graphic appears on each and every one of your contact records. Don't confuse this with a Picture field; a Picture field varies for every one of your contacts. You can add your *chef-d'oeuvre* to your layout by following these easy steps:

1. **From the Layout Designer, click the Drawing button in the toolbox and then choose the Image tool.**

2. **Using your mouse, draw a shape on your layout to match the graphic you want to insert.**

   The Open dialog box opens.

3. **Navigate to the graphic you want to insert, select it, and click Open.**

   The graphic now appears on your layout. You can drag the graphic to a new, improved location by placing your cursor on the graphic. When your cursor turns into a plus sign, drag the graphic to the appropriate spot on your layout.

Creating a circle in a square

Admittedly, no one would ever confuse me with Picasso. However, some of you might be of a more artistic persuasion, or just want to take advantage of some of the drawing tools to add a little clarity to your layout. By creating a square that is slightly larger than a grouping of several of your fields, you are in essence creating a frame that serves to highlight those fields.

If you click the Drawing button in the toolbox, you'll notice the Rectangle and Ellipse options; these are just fancy words for *square* and *circle*. At any rate, by clicking either of these options, you can draw a square or circle (okay, a rectangle or an ellipsis) on your layout. After they're drawn, you can head over to the Properties window and change the color of your newly created shape. This is a great way to emphasize a group of fields, particularly if your layout is starting to look cluttered.

Did your newly created circle or square plunk itself down on top of your existing fields? Although this leads to an interesting work of art, you probably prefer to have the graphic behind the fields. Don't panic; simply right-click the graphic in question and choose Send to Back.

Adding text boxes

If a picture is worth a thousand words, a text box might just be worth a million. Inconsistent data input is a sure-fire way to decrease the productivity of your database. This lack of uniformity is often caused not by lack of knowledge but rather by lack of communication. Adding a text box to your layout is a great way to help users input key pieces of information in the right place and to help organize the groups of data on the layout. Use your text boxes to create a heading for a group of fields or to include data input instructions to your users.

1. **From the toolbox, click the Drawing button and then choose the Text tool.**

   Your cursor now looks like a plus sign instead of the normal arrow.

2. **Find the spot on the layout to add a text box, hold down your left mouse button, and drag the cursor to create a box.**

3. **Use the Properties window to customize your text box.**

   Here's where you can really have fun. As long as the new text box is selected, you can change the text, font attributes, font color, and background color of the text box.

I'm a firm believer in doing things the easy way whenever possible. If you find yourself longing to have several text boxes all formatted the same way, create the first text box, customize it just the way you like it, and then clone it by right-clicking it and choosing Copy. At that point, you can paste it on your layout — and the only thing you have to change is the text.

Building a table

Some of you may find yourselves running out of room on your layouts because you needed to add so many customized fields. As an alternative to the traditional concept of listing all your field labels next to your actual fields, you might consider arranging your fields in table format, as shown in Figure 16-7. The idea here is to save room and allow you to easily fill in vital information.

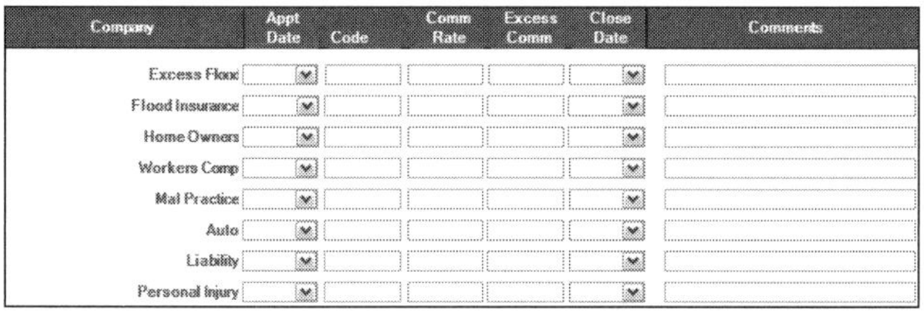

Figure 16-7: A layout formatted as a table.

Company	Appt Date	Code	Comm Rate	Excess Comm	Close Date	Comments
Excess Floor	⌄				⌄	
Flood Insurance	⌄				⌄	
Home Owners	⌄				⌄	
Workers Comp	⌄				⌄	
Mal Practice	⌄				⌄	
Auto	⌄				⌄	
Liability	⌄				⌄	
Personal Injury	⌄				⌄	

Consider building a table if you have several products and need to track the purchase date, serial number, and expiration date for each one. Or maybe you're a realtor and want to list the dimensions of several rooms. Not all databases can take advantage of a table format but those that can free up a lot of space on their layout.

Chapter 17

Zen and the Art of Database Maintenance

*I*n this chapter, I show you how to take care of your motorcycle . . . er, I mean your database. Would you believe that your ACT! database is very similar to a motorcycle? Both are made up of many moving parts that require maintenance. Failure to provide routine maintenance can result in big problems — for a motorcycle as well as for your database. If something does go wrong, having a backup is nice and, in most cases, necessary to keeping your job. Sometimes your motorcycle gets dirty; likewise, your database is prone to clutter. You'll sometimes have to bite the bullet, roll up your sleeves, and do a little cleaning — and clear out old or duplicate contact records from ACT!.

Regular maintenance keeps your database running efficiently. When you don't provide routine maintenance for a motorcycle, things get corroded; when you don't provide maintenance for your database, your records become corrupted. Quite simply, a *corrupted database* is one in which weird things start happening. No, you won't see a ghost, but you might not see a note that you know you created the day before. Or that note just might pop up again later — in the wrong place!

Understanding the Need to Check and Repair

I love to change the messages on my voice mail, and one of my favorite choices is, "Have you checked and repaired your database today?" Users often offer up a variety of excuses for why they didn't perform routine database maintenance. These excuses range anywhere from "I didn't have time" to "I didn't know I was supposed to." Of course, many of you give these excuses *after* your database has already been damaged. By then, of course, it may be too late for checking and repairing.

Determining the maintenance frequency

If you are a little old lady who uses your database only once in a blue moon, you may get away without maintaining your database. However, if the data in ACT! is extremely important to you, you want to perform your maintenance on a routine basis. At a minimum, I recommend your database receive a bit of tender loving care at least once a week.

My general rule is that the frequency of maintenance is directly tied to the amount of use that your database is receiving. There is no such thing as doing too much maintenance — only too little! Here are some situations that warrant more than weekly maintenance:

- ✔ You have a multi-user database.

    When ACT! is being used over a network the database is subject to more use — and abuse. The chances of having inaccurate and incorrect information increase exponentially with the number of users entering data into the database.

- ✔ You have a large database.

- ✔ You add new fields to your database.

- ✔ You make changes to the drop-down lists in your database.

- ✔ You add or delete numerous contact records to your database.

- ✔ You import another database into your existing ACT! database.

- ✔ You add — or delete — users to your database.

- ✔ You experienced a power outage.

- ✔ You had network problems.

- ✔ You suspect that your database is corrupted.

- ✔ You had a really lousy day when everything seemed to go wrong.

A little shopping list of database horrors

What are the warning signs of a corrupted database? Database corruption comes in many shapes and sizes. The following is a list of some of the more common indications of a corrupted ACT! database:

- ✔ While trying to open a database, you receive an error message or ACT! stops responding. Smoke might be seen rising from the back of your CPU.

- ✔ You receive error messages while working in ACT!.

- ✔ You can't log into the database as a particular user.

- ✔ Information appears to be missing, or mysteriously appears attached to the incorrect contact record.

- ✔ You notice a significant increase or decrease in the number of contact records in your database.

- ✔ Your database is acting funny or running slower than usual.

If you notice one — or heaven forbid, more than one — of the preceding warning signs, I'm sorry to say that the time has come to either perform CPR on your fainthearted co-workers or perform some simple database maintenance. In the next section, I give you the details on performing the simple database maintenance (that is, checking and repairing). You're on your own with the CPR.

Sometimes determining whether the corruption is in the *database* or in the ACT! *program* itself is difficult. To determine this, try opening the Act7demo database that's installed on your computer when you installed ACT!. If the Act7demo opens and runs correctly, the problem lies with your database. If you encounter the same problems in the Act7demo database that you're having in your own database, you might need to reinstall ACT!.

Performing Routine Maintenance

The old adage, "If it ain't broke, don't fix it!" does not apply to ACT!. Proper maintenance enables your database to run efficiently and improves performance. Some of the maintenance takes on a rather "behind the scenes" approach; users don't detect that maintenance has been performed. They know, however, that the maintenance hasn't been done if they start running into problems with the database. The other type of maintenance involves actual data cleanup; astute users can detect that changes have been made to the database.

Only the database Administrator can perform routine maintenance to ensure that your database continues to chug away without any problems. That's probably to ensure that everyone knows who to point at if things go wrong. Some maintenance tasks require that all users log off of the database so that the database can be locked, but those can be scheduled for off-peak or even overnight hours.

In ACT!, basic maintenance is referred to as *checking and repairing.* The system Administrator can run the Check and Repair tool regularly to ensure a healthy database, which consists of two procedures: the Integrity Check and the Re-index. These procedures are very similar to the Scan Disk and Disk Defragmenter procedures that you might already perform on your PC. The Integrity Check scours the database for errors and repairs them if found. After any found errors are repaired, Re-index squeezes out all the little empty spaces that are left in your database when you delete contact records in order to ensure maximum performance.

Yikes! Performing the Check and Repair sounds really important so you're probably thinking that it must be really hard. Wrong! Here's all you need to do:

1. **Log in as an Administrator and make sure that all other users are logged off the database.**

   If the Check and Repair command is grayed out from ACT!'s Tools menu, you don't have sufficient administrative rights to perform that option. You might want to jog your database Administrator's memory a bit to remind him that his salary is directly proportional to the efficient performance of your database!

2. **Choose Tools➪Database Maintenance➪Check and Repair.**

   The Check and Repair Database window opens, as shown in Figure 17-1.

Figure 17-1:
Checking
and
repairing a
database.

3. **Select both the Integrity Check and Re-index options and then click OK.**

   Your computer makes a few whirring noises, and a snazzy indicator bar appears momentarily on-screen. Try to look important during this time so as to justify your administrative salary.

Backing Up the ACT! Database

You probably already know the three rules of real estate: location, location, location. Similarly, the three basic rules of computing are backup, backup, backup! With the proliferation of viruses, as well as the poor construction of many computers, backing up on a daily basis is imperative. Failure to do so can result in loss of data — as well as time and money! Having a recent backup enables you to recover quickly when the unexpected happens. It might also ensure that you receive a paycheck at the end of the week.

Only *Administrators* and *Managers* of the ACT! database get to back up a database. And, after it's backed up, only Administrators can restore a database. Because every database requires an Administrator, you automatically landed the job if you are the only user of the database. If you need to back up the database and find that the backup option is grayed out on the File menu, you must find a database Administrator and wheedle him or her into changing your permissions. In Chapter 3, I explain the various ACT! user permissions.

If you're going to be making major changes to your database, such as importing new records, deleting old contact records, or modifying existing fields, I recommend creating a backup before you start — just in case!

You can set a reminder for backing up your database; I tell you how to do it in Chapter 3.

When you create an ACT! database, ACT! thoughtfully automatically creates several folders for you. In addition to a database folder that houses the main database files, ACT! creates subfolders for your attachments, layouts, queries, reports, and templates. When you back up your database, ACT! compresses all the data into a Zip file.

Very often, the ACT! database resides on a network drive and is backed up to a tape drive on a daily basis. In this case, backing up your database using ACT! is not necessary. However, you might be feeling a false sense of security knowing that this backup is taking place. Don't find out too late that your tape backup was backing up the ACT! program and not the ACT! data files themselves. Make sure that the database folder and all the subfolders are included as part of your backup. Feeling scared? Remind your IT person that his job security is directly related to the security of your database.

If you use backup software or store your data on an Internet site, remember that an ACT! database consists of more than a single file. You must back up all files whose filenames begin with the name of the database, as well as any related folders that contain your various supplemental documents.

Performing the basic ACT! backup

REMEMBER

You must have Administrator or Manager security level to back up your ACT! database. Open the ACT! database that you want to create a backup copy of and follow these steps:

1. Choose File⇨Back Up⇨Database.

The Back Up dialog box appears displaying the location for the backup database, as shown in Figure 17-2.

Figure 17-2:
The Back
Up dialog
box.

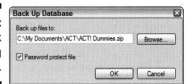

2. To back up the database to a different location from what's showing, click the Browse button, select a new location for your backup file, and then click Save.

3. Select the option to password protect your database (optional).

Just in case you feel like spies are lurking about, you might want to password protect the backup file. However, you might not feel the urge to do so knowing that only database Administrators can use the file.

4. Click the OK button.

An indicator bar appears, letting you know that ACT! is creating your backup. The time required to complete your backup varies depending on the size of your database and the supplemental files that are included in your backup. When the backup is complete, a message appears telling you that your backup was completed successfully!

Backing up to various media

Backing up a database is easy. The hard part is knowing where to place your backup. For nearly 20 years, computer users relied on the floppy disk as their backup method of choice. You may as well kiss those floppies good-bye because they just aren't big enough to hold your backup. By default, ACT! places your backup file on your computer's hard drive. That's great if your hard drive is ultimately being backed up, but not so great if it isn't — and your computer grinds to a painful halt. Here are a couple of good alternatives to your backup housing dilemma:

✔ **Zip drive:** I know this sounds confusing but you can place your backup Zip file on a Zip drive.

✔ **USB storage drive:** These tiny powerhouses can store the equivalent of a hundred floppy disks on a device the size of your thumb.

✔ **CD/DVD drive:** These puppies come installed on most of the new PCs.

✔ **External hard drive:** The price of external hard drives has plummeted in recent years; you might want to purchase one to store *all* your data files.

Restoring a backup copy of your database

A backup is no good if you don't know how to use it to restore your data. Although I hope you never have to use a backup copy, follow these steps to restore a copy of your database:

1. **Choose File⇨Restore⇨Database.**

   The Restore Database dialog box opens, as shown in Figure 17-3.

Figure 17-3:
Restoring a
backup.

2. **Select one of the restoration options and click OK.**

   • **Restore:** Restores all files to their original locations; this restore option is most commonly used when data is lost or corrupted.

   • **Restore As:** Allows you to restore the database to a new location with a new filename; this option works well when you want to copy a database or move it to another computer.

   • **Unpack and Restore Remote Database:** Allows you to install a database that synchronizes back to the main database.

3. **Click the Browse button to navigate to the location where the backup file is stored; click Save and then click OK.**

   You'll notice that all your backup files ends with the .zip extension.

Many of you are familiar with the .zip extension because you have worked with the WinZip software. Do not be tempted to unzip an ACT! backup file using WinZip. The files aren't placed in the correct locations, and the backup file probably is rendered useless!

4. Type the backup file password if prompted and click OK.

5. Type the Administrator's name and password and click OK.

Yikes! ACT! shows you the scary warning message that you see in Figure 17-4. The warning explains in no uncertain terms that if you continue, your database will be overwritten with older files. If your current database is a corrupted mess, that's a good thing; if your database is perfectly fine, that could be a bad thing!

Figure 17-4:
Scary
restoration
warning
message.

6. Click Yes to acknowledge that you want to continue.

Your computer whirs and hisses for a few moments and soon the restored database opens.

Backing up personal supplemental files

Your ACT! database comes with a set of database supplemental files that include your layouts, and report and document templates. (Turn to Chapter 3 for more info about supplemental files.) The database supplemental files are included in the regular ACT! backup. ACT! also allows you to keep a set of personal supplemental files. These files can include saved documents and reports that you create using an ACT! template, as well as any file attachments that are of a more personal nature that you might not want to include as part of the database. All database users have access to the database supplemental files, but you are the only one with access to your personal supplemental files.

Because the personal supplemental files are not a part of the ACT! database, you need to back them up separately from the rest of the database. Don't worry — the personal supplemental files are backed up in pretty much the same way that you back up the rest of the database:

1. **From any ACT! screen, choose File⬄Back Up⬄Personal Files.**

   The Back Up Personal Files dialog box opens, as shown in Figure 17-5.

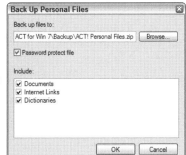

Figure 17-5:
Backing up
personal
data files.

2. **Browse to the location to which you want to save your files and click OK.**

3. **Check the Password Protect File check box if you want to password-protect the backup copy of your personal files.**

4. **Indicate whether to include your personal documents, Internet Links, and spelling dictionaries in your backup, and then click OK.**

That was fairly easy. If you indicated that you wanted password protection you're prompted to enter in the password. When the backup is complete, you get a congratulatory confirmation message.

Performing Spring Housecleaning

The good news is that if you're reading this, you're probably the Administrator of the ACT! database; after all, if you're not the Administrator, you don't have the necessary permission to perform most of the administrative tasks. The bad news is that with the job title comes quite a bit of responsibility — and hopefully a large salary.

In addition to performing the obvious mechanical maintenance chores, you probably want to do a little bit of extra house, er, database cleaning from time to time. Having blank, duplicate, or incorrect contact information serves no purpose other than to make your database perform less efficiently. So bite the bullet, roll up your sleeves, and get cleaning.

Before you perform *any* type of maintenance, I strongly recommend that you back up your database so that you can retrieve any data you accidentally delete.

Weeding out duplicate contacts

Finding pesky duplicates in your database is tricky but not impossible. Because having multiple records for the same person or company is common, ACT! allows you a way to easily check for duplicate records based on predefined criteria. You can then create a lookup of the duplicate records and delete them. You can also change the criteria used to find these duplicate records.

By default, ACT! looks for duplicate contact records based on the company name, contact name, and phone number. If the contents of these three fields are identical for two or more contacts, ACT! views them as duplicates.

1. **From any ACT! view, choose Tools⇨Scan for Duplicates.**

   As you can see in Figure 17-6, you can now specify how ACT! checks for duplicate contact records in the Duplicate Checking dialog box.

Figure 17-6: Defining duplication criteria.

2. **In the Duplicate Match Settings area, choose the three fields you want ACT! to use to search for duplicate contact data.**

3. **Click OK.**

   If ACT! finds any duplication in your database, the Contact List opens along with a dialog box informing you that duplicates were found and asking if you would like to combine them. From this list, you can delete records, keep records, or combine duplicate records.

4. **If you want to combine duplicates, click Yes to continue at the prompt.**

   The Copy/Move Contact data window opens. This is the first of six windows that you go through when merging duplicate contacts. Merging duplicates is a slow, grueling task; remember that once two contacts are merged together, there is no "unmerge" function.

As you progress through the wizard you perform the follow six tasks:

- Select a pair of duplicates.

- Decide whether you want to copy the information from the first contact record to the second contact record — or vice versa.

- Depending on your choice, one of the contacts becomes the *source,* and the other one is the *target.* By default the new, merged contact contains all the target information. If you want to retain any source field information, click in the field and then click the Copy button.

- As you see in Figure 17-7, you indicate in the fourth step if you want to move additional information from the source to the target or have the information remain duplicated on both records.

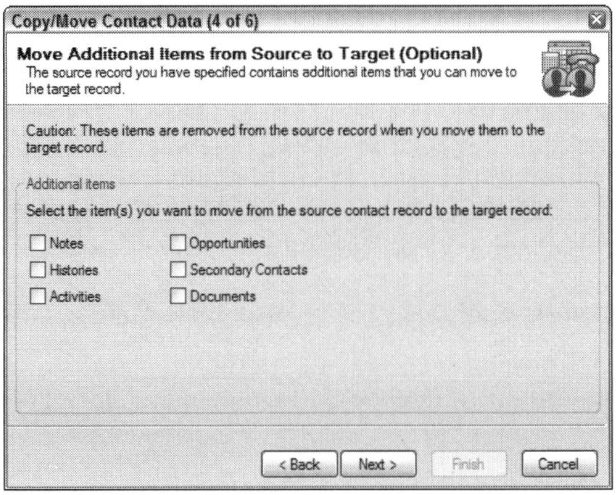

Figure 17-7:
Moving
additional
information
from the
source to
the target
record.

> **Copy/Move Contact Data (4 of 6)**
>
> **Move Additional Items from Source to Target (Optional)**
> The source record you have specified contains additional items that you can move to the target record.
>
> Caution: These items are removed from the source record when you move them to the target record.
>
> Additional Items
> Select the item(s) you want to move from the source contact record to the target record:
>
> ☐ Notes   ☐ Opportunities
> ☐ Histories   ☐ Secondary Contacts
> ☐ Activities   ☐ Documents
>
> < Back   Next >   Finish   Cancel

- Indicate whether to keep or delete the source record. For your convenience, ACT! recaps the information to make your decision easier.

- If you decide to delete the source record, click Yes on the scary warning that confirms that you might be losing information. Your two duplicate records merge into one.

You cannot restore deleted records. If you inadvertently deleted important information, run — don't walk — to your backup file and restore your information. For many of you, merging two contact records together is only the tip of the iceberg. You need to repeat the merge process again for each pair of duplicates in your database. And, after you complete the process, you might want to start over again by changing the duplicate checking criteria.

As I stress throughout this book, having some semblance of uniformity is very important. Lack of uniformity is a great way to sabotage your database. A search for all your clients in *Ft.* Lauderdale does not include those clients in *Fort* Lauderdale. In the same way, a company or contact might be duplicated if it is entered into your database in two different ways. For example, you might have *John Q. Public* and *John Public,* or *ABC Company* and *ABC Co.* ACT! doesn't recognize any of these examples as duplicates.

You can change the criteria that ACT! uses to look for duplicate records. To find the duplicates that I mention in the preceding paragraph, you need to use a different criterion for your search. Changing your search parameters to search for duplicated phone numbers might just give you the results that you're looking for.

Removing old data

ACT! users tend to be extremely loyal; it's not unusual to run into ACT! fanACTics who have been using ACT! religiously for over 15 years. Over time, the amount of information that is stored in ACT! gets larger and larger; over a period of time that information may become less and less important. ACT! provides you with a simple tool for clearing the clutter from your database; I just wish I had a similar tool to clear the clutter from my closet!

1. **From any ACT! screen, choose Tools➪Database Maintenance➪Remove Old Data.**

   The Remove Old Data window opens, as shown in Figure 17-8.

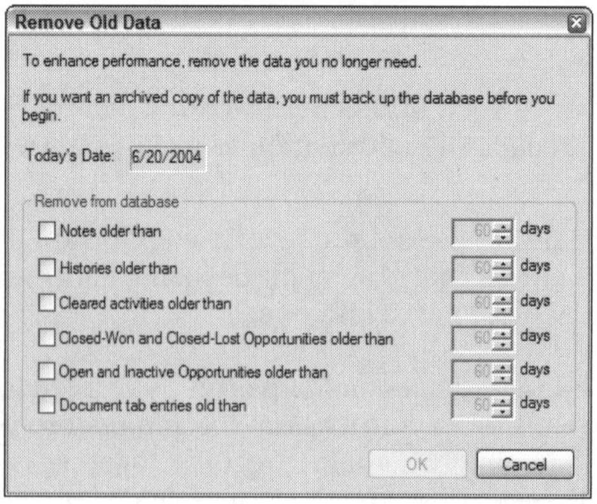

Figure 17-8: The Remove Old Data window.

2. **In the Remove from Database area, select the type of data you want to remove and indicate the number of days that you want to use to remove that data.**

   If you want to get rid of data that is older than a year, indicate 365 days; if you want to get rid of data that is more than two years old, indicate 730 days.

3. **Click OK.**

Like a champ, ACT! searches, scrubs, and ultimately removes any data that matches your selection criteria.

Deleting a database

You may be wondering why you ever want to delete your database. That's good thinking because you're right — you don't want to delete your database. However, you might have inherited several databases that you no longer use, or perhaps you created a database or two for specific, temporary purposes. In general, allowing users to have access to more than one database is not a good idea; chances are pretty good that one of your users ends up in the wrong database. Having a multitude of extraneous databases can also put an extra strain on your resources and slow down your general performance.

Before deleting a database, I recommend backing it up, just in case. You might also consider moving the database to another location for safekeeping rather than deleting it.

Deleting a database is ridiculously simple and, once deleted, impossible to undelete. Proceed with caution.

Okay, are you ready? Take a deep breath and follow these steps to delete the database:

1. **Open the database you wish to delete.**

   ACT! deletes the currently opened database. Be sure to close all other databases. In previous versions of ACT! it was not possible to delete the open database — only closed ones. Govern yourself accordingly!

2. **From any ACT! screen, choose Tools⇨Database Maintenance⇨Delete Database.**

   The Delete Database window opens, verifying that you absolutely want to delete, destroy, and make the current database disappear forever.

3. **Click Yes to bid your database adieu.**

Ironically, ACT! gives you two options to change your mind: No or Cancel both serves to keep your database safely in place.

Copying or moving contact data

One of the neat utilities included with ACT! is the ability to copy or move selected field information from one record to the next. One example of this might occur if an existing contact leaves a company to work at another company. You might create a new record for the individual and then realize that his previous record still contains pertinent information, such as his home phone number and birthday. By using the Copy/Move command, you can move that specific field information from his old contact record to his new one. You can then edit the original contact record with the contact details of the new, replacement person.

ACT!'s Copy/Move Contact Data function works almost exactly like the Scan Duplicate function. The only difference is that unlike with the duplication procedure, you're not presented with a list of contacts to start with. The onus is on you to select two records whose field information you want to copy or move.

1. **From any ACT! screen, choose Tools⇨Copy/Move Contact Data.**

Look familiar? It's the Duplicate Checking dialog box (refer to Figure 17-6).

2. **Click Next to proceed through the wizard screens.**

Proceed through the wizard while remembering a few key points:

- The *source record* is the record you want to copy data to.

- The *target record* is the record that contains the data that you want to copy.

- You have the option to copy or move data on a field-by-field basis.

- You have the option to keep or delete the original source record.

Performing a global edit/replace

Another way that you can keep your database working well is by ensuring that all fields contain consistent information. You might notice that some of your contacts have the city listed in all capitals while others don't. You might see that some contacts are listed in *Florida,* whereas other contacts reside in

FL or *Fla*. This lack of consistency makes it extremely difficult to query your database. Like a forgiving mother, ACT! provides you with the ability to correct the error of your ways. After you pinpoint your inconsistencies, you can standardize them in one fell swoop (rather than by correcting each field on an item by item basis); just do this:

1. **Perform your lookup.**

   In the preceding example, you might create a lookup of *FLA* and then add *Florida* to the mix. If you need help, flip to Chapter 7 and review the section on lookups.

   Unless you're planning on changing field data for every contact in your database, make sure you perform a lookup *before* proceeding. These changes are irreversible! For example, say you notice 27 instances of *Fla* that you want to change to *FL*. If you fail to do a lookup first, you end up changing the State field for *every* contact in your database to *FL* rather than just for the original 27 that you intend to change. Unfortunately, unless you have a backup handy, you're stuck with the changes because, again, these changes are irreversible.

2. **From any ACT! screen, choose Edit⇨Replace Field.**

   You're now looking at the Replace Data dialog box, shown in Figure 17-9. If you prefer, you can choose one of the other two options as well:

   • **Swap Field:** This option swaps the information between two fields.

   • **Copy Field:** This option copies information from one field and repeats it in a second field.

Figure 17-9:
The Replace
Data dialog
box.

3. **Select your desired field from the Replace Contents Of drop-down list.**

   You can select from virtually any of your contact fields with the exception of the system fields.

4. **Enter the desired information in the Value field.**

   In this example, you type **FL** in the field. To make life even easier, ACT! supplies you with the appropriate drop-down list based on the field you indicated in Step 3.

5. Click OK.

6. Read the warning that appears.

Generally speaking, when life — or ACT! — gives you a warning, it's a good idea to heed it. ACT! is politely asking you to verify that you intend to change all the contact records in the current lookup (see Figure 17-10). If you're not sure as to the exact number of contacts in the current lookup, click No, return to the Contact Detail window or Contact List, and read the record counter in the top-left corner.

Figure 17-10: Last chance warning before replacing all your data.

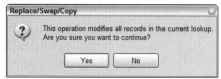

7. Click Yes.

ACT! might have to think about this for a moment depending on the number of contact records in your lookup. When it finishes, you'll notice that the field that you indicated in Step 3 has now changed for each of the contact records in your lookup.

A few more housekeeping tips

So far, I've talked about ways that ACT! can mechanically maintain the integrity of your database. However, you, as the Administrator, can do a few things to help ensure a healthy database:

- ✔ If your organization has customized the database, limit the number of users who have permission to edit layouts and add new items to the drop-down lists.

- ✔ Periodically clear unwanted items from the drop-down lists. Insist that the users routinely pick items from the drop-down lists when entering new data.

- ✔ To avoid duplication of contacts, emphasize the importance of querying the database for an existing contact before entering a new one.

- ✔ Delete any fields not being used.

✔ Delete outdated attachments, layouts, reports, templates, and queries.

✔ Be cognizant of field length. If you have a field that holds a Yes or No value, consider trimming the field length down to three characters.

✔ Save contact records you rarely use to a different database, and then remove them from the main database. Use a Contact Activity lookup to locate infrequently used records.

✔ If you synchronize with remote databases, review and purge your synchronization logs often.

Chapter 18

ACT!ing with Synchronizations

*O*ne of the most exciting new changes in ACT! 2005 is the change in synchronization procedures. In the past, synchronization was a very delicate — and technical — operation; if not done correctly you had a great chance of corrupting your database. With the advent of ACT! 2005, the synchronization process has been streamlined. Although many steps are involved, they are not hard or complicated.

The synchronization procedure I follow in this chapter refers to the method used with ACT! 2005. I'm also assuming that remote users are connecting their computers to the main computer's network in order to synchronize. In most cases, that involves bring in the remote user's laptop and connecting it to the network. Although connecting to the host computer using other methods (such as a VPN or terminal services) is possible, it's beyond the scope of this book.

What in the World Is Synchronization?

To understand synchronization, you need to know the following terms:

▶ The *master* database is the main database that contains all of your data.

▶ The *remote* database is a separate database being used by another user, generally in a different location.

ACT! users commonly confuse backing up and restoring data with a true data *synchronization*. If you back up your database and restore it on a remote user's computer, the remote user now has a carbon copy of your database. This method works fine if the remote user doesn't want to make any changes to his database. However, if you both make changes to your respective databases, you have no way of merging those changes. If you back up your database and restore it once again to the remote user's computer, you wipe out any changes he has previously made.

Synchronization means that you can make changes from either the master or the source database. It's the exact same concept that's used when you synchronize your PDA to your computer. After synchronizing, changes made in the master database are seen in the remote database and vice versa.

Why synchronize?

You may want to synchronize your data for several reasons:

- ✔ You want to share your database information with other remote users in your organization and vice versa.
- ✔ Your database is located on an office server, but you need to keep your information on a laptop for traveling purposes.
- ✔ You may want some of your users to have access to only portions of your database for security purposes; ACT!'s synchronization allows you to send and receive changes based on selected contacts so that your remote user's database contains only a portion of the entire master database.

The synchronization cycle in a nutshell

Here's what happens during the synchronization cycle:

- ✔ Any changes that you made to your remote database are compiled into a packet and sent back to the master database.
- ✔ When the master database "hears" the remote database, it accepts the changes and sends out any changes that occurred in the master database that affect the remote user.
- ✔ As other remote users sync to the master database, they can also receive any contact changes that affect them, including ones made by other remote users.

Things that change during a synchronization

When you synchronize your data, you merge any changes that you made to your database with changes made by your remote user(s), including the following:

- **Contact information:** If you change a contact's telephone number and the remote user changes the address, ACT! merges both changes into the original contact record. If you change the same contact's telephone number and the numbers do not match, ACT! applies the most recent change.

- **Notes and histories:** If you both add notes, the contact record now reflects all the notes and histories of both the master and remote users.

- **The Task List:** Any tasks that either you or the remote users create now appear in both the master and the remote databases. You can even schedule an activity for your remote users.

- **Calendars:** Synchronization allows you to share the calendars of all the users in your organization.

- **Field definitions:** If the master database has added, removed, or changed fields, these changes are sent out to the remote users.

- **Drop-down lists:** Changes made in the master database to field drop-down lists are sent to remote users.

- **Layouts:** New or customized contact, company, and group layouts synchronize to remote users.

- **Templates:** Letters, reports, envelopes, and labels synchronize to remote users.

- **Attachments:** All documents attached to the master and remote databases synchronize; documents stored in your personal folders don't synchronize.

Performing a Synchronization in Three ACT!s

The synchronization process consists of four parts: understanding the sync process, setting up the master database, setting up the remote database, and the actual sync process.

If you feel you are not up to the task, you might want to contact your local ACT! Certified Consultant who arrives at your office wearing his or her Superman costume. If you look carefully, you might even see his pocket protector under his T-shirt. Anyway, your friendly ACC can probably save you hours of frustration — and ensure that your database doesn't become corrupted! You can find a list of ACCs by choosing Help⇨Service and Support⇨ ACT! Consulting.

ACT! 1: Doing your homework

Many of you may find that your knees are shaking. Relax, take a deep breath, and plot your strategy. Before bravely forging ahead and attempting to sync, you can do a little preparation.

If you were a Boy Scout, you learned to be prepared. Now that you are a savvy user of ACT!, being prepared is even more important. Here are some tips that make your synchronizations run more smoothly:

- **Enter your data consistently.** I know I sound like a broken record, but it is worth repeating: Enter your data consistently. For example, if you enter a contact's company name as *Tech Benders, Inc.* and someone else enters it as *Tech Benders,* you have duplicate contact records when you synchronize data. To help enter data consistently, rely on drop-down lists whenever possible.

- **Determine which contacts to include in the remote user's database.** This decision might involve setting up a query to identify those contacts. If Joe is to receive all the contacts in the Southwest region, consider adding a region field to your database — or at the very least, identify those states included in the Southwest.

- **Use the same criteria to search for duplicate records.** ACT! matches contact records using a *Unique ID,* which is an identifier assigned to each record in your database. If you set up the synchronization procedure correctly, identical contacts in all databases have the same Unique ID. If both you and your remote users add the same contact to your databases, each contact is assigned a different Unique ID. If the Unique IDs of two records do not match, ACT! matches duplicate records using the criteria you specify. To ensure that the synchronization process does not create duplicate contact records, both databases need to use the same criteria for determining duplicate records.

You can find out how to modify your duplicate record match criteria in Chapter 17.

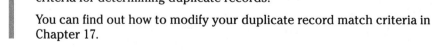

✔ **All users must have the same version of ACT!.** You can't synchronize an ACT! 2005 database to an ACT! 6 database. You also can't synchronize an ACT! 2005 database to an ACT! 2005 Premium database. Make sure that all databases have the most recent version of ACT!:

- To display your current version, choose Help⇨About ACT!.

- To update your version of ACT!, choose Help⇨ACT! Update.

✔ **Perform spring-cleaning on your database.** Scan for duplicate records and clean up your database *before* starting the synchronization process. Turn to Chapter 17 to do so.

ACT! 2: Setting up the main database

You must follow a number of steps in order to set up a remote database. Sound like a lot of work? Don't worry; only Administrators and Managers need apply because other users don't have the appropriate rights to set up synchronization. And, if you are an Administrator or a Manager, you can stop hiding under your desk; although there are a lot of steps, they are all very easy to follow.

Enabling synchronization

The first thing you need to do is to turn on the synchronization. Follow these steps:

1. **From any ACT! screen, choose Tools⇨Synchronization Panel.**

   The Synchronization panel opens, as shown in Figure 18-1.

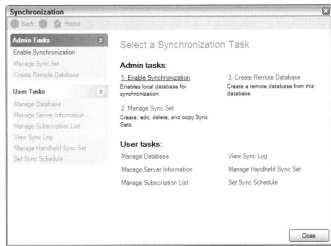

Figure 18-1:
The Synchronization panel.

> **2. Click the Enable Synchronization option in the Admin Tasks area and then click Yes in the ACT! message dialog box.**

Admit it — it doesn't get much easier than that!

Defining a sync set

The *sync set* is the main list of contacts that the remote user receives. An Administrator or a Manager of the remote database creates the sync set. On the simplest level, the sync set consists of all contacts that the remote user has permission to access. However, the Administrator might set up additional criteria to limit the number of contacts that the remote user can access. After you set the criteria, the remote user has the opportunity to add additional contacts that he has permission to access to his database. Contacts that are added to the remote database by the remote user would automatically become part of the remote users sync set and the remote user has rights to access the additional contacts.

Consider these key elements before creating a sync set:

- ✔ A sync set is only a starting point; remote users can add additional contacts to their databases from the master database.
- ✔ A sync set can include only contact records that the remote user has permission to access.
- ✔ A sync set always includes all the master database Record Manager contacts as well as all group and company records. The groups and companies populate only those records that the remote user has access to.
- ✔ Master database Administrators and Managers can create sync sets based on a query.
- ✔ An Administrator or a Manager can copy, edit, or delete sync sets.
- ✔ More than one remote database can use a sync set; however, each remote database has only one sync set.

Follow these simple steps to create a sync set:

1. **From any ACT! screen, choose Tools⇨Synchronization Panel.**

   The Synchronization panel opens (refer to Figure 18-1).

2. **Click the Manage Sync Set option in the Admin Tasks area.**

3. **Click Create New Sync Set and click Next.**

   Okay, I know you have several choices here, but for the purposes of this section, create a brand new sync set. Just remember that you can always go back and copy, edit, or delete your sync set later.

4. Give your sync set a name, an optional description, and then click Next.

What you decide to call the sync set is a big deal because you need to recognize it by name later on down the road. If the sync set consists of the contacts used by the remote sales guys, you might name the sync set something clever like "Remote Sales Guys."

5. Select the names of the remote users who will use the sync set, click the right-pointing arrow and then click Next.

The remote user must be an active user of the master database, even if he doesn't have permission to access all records.

6. Decide on one of the following options:

- If you want to synchronize all the available contacts to the sync users, select the Synchronize All Available Contacts option, click Next, and then click Finish.

- If you want to further limit the contacts the remote user sees, select the Define Sync Set Criteria option and then click Next.

The Sync Set Criteria window opens, as shown in Figure 18-2.

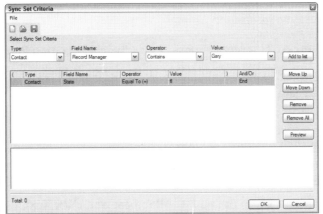

Figure 18-2:
Determining sync set criteria.

7. Choose the criteria you want to set the sync to:

- You only have one choice of field type — contact.

- In the Field Name drop-down list, select one of the available contact fields.

- In the Operator drop-down list, select one of the available items, such as Contains or Equal To (=).

- In the Value drop-down list, select one of the available items that correspond to the selected field name.

8. **Click the Add to List button.**

   As you add a criterion, it appears in the bottom section of the window. Notice in Figure 18-2 that I am creating my sync set to include all contacts in Florida that are managed by Gary.

9. **To select more than one criterion, repeat Steps 7 and 8.**

   You might need to use the And/Or column to help you build the query. *And* indicates that a contact must match *all* criteria; *Or* indicates that a contact can match *any one* criterion.

10. **Click the Preview button to see a list of all the contacts that match the criteria you indicated.**

    You even see the total number of records that are included in the sync set.

11. **When you're happy with your results, click OK and then click Finish.**

    If necessary you can create or edit additional sync sets or click Home to return to the main Synchronization dialog box.

Creating the remote database

After you enable synchronization and create a sync set, you're ready to create the remote database(s). Once again, you return to the scene of the crime — the Synchronization panel:

1. **From any ACT! screen, choose Tools⇨Synchronization Panel.**

   The Synchronization panel opens (refer to Figure 18-1).

2. **Click Create Remote Database in the Admin Tasks area.**

   Like with most of the other ACT! tasks, you now follow a wizard through the next several steps. Probably the hardest thing you have to do is click Next at each juncture.

3. **Give the remote database a name, click the Browse button to save the new database to a different location if necessary, and click Next.**

4. **Select a sync set to use with the database and click Next.**

   You see the sync set you created earlier sitting there waiting for you.

5. **Indicate the following choices and click Next.**

   • Allow database supplemental files to synchronize.

   • Allow attachments to synchronize.

   • Set the number of days that the synchronization expires. This ensures that the remote user synchronizes on a timely basis or risks having the database expire. After a database expires, the remote user can't synchronize until the Administrator of the main database creates a new database for the remote user.

6. **Give the database an optional password and click Finish.**

7. **Choose Tools⇨Synchronize⇨Accept Incoming Syncs.**

   The final step sets the master database in a wait-and-see mode. As the Administrator, your job is almost finished. Time to sit back, pat yourself on the back, and figure out a way to get that database to the remote user.

Delivering the remote data

Your job as the grand poobah of remote database creation is just about done; all good things must come to an end. The only thing you have left to do at this point is to get that new database, along with all the associated files and attachments, out to the remote users. But wouldn't you know, ACT! has solved that problem for you already. When you create the remote database, you actually create a special backup file; unlike a traditional backup file, this one comes with the .rdb extension. You can simply e-mail the file to the remote user, or burn it to a CD and send it via snail mail.

ACT! 3: Setting up the remote database

When you set up the remote database and send it off by carrier pigeon to your remote user, the ball is in the other guy's court. Relax and go float in the pool — just make sure to keep the cell phone on in case the remote user has a question. And don't forget the sunscreen!

Restoring the remote database

If you are the remote user, you have a few chores to do. Thankfully, none of them are very hard. The first thing you need to do is restore the remote database that the Administrator of the master database sent. This procedure works pretty much the same way as the restore procedure that I discuss in Chapter 17; the main difference lies in the fact that the remote database has a different backup extension than a traditional database backup file.

Traditional backup files have the .zip extension. Remote database backup files have the .rdb extension. Could it be that RDB stands for *Remote Database?* You be the judge!

You, as the remote user, can follow these steps to set up the database:

1. **Save the .rdb file that you receive from the master database Administrator into an appropriate spot on your hard drive.**

   My suggestion is that you jot down the location so that you don't have to call the Administrator and ask for help. My experience is that Administrators get very cranky when interrupted in mid-swim.

2. From any ACT! screen, choose File⇨Restore⇨Database.

The Restore Database window appears.

3. Select the Unpack and Restore Remote Database option and then click OK.

The Unpack and Restore an ACT! Remote Database window opens.

4. Click the Browse button next to the Select the Remote Database File to Restore field to locate the remote database (.rdb) backup file.

5. Click Browse to select a location for the restored database.

If you're not going to store the database on a network, you'll probably find that the default location, located in your My Documents folder, fills the bill nicely. If you're sharing the database, save it to a place on your network.

6. Select the Share This Database with Other Users option if you are sharing the database with other users.

7. Click OK.

If the database you are restoring is password protected, type your secret password and click OK. Don't know the password? Your Administrator might just have to finish his swim and supply you with it!

After you restore the database, you can open and begin using it just like any other ACT! database. You can also begin to synchronize your data at any time.

Depending on the access rights given to you by the master database Administrator, you might not be able to perform various functions, such as backing up your database. The same user rules apply to the remote database as to the master database; you can't delete contact records, notes, and other things created by other users.

Synchronizing data

The remote user is the keeper of the synchronization key and the only one who can initiate a sync. You'd think that having such a big responsibility would entail a lot of work. Fortunately for you, it doesn't.

1. From any ACT! screen, choose Tools⇨Synchronize.

2. Click the Synchronize Now option.

When you synchronize the database, two things happen:

- Any changes made in the remote database now appear in the master database.

- Any changes made in the master database associated with contact records included in the remote user's sync set now appear in the remote database.

The synchronization can take a few minutes depending on the number of changes that have been made to both the remote and the master databases. You see an indicator bar roll across your screen and then a congratulatory message celebrating the fact that you have performed a successful synchronization. You're also asked to refresh your database so you don't drive yourself crazy looking for changes that might take a moment to appear.

Setting up automatic synchronization

In the standard edition of ACT!, the master database cannot receive sync packets if other users are logged on to a multi-user database. Of course, one way to get around this limitation is to come in at dawn — or stay until midnight — to perform your synchronization. For most of you, this option is not what you have in mind! As the remote user, you might prefer to have ACT! perform your synchronization automatically for you while you're at home snoozing.

Here's how you set up an automatic synchronization:

1. **Open the remote ACT! database.**

2. **Choose Tools➪Synchronization Panel.**

   The Synchronization panel opens (refer to Figure 18-1).

3. **Click Set Sync Schedule in the Users Tasks area.**

   The Sync Schedule window opens, as seen in Figure 18-3.

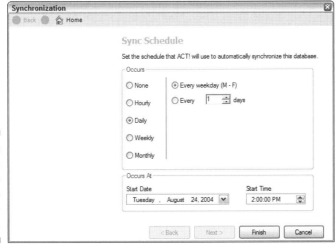

Figure 18-3: Scheduling an automatic synchronization.

   4. **Indicate your scheduling preferences.**

   • **Occurs:** Indicate the frequency with which you want the synchro-
     nization to occur.

   • **Occurs At:** Indicate the date and time you want to commence using
     the automatic synchronization.

   5. **Click Finish.**

You must leave both the master and remote databases open so that
synchronization updates are sent and received automatically at the specified times. And only one person can access each database at the time
of synchronization.

Adding contact records to a sync set

Because a sync set is created based on a query and may be used for more
than one remote user, you might find that your database is missing some contacts. These contacts represent people that you might have access to but
who didn't match the criteria the Administrator used for the sync set.
Ironically, these contacts actually reside in the remote database even though
you can't access them.

Sound confusing? To put it a little simpler, if you find that you're missing one
of your contacts, you can add it to the database:

   1. **Choose Tools⇨Synchronization Panel from any ACT! screen.**

      The Synchronization panel appears (refer to Figure 18-1).

   2. **In the User Tasks area, click Manage Subscription List.**

      You now see a list of all the contacts that you can access. The contacts
      that are a part of the sync set are indicated with a check mark.

   3. **Click Add Contacts to Sync Set in the Subscription Tasks area.**

      The Contacts window opens, as shown in Figure 18-4.

   4. **Select the contact(s) from the list on the left, and then click the right
      arrow button to add them to the remote database.**

   5. **When you finish, click OK and then click the Finish button in the
      Manage Subscription List window.**

The additional contacts appear in your database after your next
synchronization.

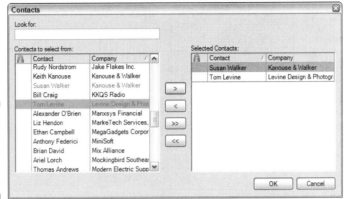

Figure 18-4:
Adding
contacts to
the remote
database.

Maintaining the Synchronization

Wow! The worst is over. Your remote database is synching back to the master database and life is beautiful. But meanwhile back at the ranch — or at least at the master database — the Administrator's job continues. You may want to check a few minor details from time to time. Or you may decide that the fun is over, and you no longer want to continue syncing.

Viewing the last data synchronized

The synchronization process goes so smoothly that you might be left wondering what, if anything, actually synchronized. Sure enough, you can easily determine that by creating a lookup. Here's all you need to do:

1. **From any ACT! screen, choose Lookup⇨Advanced⇨Last Synchronized.**

   The Last Synchronized window opens, as shown in Figure 18-5.

2. **Specify the Lookup criteria:**

   - **Last Session or Date Range:** You can view either the last contacts synchronized or the contacts that synchronized during a specific date range.

   - **Record Type:** Indicate whether you want to find contact, company, or group records.

   - **Look In:** Specify whether you want to find notes, opportunities, histories, and/or activities that changed during the last synchronization.

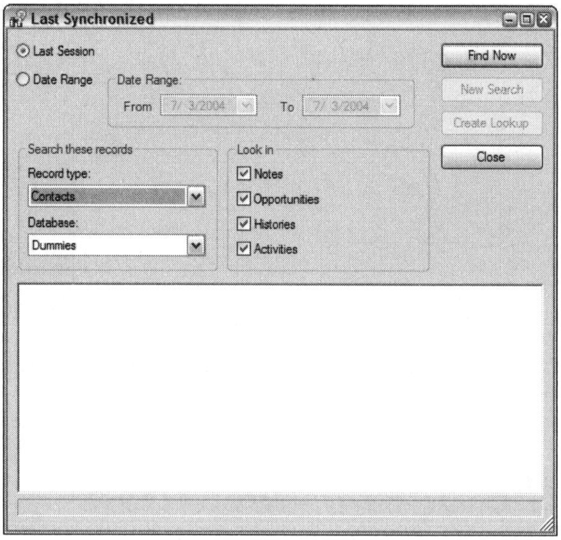

Figure 18-5:
Creating a
lookup of
the last
records
synchro-
nized.

3. **Click the Find Now button.**

   The contact records that changed during the last synchronization are
   shown in the lower section of the Last Synchronized window.

4. **Click the Create Lookup button.**

   The Contact List now displays a list of all contacts that changed during
   the last synchronization.

Looking up the Sync Set lookup

As an Administrator, you probably rush through your day; chances are you
occasionally forget something: lunch, your head — or maybe the contacts
included in a sync set. You can easily create a list of all the contacts that are
part of a sync set by choosing Lookup➪Advanced➪Sync Set. The Contact
List magically appears, displaying all the contacts included in the sync set.
The difficult part is figuring out what to do for lunch!

Viewing and printing sync settings

You might want to review the sync settings of your database that were created for each of the remote databases. Again, this feat is easy to accomplish:

1. **From any ACT! screen, choose Tools⇨Synchronization Panel.**

   The ever-familiar Synchronization panel appears (refer to Figure 18-1).

2. **Click Manage Database in the User Tasks area.**

   The Synchronization window opens.

3. **Select the name of your database and click View Settings in the User Tasks area.**

   As you can see from Figure 18-6, you see the names of both the master and remote databases, the sync server port, and the expiration period of the database.

4. **If you want to print out the results, click Print and then click Finish.**

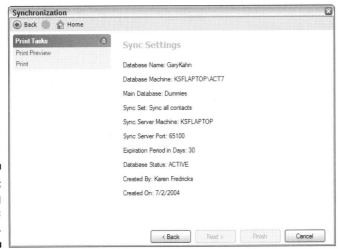

Figure 18-6:
Displaying the sync settings.

Stopping the synchronization process

All good things must come to an end, and so it is with your remote database. You can severe the ties that bind the master database to the remote one in three ways. After the synchronization stops, the only way to get it going again is to completely create — or re-create — the remote database.

✔ **Letting the expiration date expire:** Remote databases are assigned an expiration date when they are created. If the remote user fails to synchronize during the allotted time period, the remote database no longer can sync to the master database.

✔ **From the master database:** The master database can disable synchronization for a remote database and optionally allow one last synchronization before disabling the remote database. The remote database receives a notification that synchronization is disabled and is allowed one last synchronization session.

✔ **From the remote database:** A user with Administrator rights can disable the remote database so that it no longer synchronizes to the main database. After a remote database is disabled, it is no longer a remote database. The database can still be used as a standalone database.

To disable either a master or remote synchronized database, follow these steps:

1. **From any ACT! screen, choose Tools⇨Synchronization Panel.**

2. **In the Admin Tasks area of the Synchronize panel, click Disable Synchronization.**

3. **When prompted, click Yes to disable the synchronization.**

Re-creating a remote database

You may find yourself needing to send out another sync set to a remote user. For example, the remote user might have forgotten to synchronize and finds that his database has expired. Or maybe the remote user's computer died a slow and painful death and needs to be replaced. In any case, there is a simple way to re-create a remote database:

1. **From any ACT! screen, choose Tools⇨Synchronization Panel.**

2. **Click Manage Database in the User Tasks area of the Synchronization panel.**

3. **Select the remote database you want to re-create, click Recreate Database and then click Yes.**

4. **Click the Browse button to specify a location to save the newly re-created database and then click OK.**

   ACT! whirs and hisses as it busily sets up the remote database again. ACT! doesn't complain about having to do this chore a second time. In fact, you're even rewarded with a happy message confirming that you have indeed re-created the remote user's database.

5. **Click OK.**

Part V

Commonly Overlooked ACT! Features

The 5th Wave   By Rich Tennant

"For 30 years I've put a hat and coat on to make sales calls and I'm not changing now just because I'm doing it on the Web from my living room."

In this part . . .

If you aren't content with relying on the basic ACT! functions to keep your life organized and you want to squeeze every last drop of functionality out of ACT!, here's the place to find some of the best-kept secrets of ACT!. Want to surf the Net or edit your documents without leaving the comforts of ACT!? Interested in keeping a record of your ongoing sales activities? Want the functionality of a high-priced relational database — without mortgaging the farm? ACT! can help you accomplish these goals, and Part V shows you how.

Chapter 19

Integrating ACT! with Microsoft

- -

- -

*F*ace it. Microsoft is everywhere, and most probably you are running more than one of its products on your computer. Like many other software products, ACT! 2005 has taken the "if you can't beat 'em, join 'em" philosophy. ACT! fully integrates with four of the most popular Microsoft products — Outlook, Internet Explorer, Word, and Excel.

Although other Microsoft products don't fully integrate with ACT!, you don't need to stop using them. For example, you can easily store PowerPoint presentations on the Documents tab for easy access.

Changing Your Outlook on Life

A common misconception I hear from potential ACT! users is that they don't need ACT! because they're using Outlook. You might snicker at that suggestion because by now you realize that Outlook is a PIM (personal information manager) whereas ACT! is a true contact manager. I like to think of ACT! as Outlook on steroids; try doing a mail merge, customize fields, or log in notes in Outlook and you'll see what I mean.

Still, some ACT! users find themselves needing to use Outlook for a variety of reasons:

- ✔ His company is currently using Outlook to maintain the company calendar.

- ✔ She might use Outlook to keep track of personal addresses and information that doesn't belong in ACT!.

Fortunately, you can teach ACT! and Outlook to share both their address books and calendars with one another.

Sharing ACT! and Outlook address books

When using both ACT! and Outlook address books, you need to be aware of how the integration works:

- ✔ You can import all your Outlook contact information — including appointments, tasks, notes, and journal entries — into ACT!.
- ✔ You can view all ACT!'s e-mail addresses in Outlook.
- ✔ You can view all Outlook's e-mail addresses in ACT!.
- ✔ You don't see new Outlook contact information, appointments, tasks, notes, and journal entries unless you reimport your Outlook data.

Importing Outlook into ACT!

ACT! very nicely includes Outlook as one of its import options. After all, more people switch from Outlook to ACT! than from ACT! to Outlook. Here's all you need to do to import the Outlook data:

1. **From any ACT! screen, choose File⇨Import.**

   Backing up your database is a good idea before attempting to try something as tricky as a data import. Chapter 17 explains how to create an ACT! backup.

   The Import Wizard opens with a nice welcoming screen that you can skip over by clicking Next.

2. **Select Outlook as the type of data you want to import and click Next.**

3. **Specify that you want to import contact records and click Next.**

   Your contact records include the good stuff, such as the person's name, company, address, phone number, and shoe size.

4. **Specify your import options and click Next.**

   The Specify Import Options screen opens, as shown in Figure 19-1.

   - **Outlook Contacts:** Imports your Outlook contacts into ACT!.

   - **Exchange Contacts:** Imports your Exchange contacts into ACT!. Use this option only if you work for a large company that shares your Outlook information on a network.

   - **Appointments and Tasks as ACT! Activities:** Converts your Outlook appointments and tasks into ACT! activities.

- **Notes as ACT! Notes:** Converts your Outlook notes into an ACT! note.

- **Journal Entries as ACT! Notes:** Imports your Outlook journal entries as ACT! notes.

5. **Map your Outlook fields to ACT! fields and click Next.**

   I personally love it when my software does all my work for me. ACT! has already "translated" the existing Outlook fields into ACT! fields. For example, Outlook's Business Address Postal Code becomes ACT!'s Zip Code field.

6. **Click Finish.**

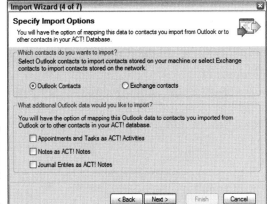

Figure 19-1:
Outlook to
ACT! import
options.

Configuring Outlook's address book to include ACT!

Using Outlook for your personal e-mail? You can view e-mail addresses stored in Outlook from ACT! and vice versa. Although ACT! automatically detects your default Outlook address book(s), Outlook isn't quite that bright; you have to tell Outlook where to find your ACT! data. Follow these steps to do so:

1. **In Outlook, choose Tools⇨E-mail Accounts.**

   The E-mail Accounts Wizard opens.

2. **Select the Add a New Directory or Address Book option and click Next.**

3. **In the Directory or Address Book Type window, select the Additional Address Books option and then click Next.**

4. **Select the ACT! 2005 Address Book option, and click Next.**

   The ACT! 2005 Address Book dialog box opens, as shown in Figure 19-2. You can specify three ACT! databases if you like.

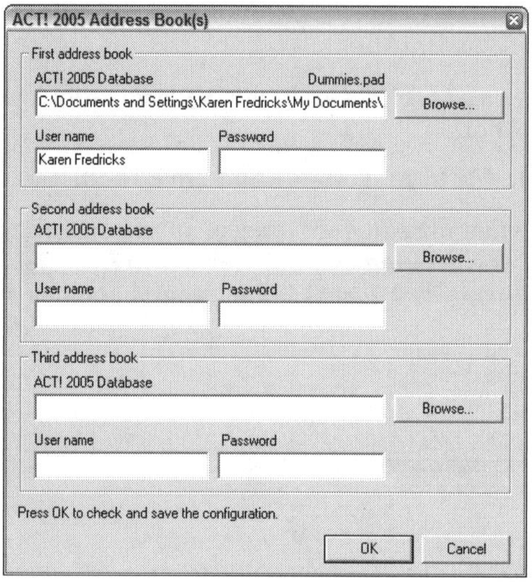

Figure 19-2:
Adding
ACT!
address
books to
Outlook.

5. **Click Browse to locate and select your ACT! database in the First Address Book section.**

6. **Enter your ACT! user name and password and click OK.**

   You receive a message telling you to exit Outlook and then reopen it again for your changes to take effect. So . . .

7. **Exit Outlook and reopen it again so your changes take effect.**

Using ACT! with Outlook's e-mail

After you configure Outlook to play nicely with ACT!, you can create history that appears on the contact's History tab in ACT!. You can do this for either received messages or for messages that you are creating.

Creating ACT! history from an e-mail received in Outlook

If you want to attach an Outlook e-mail message to a contact's History tab, follow these steps:

1. **In Outlook, open the message to which you want to attach history.**

2. **Choose an option from the ACT! History drop-down list.**

   Don't see the ACT! History option? Right-click the Outlook toolbar and select ACT! History.

3. **Click the Attach to ACT! 2005 Contact(s) button on the Outlook toolbar.**

   Not sure what the button looks like? There should be a vaguely familiar button on the right end of the toolbar — it's the graphic associated with

ACT!. If you have added more than one ACT! address book to Outlook, you're prompted to select the database in which the contact is stored.

4. **Select a contact in the Attach E-mail to Contact window and click OK.**

A link to the e-mail message appears on the contact's History tab.

Creating ACT! e-mails in Outlook

If you're in Outlook and feel the overwhelming desire to send e-mail to your ACT! contacts, you can do so by following these steps:

1. **Create a new message in Outlook.**

2. **Choose an option from the ACT! History drop-down list.**

Don't see the ACT! History option? Right-click the Outlook toolbar and select ACT! History.

3. **Click the To button on the new mail message.**

The Select Names dialog box opens, as shown in Figure 19-3.

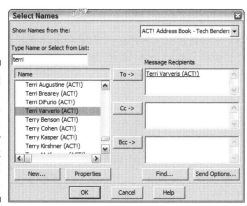

Figure 19-3: Selecting a contact to associate with a new Outlook e-mail message.

4. **Select the name of your ACT! database from the Show Names from The area.**

5. **Select a contact in the Type Name or Select from List drop-down list.**

To speed up the process, type the first couple of letters of your intended recipient's first name.

6. **Click OK.**

Your message looks pretty much like what you see in Figure 19-4. Click the Send button and you're ready to go. Once again, you get to sit around twiddling your thumbs while ACT! slaves away, creating a history of the sent e-mail on the contact's History tab.

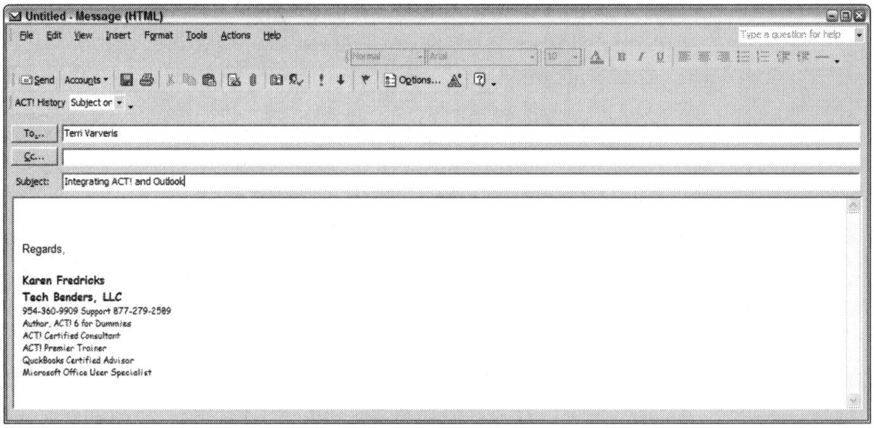

Figure 19-4:
Recording
ACT! history
in a new
Outlook
e-mail
message.

E-mailing to Outlook contacts in ACT!

Sending an ACT! e-mail to one of your Outlook contacts is almost too easy. All you need to do is follow these steps:

1. **Generate a new ACT! e-mail message by clicking the E-Mail icon on ACT!'s Navigation bar and then clicking New.**

   The new message window appears.

2. **Click the To button.**

   The Select Recipients dialog box opens, which looks a lot like the Select Names dialog box (refer to Figure 19-3).

3. **Select Microsoft Outlook from the Address Book drop-down list.**

   You now see a list of all your Outlook contacts. To speed up the process, you might consider typing in the first couple of letters of the person's first name in the Type In/Choose Name drop-down area.

4. **Select the desired name from the list and click OK.**

Sharing ACT! and Outlook calendars

After you bring your Outlook data into ACT! — including your activities — you'll want to keep both your ACT! and Outlook calendars up to date by synchronizing your calendars. (See the section "Importing Outlook into ACT!," earlier in this chapter, if you still need to import your Outlook data.)

Synchronizing your ACT! and Outlook calendars

To keep your ACT! and Outlook calendars the same, follow these steps:

1. **From any ACT! screen, choose Tools⇨Outlook Activities⇨Update Activities.**

   The Update Calendars dialog box opens. Figure 19-5 shows you the various options from which you can choose.

Figure 19-5:
Synchro-
nizing your
ACT! and
Outlook
calendars.

2. **In the Update area, select the type of update you want to perform — ACT! to Outlook, Outlook to ACT!, or a two-way sync.**

3. **Select a date option in the For These Dates area.**

   If you chose the Date Range option, you're to select a starting and ending date. Always synchronizing from today forward to speed up the process is a good idea.

4. **Click Update.**

If you are using ACT!, Outlook, and a PDA, you need to make a decision as to which program to use in order to sync your handheld device. If you attempt to synchronize both ACT! and Outlook to your PDA chances are quite high that you end up with duplication of your contacts and activities. You're safer synchronizing ACT! and Outlook through ACT! and then synchronizing your PDA to just one of your databases.

Removing Outlook activities from ACT!

After you synchronize your Outlook and ACT! activities, you might want to remove them. If you realize immediately that your synchronization didn't work entirely as planned, you can always restore an ACT! backup. You can also simply remove any synchronized activities.

1. **From any ACT! screen, choose Tools➪Outlook Activities➪Remove Activities.**

   The Remote Activities dialog box appears.

2. **Select the appropriate option:**

   - To remove ACT! activities from Outlook, select the ACT! Activities from Outlook check box.

   - To remove Outlook activities from ACT!, select the Outlook Activities from ACT! check box.

   - To remove both types of activities, select both check boxes.

3. **Click OK.**

This procedure removes only Outlook activities added to your calendar through the synchronization process. It has no effect on Outlook activities imported to your database through importing.

Displaying Outlook activities in ACT!

You can view — or not view — your Outlook activities in ACT! in a number of ways. Your Outlook activities appear on your Task List, calendars, and even on the Activities tab.

Viewing Outlook activities on the ACT! Activities tab

A major difference between ACT! and Outlook is in the way that the two programs schedule activities. I consider Outlook to be somewhat of a free-for-all; scheduled activities are not generally associated with a specific contact. Not so with ACT!; Chapter 9 shows you how every activity *must* be associated with a contact record.

Because of this difference in scheduling procedures, you don't find your Outlook activities on the Activities tab of an individual contact. You do, however, see all your Outlook activities on the Activities tab of your own My Record contact.

1. **Display your My Record contact by choosing Lookup➪My Record.**

2. **Click the Activities tab.**

   You'll notice that your Outlook activities have a unique icon displaying in the Type column. The discerning eye also notes that all your Outlook activities display in a fetching shade of blue, and all your ACT! activities are in black.

Now, here comes the really cool part: You can edit every one of those synchronized activities. For example, even though all the Outlook activities appear on the Activities tab of your own My Record, you can edit the activity with a simple double-click and change the Schedule With person to any one of your contacts. By doing that, the activity disappears from your own record and reappears on the other contact's record.

Viewing Outlook activities from ACT!'s Task List

Viewing your Outlook activities in your Task List requires a bit more fiddling, but I know you're up to the (Task List) task. Please, no groaning!

1. **Click the Task List icon on ACT!'s Navigation bar.**

2. **Click the Options button on the Task List toolbar and select Show Outlook Tasks.**

   What? You don't see a Task List toolbar? Click the Show Filters button — and read all about list filters in Chapter 5. You see the same Outlook icon and colors that you see on the Activities tab.

Viewing Outlook activities in ACT! calendars

By now, it probably comes as no surprise to you that your Outlook activities magically appear on all your ACT! calendars. In fact, it probably would have been a surprise if I had said you can't see them.

1. **Click the Calendars icon on ACT!'s Navigation bar.**

   The daily calendar pops open. Because your Outlook activities appear on all your calendars, feel free to select Work Week, Weekly, or Monthly from the Calendar toolbar.

2. **Click the Options button and select Show Outlook Activities.**

   The nice thing about ACT! is the consistency that you see throughout the program. If the Options button is MIA, remember to click the Show Filters button.

Viewing ACT! activities from Outlook

All your ACT! activities that you synchronize to Outlook are now accessible — and editable — in Outlook. Because ACT! and Outlook activities are created differently, your ACT! activities look a bit different when you view them in Outlook. The main difference lies in the association between activity and contact that Outlook doesn't have. However, an ACT! activity opened in Outlook displays all the associated contacts in the Details area, as you can see in Figure 19-6.

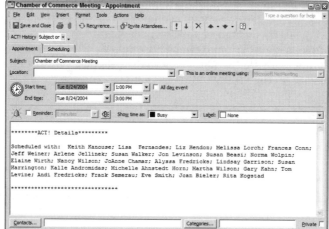

Figure 19-6:
An ACT!
activity
displayed in
Outlook.

Exploring the Internet

The Internet Services button sits on the bottom of the Navigation bar; when you click it, Internet Explorer opens, albeit with a different home page than you're used to seeing. You'll notice that all your favorites are intact and that you can navigate through the Web until the cows come home.

Because ACT! is all about contacts, it only seems logical that you might want to view a contact's Web site. Accomplish this feat of daring by following these steps:

1. **Click the Web site address that you entered into the contact record.**

   You've probably already noticed that the Web site appears to be blue, and that when you hover the mouse over the field, your cursor turns into a pointing hand indicating that this is a link. If you click the link, you're hurled into the exciting world of the Internet.

2. **Internet Explorer launches and displays the contact's Web site.**

3. **After you peruse the site and are ready to continue working in ACT!, close the browser.**

Taking advantage of Internet Links

If you're like me, you like to take advantage of the abundance of information on the Internet. Even more important to me — and probably to you, too — is the ability to find information about contacts. As its name implies, ACT!'s Internet Links link your contact information to a site on the Internet. Among the most frequently used informational sites are the various Yahoo! pages that help you find information on anything from a local weather report to driving directions and maps. By using an Internet Link in ACT!, you can access these sites in a new, unique way: Yahoo! searches for your information based on the information in the current contact record.

If one of your contacts is located in Boca Raton, Florida, you can go to that contact's record and click the <u>Yahoo! Weather</u> link to find the local Boca Raton weather report. If your My Record has you listed in the city of Miami and you're currently on the record of a contact located in Fort Lauderdale, the <u>Yahoo! Driving Directions</u> link supplies you with the driving directions to get there.

You can program an Internet Link between your ACT! information and virtually any site on the Internet. However, creating a new Internet Link is doable, but rather complicated. To make life easy for you, Stan Smith, a generous spirited ACT! Certified Consultant from Birmingham, created links to nine popular Yahoo! pages that you can download free by visiting `http://tech benders.com/act4dummies.htm` and downloading the NetLink package. Who said there's no such thing as a free lunch?

Using one of the Internet Links

After you create — or borrow a pre-existing — Internet Link, you get to use it. And that's definitely a very simple process.

1. **In ACT!, display the contact record containing the information that you want to use.**

2. **Choose View⇨Internet Services⇨Internet Links.**

   You see a menu featuring the Internet Links installed on your computer.

3. **Choose the site that you want to link to.**

   Depending on the site that you're linking to, you might be asked to confirm the information that you've selected in ACT!. Internet Explorer then displays the results; the My Record information appears on the left side of the screen, and the contact's information is on the right.

   Internet sites are extremely volatile — here today, gone tomorrow. If an Internet Link fails to function, maybe the site has changed its content information or disappeared from the scene altogether.

Excelling in Excel

At the risk of sounding like a nerd, my accounting background has turned me into an Excel junkie. Apparently I'm not alone because ACT! supplies you with numerous opportunities to interface with Excel.

Excel, the Opportunities List, and pivot tables

Because the Opportunities List deals with numbers and dollar amounts it is probably the list that you'll most often want to see in Excel. And, just like with the Contact, Group, and Company lists, one click is all it takes.

Remember: You can list only one product in the Product Name column of the opportunity in either ACT! or Excel. Opportunities with multiple products list the first product name followed by an ellipsis (. . .).

Now here comes the cool part: When you export the Opportunities List to Excel, your information is automatically translated into a pivot

table and chart. What exactly is a pivot table? Well, according to Microsoft, "in a pivot table, each column or field in your source data becomes a pivot table field that summarizes multiple rows of information." What that means is that you get some neat looking tables like the one you see in the following figure and that you can manipulate those charts to your heart's content.

After Excel opens with your Opportunities List, just click the Opportunities pivot table or the Opportunities Pivot tab to introduce yourself to the exciting world of pivot tables!

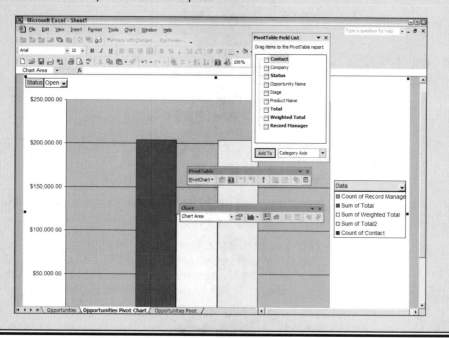

Exporting a list to Excel

Very often, ACT! users want to export a part of their database to Excel. Perhaps they need to get information to a non-ACT! user. Or maybe they want to manipulate the data in a different way. It could be that they need to import their ACT! information into another program, and Excel is the vehicle of choice.

If you look closely, you find hints of Excel throughout ACT! 2005. Specifically, if you look really close to the Contact List, Group List, and Company List icon bars, you see an icon that looks like a mini-spreadsheet. Figure 19-7 shows the icon. If you pause your mouse on it for a second, you see that the button is called Export to Excel.

Figure 19-7:
The Export
to Excel
icon.

Funnily enough, the button works exactly as you would suspect. Click it and Excel opens, displaying the list view that you're currently in. Don't see the field you're looking for? Is Excel showing you a field you didn't want? No problemo. If you customize the list to show just the fields you want (find out how to do that in Chapter 6), Excel displays those very same fields.

Because other programs can easily use Excel data, only Standard, Manager and Administrator ACT! users can export list data to Excel.

Importing a product or drop-down list into ACT!

I've never figured out whether I'm lazy or smart — or a little of each. Whatever, I love to use shortcuts to save myself valuable time. If you're a new user of ACT!, you might have already developed a rather lengthy Product List in another piece of software. For example, you might have created a Price List using Excel or created an Inventory List in your accounting software. If I didn't like you so much, I'd tell you to start typing, but instead I tell you how to export that list from Excel into ACT!.

To import data into ACT!, follow these steps:

1. **Save the Excel file as a comma-delimited file.**

2. **In ACT!, choose Tools⇨Define Fields⇨Manage Drop-Down Lists.**

3. **Select the field into which you want to import the data, click Edit Drop-Down List, and click Next.**

4. **Choose the Import Drop-Down List Items option.**

   From here, browse to the place where you saved the .csv Excel file and watch while ACT! brings in your list of information — and saves you a lot of typing.

Mapping ACT! fields to Excel

Another excellent ACT! feature (pun intended) is the ability to map specific ACT! contact, group, or company fields to Excel cells. Here's what you need to know to accomplish that feat.

1. **Add an Excel spreadsheet to the Documents tab.**

2. **Click the Documents tab, select the spreadsheet, and then click Edit Document.**

   The spreadsheet opens. You'll notice that after you install ACT!, Excel is now the proud owner of a new ACT! menu just like the one in Figure 19-8.

Figure 19-8:
The ACT!
menu in
Excel.

If you prefer, you can attach a spreadsheet to ACT! while you're in Excel by choosing ACT!⇨Attach to ACT!.

3. **In Excel, select the Excel cell you want to map to an ACT! field.**

4. **Choose ACT!⇨Map to Contact (or Company or Group).**

   The Map Fields dialog box opens. As you scroll through the list you'll notice that all of the fields are in it.

5. **Select the ACT! field you want to map to the selected Excel field and click Add.**

   You can easily add as many fields as you want by selecting an Excel cell, choosing an ACT! field, and then clicking the Add button to "map" the two together. Each ACT! field name appears in angle brackets in the Excel cell.

6. **Save and close the spreadsheet when you finish.**

7. **In ACT!, select the spreadsheet on the Documents tab and then click the Map to Excel button.**

   The fields automatically update with the corresponding field entries when the document opens.

What's in a Word?

ACT! can use Word as the default word processor (see Chapter 3 to appoint Word as your word processor), and you attach documents to the Documents tab (see Chapter 5). What you might not have noticed, however, is that when you install ACT!, it adds an ACT! menu to Word (as shown in Figure 19-9).

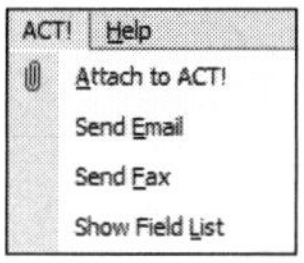

Figure 19-9:
The ACT!
menu that
appears in
Word.

You can use Word's ACT! menu to help you with several tasks.

Attaching a document to a contact record

Follow these steps to attach a document to a contact's Document tab:

1. **Open or create a document in Word.**

2. **From Word, choose ACT!⇨Attach to ACT!.**

   The Select Contacts window opens.

3. **Select the contact to whom you want to attach the document and click OK.**

   In essence, you've created a link to your document. If you look carefully, you'll notice something new on the Documents tab — an icon that matches the type of document you've just added. So, if you added a Word document, you see the familiar-looking Word icon smack dab in the middle of your Documents tab as well as the name and path of the attached file. Go ahead, make my day: Click the icon. The attached document miraculously opens in all its glory.

Sending a document as an e-mail

In this age of viruses, you're probably hesitant to send too many attachments knowing that the recipient might not even open it. If you're using Word to create your documents, here's a simple way to convert the document into the body of an e-mail:

1. **Open or create a document in Word.**

2. **From Word, choose ACT!⇨Send Email.**

   The Select Contacts window opens.

3. **Select the contact you want to send the e-mail message to, click the right arrow button, and then click OK.**

   The New Message window appears.

4. **Type the subject and then click Send.**

   Through the wonders of modern science — or at least the wonders of ACT! — a history of your sent e-mail appear on the contact's History tab.

Sending a document in a fax

If you want to fax a Word document, follow these steps:

1. **Open or create a document in Word.**

2. **From Word, choose ACT!⇨Send Fax.**

   The Select Contacts window opens.

3. **Select the contact you want to send the fax message to, click the right arrow button, and then click OK.**

   Your fax software now opens. At this point, you need to follow the instructions of your fax software with one big difference — ACT! creates a history of your fax.

The ability to fax using ACT! is dependent on having access to fax software and a phone line. The various options for sending a fax depend on the fax software installed on your computer. If the fax option is grayed out, you can't fax because your machine is lacking the proper software.

Showing ACT!'s mail merge fields

Sometimes in your zealousness, you might close the list of mail merge fields that opens when you edit or create a template (see Chapter 13 to find out how to create a template). Not to worry — getting them back is easy enough.

In Word, choose ACT!⇨Show Field List. The Add Mail Merge Fields dialog box reappears — and you can continue adding fields to your template.

Chapter 20

ACT!ing on Your Opportunities

*I*n this chapter, I lead you through the entire sales process using ACT!. I show you how to create an initial opportunity, make changes to it as the sale makes its way through the sales funnel, and view your opportunities by using the Opportunity List and various ACT! reports.

Creating Opportunities

ACT! was originally created by a sales person for sales people. Ironically, many users of the earlier versions of ACT! found the program a bit lacking when it came to tracking sales opportunities. Happily, ACT! 2005 includes a totally revamped Opportunities module.

In ACT!, an *opportunity* is a potential sale to a contact. Each opportunity must be associated with a contact. All sales information for a contact appears on the Opportunities tab of the contact record. (Figure 20-1 shows an example of the Opportunities tab.) When you create an opportunity, you can list the names of your products or services, specify a sales stage and forecasted close date, and even make use of eight customizable fields. Click a button, and ACT! generates a quote. You can even schedule a follow-up activity for the opportunity.

After creating an opportunity, you can go to the Opportunity List where you can see all your opportunities listed together or view the contact's, group's, or company's Opportunities tab. As if that isn't enough, you can choose from a slew of sales reports, including a sales graph. Whew!

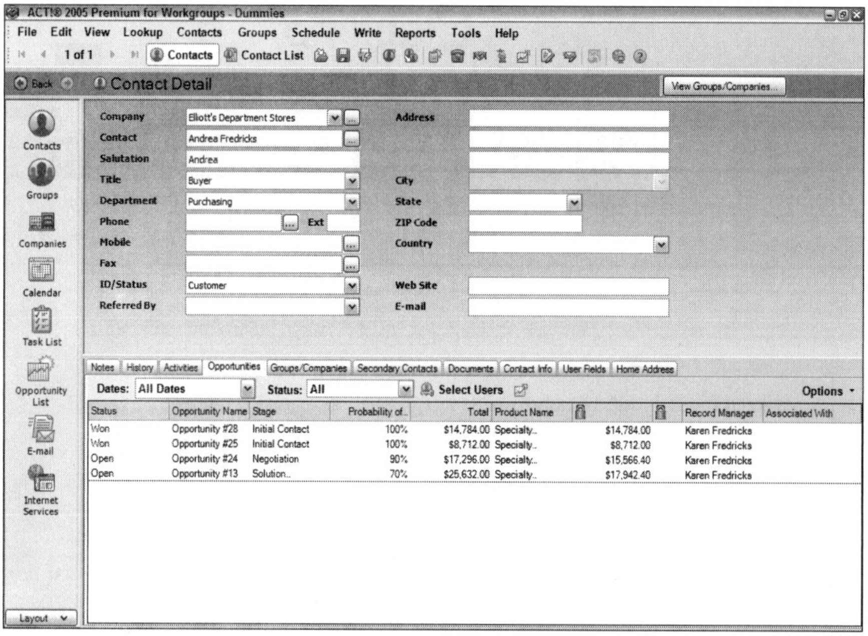

Figure 20-1:
The
Opportu-
nities tab.

By automating the sales process using ACT!, you have a better chance at closing more sales. First of all, if you're following up on your activities as I show you in Chapter 9, you have significantly fewer contacts falling through the cracks of your database. Secondly, you can adjust your predictions as the opportunity moves through the sales stages. Most importantly, you can generate reports based on your projected sales, allowing you to focus on the deals that you think you have the best chance of closing.

Initiating the opportunity

So why are you sitting around reading a book? It's time for you to go out there and make some money. Here's how you're going to make your first million:

1. **Go to the Contact Detail window by clicking the Contacts icon on the Nav bar.**

2. **Perform a lookup to find the contact for whom you're creating an opportunity.**

   What? A little rusty on those lookups? Fear not — and head to Chapter 7 for a quick refresher.

3. **Create a new opportunity by clicking the Opportunities tab and then clicking the New Opportunity icon.**

   If you have a bit of trouble locating the New Opportunity icon, it's understandable; it's the icon on the Opportunities tab that looks like a graph. You also know you're on the right track when you pause your cursor over the button; a ToolTip proclaiming New Opportunity shows up.

   The Opportunity dialog box opens, as shown in Figure 20-2.

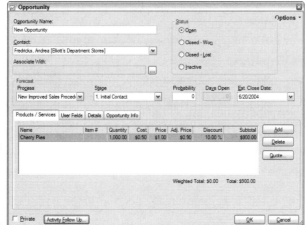

Figure 20-2:
The
Opportunity
dialog box.

4. **Give the opportunity a name.**

   After you create the opportunity, you track it down by doing a Name lookup, so you may want to assign a name that starts with the company name that you're doing business with. If you don't give the opportunity a name, ACT! assigns one for you automatically: New Opportunity.

5. **Associate the opportunity with a contact.**

   After all, ACT! is contact-centric and needs to associate each opportunity with a given contact.

6. **Assign a sales status.**

   This option is a fairly simple one. All new opportunities are assigned the Open status.

7. **Assign a sales process.**

   Here's where ACT! really forces you to get organized. Although not necessary, you possibly have more than one Process List with your opportunities. You might use one for the pre-sales steps that you want everyone in your organization to follow and another for the steps that you need to follow once you land that large deal.

Each process comes with its own list of stages. Your homework is to verbalize your sales processes and translate them into ACT! (see Chapter 15). Doing so keeps you organized, lets you know where you stand in the scheme of things, and allows you to generate some useful sales reports later on down the road.

8. **Assign a sales stage.**

   If you're hearing a nagging voice in the back of your head, it's because I'm nagging you. An important concept in computing is Garbage In, Garbage Out (GIGO). You want to set the sales stage so you know where this opportunity lies in your sales pipeline and so that this opportunity doesn't fall by the wayside. And, you'll want to go back and change the stage as the opportunity progresses through your sales cycle.

9. **Enter a probability of closing.**

   This step could be rather easy because you can assign probabilities to each sales stage when you set up the sales process. Feel free to over-write the probability percentage based on your own hunches for each opportunity.

10. **Enter the estimated close date.**

    Again, you use this information for sorting and reporting later.

All that's left for you to do is fill in the Product/Services, User Fields, Details, and Opportunity Info tabs — a little time consuming, but you reap the rewards later for all your hard work now.

Product/Services tab

If you're like most people, this part is fun. Here's where you get to count the cash, bill for the beans, dream of the dollars. . . . In any event, the Products/Services tab is where you get to add all the line items for your opportunity and sit back while ACT! crunches the numbers for you.

Although the process of adding products or services to an opportunity is pretty straightforward, I walk you through it, just in case:

1. **Click the Add button.**

2. **Choose a name from the Name drop-down list.**

   If you're selling a new item, scroll to the bottom of the list and click Edit List to add it.

   Chapter 15 gives you the full lowdown on creating a Product List.

3. **Add an item number.**

   If you filled in all the appropriate item numbers when creating your Product List, this step isn't necessary.

4. **Enter the quantity.**

5. **Double-check the cost and price.**

   This information fills in automatically from your Product List. If the information is incorrect, head back to the Product List to correct it.

6. **Adjust either the adjusted price or the discount percentage.**

   If you lower (or raise!) a price, ACT! automatically calculates the discount percentage. If you prefer to tinker with the percentage, ACT! automatically adjusts the price.

7. **Get out your abacus and multiply the quantity by the adjusted price — not!**

   Throw out the calculator because ACT! does the calculation for you — and even totals up all the line items for you. You'll also notice a weighted total that multiplies the total against the probability percentage. And unlike me, ACT! never makes a mistake!

8. **Repeat Steps 1 through 7 as many times as necessary until your opportunity includes all the necessary line items.**

User Fields tab

The User Fields tab consists of eight customizable fields. Chapter 15 explains how you can customize those eight fields by renaming and customizing them. You might be a manufacturer's rep and want to indicate your eight major lines. Or you might want to indicate the eight manufacturers you deal with. Don't forget that you can query and generate reports with these fields so use them wisely. You can check out the Opportunity User Fields tab in Figure 20-3.

Giving 'em a discount

You can create discounts on an item-by-item basis by either changing the adjusted price or the discount percentage. That works pretty well for most situations, but you might prefer to add the discount rate as a totally separate line item. In order to do this, you need to add a Discount Item entry to your Product List. Because the discount amount varies, you need to manually insert the amount of the discount each time you create a new opportunity.

To create a discount item, follow these steps:

1. **From any ACT! screen, choose Tools⇨ Define Fields⇨Manage Product List⇨Add.**

2. **Type a name for the discount, such as Discount.**

To use the discount item

1. **From the Opportunities tab, add or edit an opportunity.**

2. **Add a new item and choose Discount from the Name list. If you want to make this the bottom item, you probably want to choose Discount as your last item.**

3. **In the Adjusted Price field, type in a hyphen (–) followed by the discount amount for the order.**

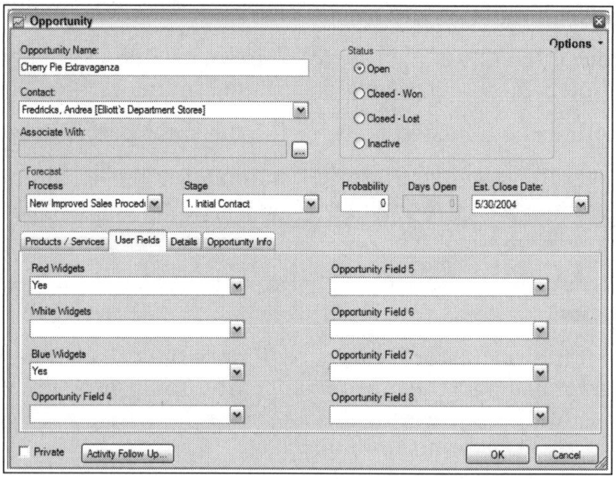

Figure 20-3:
The
Opportunity
User
Fields tab.

Details tab

In general, a database consists of many fields with each containing a single piece of information. But people are people and sometimes storing all your important information into a bunch of teeny tiny fields isn't possible. That said, you can use the Details tab to write the Great American Novel — or at least a few important tidbits of additional info — about your opportunity.

If the information that you want to include with the opportunity is in a document, such as a word processing file, you can copy the text in the other application and paste it on the Details tab.

Opportunity tab

By now your mind is probably fogging over from all the information that you're inputting. The information on the User Fields, Details, and Opportunity Info tabs are purely optional, albeit helpful. If your poor fingers are wearing down to little stubs, you can always go back and complete the rest of this information later.

Those of you with the stamina to make it this far will notice a few of the cool pieces of information stored on the Opportunity Info tab. The rest of you can sip your lemonade and gaze at Figure 20-4.

- ✔ **Open Date:** By default, ACT! assigns today's date to a new opportunity. This is where you can change it if necessary.

- ✔ **Record Manager:** By default, the name of the logged-on user appears as the opportunity's Record Manager. Feel free to change it if necessary.

✔ **Referred By:** If you go by the Christmas ham theory — the big guys get a ham and the little guys get a fruitcake at holiday time — you might just want to attribute each of your opportunities to the appropriate source.

✔ **Competitor:** If you keep one eye on the competition, here's where you can do it.

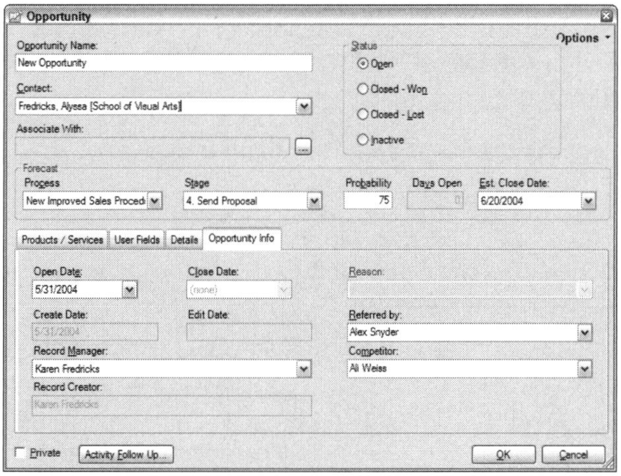

Figure 20-4:
The
Opportunity
Info tab.

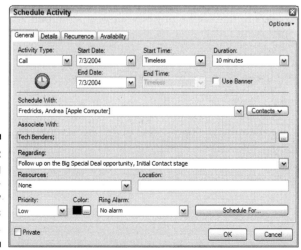

Click the Activity Follow Up button. Getting all your information into a sales opportunity is only half the fun. The other half consists of sticking to your original course of action. You get to set up your follow-up activity in the Schedule Activity dialog box. You'll notice in Figure 20-5 that ACT! inserts the opportunity name and stage into the Regarding field. Then click OK. You've just gotta love a program that does so much of your work for you!

Figure 20-5:
Scheduling
a follow-
up activity
for a sales
opportunity.

At this point, you're essentially done with creating the opportunity. Sit back, relax a moment, and then go out and start selling your heart out!

Modifying the opportunity

As your opportunity progresses, going back and modifying the sales stage is often necessary. Again, this information appears in your various reports, so updating your opportunities is vitally important. This process is painless and short:

1. **Find the opportunity that you want to update.**

   You have several choices here:

   - Create a lookup for the contact associated with the opportunity, and then click the Opportunity tab. On the Opportunities tab, double-click the opportunity.

   - From the Opportunity List, double-click the opportunity that you want to modify.

   - From any of the ACT! screens, choose Lookup⇨Opportunities and then select one of the field choices. For example, you can search by opportunity name, product, or status. ACT! then scurries through your database and opens the Opportunity List, which presents you with all opportunities that met your search criteria. Double-click the opportunity you want to modify.

   The Opportunity dialog box opens (refer to Figure 20-2).

2. **Change the information in the Stage field as necessary.**

   The purpose of ACT!'s opportunities is to allow you to track a potential sell from its inception to its final outcome. You'll probably find editing your opportunities useful as they progress through the various sales stages. This allows you to view any of your opportunities to assess exactly where you stand.

3. **Schedule another follow-up if necessary.**

4. **Click OK when you finish editing the opportunity.**

The biggest challenge for many busy people is remembering to take care of all those nagging little details. Chapter 10 focuses on the activity series. You might consider creating a sales activity series and including "updating sales stage" as one of the steps.

Closing the deal

When you close a sale, you can record the outcome and the closing date. ACT! records a history on the contact's History tab, and if you associated the opportunity with a group or company, on the History tab for the group and company as well.

1. **Find the contact for whom you're recording the outcome of an opportunity.**

2. **On the Opportunities tab, double-click the opportunity that you want to complete.**

3. **Change the status to indicate the current state of the opportunity in the Opportunity dialog box.**

   - Open

   - Closed-Won

   - Closed-Lost

   - Inactive

4. **Click OK.**

The opportunity remains on the Opportunities tab. The status changes to Won, Lost, or Inactive depending on the choice you made. The Actual Close Date updates to reflect today's date.

You Can Quote Me on That

After you create an opportunity, ACT! can convert it into a quote for you. The quote template actually consists of two pieces:

- ✔ The quote.adt file, which Word creates. You can edit the template by changing the fonts, graphics, and wording. Typically, the .adt file contains information about both you and your contact and can also contain disclaimer information.

- ✔ The quote.xlt file is created in Excel and embedded into the .adt file. It appears as a table in the center of a quote and contains numeric data, such as quantity, pricing, and totals. Because of the way that the .xlt file is created, you'll probably not want to make any changes to the file; doing so may run the risk of leaving the quote generator inoperable.

Only one quote template works directly from the Opportunity dialog box. If you create other quote templates, use them to fill in contact information, but leave the product information blank.

Because the quote template consists of both a Word document and the embedded Excel table, you must have both programs installed on your computer in order to generate quotes using ACT!. You also need to set your word processor preference to Word in order to edit the `quote.adt` template; Chapter 3 shows you how to do that. You can see a quote in Figure 20-6.

Creating a quote for an opportunity

You can literally create a quote at the click of a button. And here's how you find the button:

1. **Open an existing opportunity.**

2. **Click the Quote button on the Products/Services tab.**

3. **If you set the preferences to prompt you for a quote number, type the number in the Enter Quote Number field and click OK.**

   After a moment or so of whirring and hissing, Word opens, revealing the quote, which is all filled out and ready to go.

Figure 20-6:
Sample quote created using ACT!.

	Tech Benders			
	275 NE 48th Street			Quote #: TB1001
	Pompano Beach, FL 33064			
	Phone:			
	Fax:			

Andrea Fredricks		Phone: 800-389-1212	Date: 5/30/2004
Elliott's Department Stores		Fax: 800-183-1414	Rep.: Karen Fredricks
275 NE 48th Street		Email: andi@techbenders.com	
Pompano Beach, FL 33064			

Qty	Item #	Name	Price	Total
1000	1674	Cherry Pies	$.90	$900.00
10	8608	Balloon Bouquet	$70.20	$702.00
25		Chocolate Sampler	$9.00	$225.00

			Sub Total	$1,827.00
		Shipping & Handling		
		Taxes	0.000%	$.00
		TOTAL		$1,827.00

Comments: Office Use Only:

Thank you for your business

Chapter 3 focuses on the various ACT! preferences settings. Buried away in those settings is one that determines whether you're prompted to supply a quote number every time you generate a quote. At the same time, you can indicate the numbers and/or letters that you want to include in the beginning of each quote number. You find those settings by choosing Tools⇨Preferences⇨Quote Preferences.

Want to change the order in which your products appear on your quote? It's easy. Simply click the appropriate column heading on the Products/Services tab in the Opportunity dialog box. Want the products sorted alphabetically? Click the Name column heading. Want them sorted by price? Click the Subtotal column heading.

4. **Print and save the quote as you do any other Word document.**

Editing the opportunity quote template

As I mention earlier, you can't fiddle with the Excel portion of the quote template; doing so could cause your calculations to not calculate. You can, however, modify the Word portion of the quote template to your exacting specifications. Chapter 13 goes into greater detail about the exciting world of template modifications, but for now, here's a quick refresher course.

1. **From any ACT! screen, choose Write⇨Edit Template.**

2. **Choose quote.adt and then click Open.**

3. **Edit the template as necessary and then save it.**

When you click the Quote button in the Opportunity dialog box, ACT! automatically looks for the `quote.adt` template file. Although I advocate saving templates and reports as other, unique names when attempting to modify them, the same theory does not hold true for the quote template. If you change the name, you can't access it from the Opportunity dialog box — and your product information doesn't magically pour into it. Do not change the name of the opportunity quote!

Viewing the Opportunity List

The Opportunity List provides you with a way to view all your opportunities for all of your contacts. You can filter the Opportunity List to display only those opportunities that match your specifications. You can then print the Opportunity List. Or, if you are really ambitious, you can export the Opportunity List to Excel where you find Pivot Tables waiting patiently for you. Not sure what a pivot table is? Head back to Chapter 19 for more details.

Getting to the Opportunity List is almost too easy: Just click the Opportunity List icon on the Navigation bar. A list of opportunities appears, as you can see in Figure 20-7. The Opportunity List even comes equipped with a status bar running across the bottom that displays the total number of opportunities, the weighted total, and the grand total. You'll also notice that the Opportunity List comes equipped with its very own toolbar containing icons specifically pertaining to the Opportunity List.

Filtering the Opportunity List

If you hate to make a decision at the ice cream store, you might not appreciate the Opportunity List filters. But if you're the kind of person who loves to have things, well, exactly the way *you* want them, then you're going to love the Opportunity List!

The various filter options are located at the top of the Opportunity List window. As you change filter options, the Opportunity List changes to include the options you select. After this is set, you can click the Hide Filters button in the upper-right corner of the Opportunity List. Don't see any filters? Click the Show Filters button that appears instead.

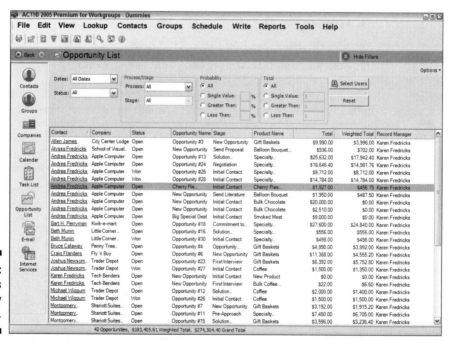

Figure 20-7:
ACT!'s
Opportunity
List.

Feel free to choose from the following Opportunity List filters:

- **Dates:** Limits the opportunities to those matching the estimated closing date that you indicate.

- **Status:** Indicates whether you want to view Open, Closed-Won, Closed-Lost, Inactive, or all opportunities. You can also choose None, which frankly doesn't make a whole lot of sense because then you don't see any of your opportunities!

- **Process/Stage:** If you set up more than one series of sales processes, here's where you indicate which one you like to see.

- **Probability:** Type the percent you want to use; you can find opportunities that only match a specific percentage, or those that are greater than or less than a given percentage.

- **Total:** Type the amount you want to use or choose whether to view opportunities that are greater than or less than a given amount.

- **Select Users:** Selects the names of the Record Managers associated with the opportunities you want to view.

- **Options:** Actually, you have only one true filtering option here; select Show Private to display your private opportunities. You'll also notice the Customize Columns options that let you add, remove, and change the order of your columns.

Resetting the Opportunity List filters

After you diligently work to set all your filters, you're probably going to need to reset them again sooner or later. You can accomplish that task in either of the following two ways:

- Click the Reset button from the Opportunity List.

- Choose Lookup⇨Opportunities⇨All Opportunities.

Printing the Opportunity List

Now comes the exciting part. Okay, it might not be your exact idea of excitement, but seeing all your hard work translated onto a nice piece of white paper can at least give you a nice sense of accomplishment. Remember all those numerous opportunity fields that you so painstakingly filled? Here's where you get to display them in all their glory.

Customize your columns before printing out a copy of your Opportunity List. I tell you how in Chapter 5.

1. **Click Quick Print from the Opportunity List toolbar.**

2. **From the Print dialog box, click OK.**

Viewing Opportunity History

Chapter 8 talks about the nifty histories created by ACT! when you change certain key pieces of contact information. You create a history for an opportunity when you create, change the status or stage, generate a quote, or change the estimated close date. You can view the opportunity history from the contact's History tab. If the opportunity is associated with a group or company, you can view the opportunity from those History tabs as well.

When you customize the eight opportunity user fields in the Opportunity dialog box, you can also modify them to become History fields so that whatever information you put into them is forever recorded on the History tab, even if you change the content of one of those fields.

Okay, do you want the good news or the bad news? Well, I can't hear your response — and don't you feel silly responding to an inanimate object — so I'll give you the bad news first. You might find the histories that ACT! creates are a bit terse. The good news is that you can edit them as much as you like by simply double-clicking the history. The Edit History dialog box opens, as shown in Figure 20-8. Edit away to your heart's content — after all, who said you couldn't change history?

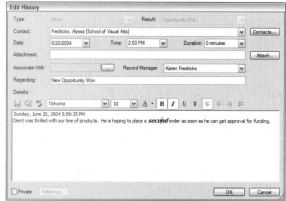

Figure 20-8:
Editing an opportunity history.

Tracking Opportunities

You poor reader, you! You work so hard in filling out the numerous opportunity fields. Knowing that you need a little break, ACT! rewards you with an abundance of sales reports and charts. Whether you need to report on a single customer or all your current opportunities, ACT! has a way of giving you the information.

You can monitor the opportunities that you have at each stage of the sales development cycle and display this information in a report or graphically in a sales funnel or sales graph.

Reporting on a single contact

The Opportunities tab provides you with the sales information on any given contact. The columns on the Opportunities tab work just like the columns in other ACT! areas, such as the History tab and the Contact List. You can change their order, sort by any column, and add new columns. You can filter the list by date and status.

You can use the information contained on the Opportunities tab to create a quick-and-dirty report in the exact way that you create a report based on the Contact List. ACT! prints the report in the same exact order as it appears on-screen — that is, what you see on-screen is what you see on paper. To print a report on a single opportunity, follow these steps:

1. **Go to the contact record of the person for whom you like to track opportunities.**

2. **Right-click the Opportunity tab or click the Options button.**

   You can use a lot of informational fields when you enter a new opportunity. You can portray each of these fields as a column on the Opportunities tab. You can customize the tab in any one of the following ways:

   • **Add a column:** Select a field from the Available Fields area and click the right-pointing arrow.

   • **Change the order of the columns:** Select a field from the Show as Columns in This Order area and then click the Move Up or Move Down buttons.

   • **Remove a column:** Select a field from the Show as Columns in This Order area and click the left-pointing arrow.

3. **Click OK when you finish adding columns.**

Reporting on all your opportunities

If you feel an overwhelming desire to chop down a few more trees in the rain forest, ACT! can help. ACT! comes equipped with a dozen opportunity reports to suit most of your reporting needs. If, for some reason, you don't find a report that suits you, at least you look busy when the boss walks by! ACT! opportunity reports provide details and summaries of opportunities, closed sales, and lost sales.

The 15 ACT! opportunity reports are

- **Totals by Status:** Lists all your opportunities subtotaled by Closed/Won and Lost sales.

- **Adjusted for Probability:** Lists all your opportunities by contact, sorted by sales stage. I'm not sure what love — or probabilities — got to do with it; they don't affect the report.

- **Pipeline:** Lists information subtotaled by sales stage; this is a great accompaniment to the Sales Pipeline graphic.

- **Opportunities by Record Manager:** Lists information on your opportunities, subtotaled by the Record Manager.

- **Opportunities by Contact:** Lists opportunities subtotaled by contact.

- **Lost Opportunities by Competitor:** Subtotals lost opportunities by competitor.

- **Lost Opportunities by Reason:** Subtotals lost opportunities by reason for losing the sale.

- **Lost Opportunities by Record Manager:** Subtotals lost opportunities by the Record Manager.

- **Opportunities by Company:** Complete information for each company with an opportunity or a closed sale.

- **Opportunities by Group:** Subtotals opportunities by group.

- **Opportunities Referred By:** The report is subtotaled by the opportunity referral sources.

- **Sales by Reason:** Opportunities listed by the reason that they're either won or lost.

- **Opportunity by Status:** Report subtotals opportunities based on Open, Closed, or Inactive status.

- **Gross Margin by Product:** Subtotals the opportunities by product showing the gross margin.

- **Gross Margin by Contact:** Subtotals the opportunities by contact showing the gross margin.

Creating an opportunities graph

The opportunities graph can show your sales forecast or your closed sales for a month, a quarter, or any period of time you choose. Many sales organizations prefer to see sales information in the form of a graph. As usual, ACT! is up to the task and can create one for you in the blink of an eye — or at least in the click of the mouse.

Here's all you need to do to see all your opportunities translated through the wonder of modern technology into a graph:

1. **Create a lookup of contacts to include in the graph.**

   Need a warm-up on performing lookups? Head to Chapter 7.

2. **Choose Reports⇨Opportunity Reports⇨Opportunity Graph.**

   The Graph Options dialog box appears, as shown in Figure 20-9.

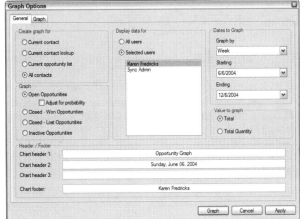

Figure 20-9: The Graph Options dialog box.

3. **On the General tab, indicate the information you to want include in your graph:**

   • In the Create Graph For area, select the Current Contact, Current Lookup, Current Opportunity List, or All Contacts radio button.

   • In the Graph area, select the type of opportunities to appear in the graph.

   • Choose the Record Managers of the contacts you're including in your graph from the Display Data For area.

   • Enter header and footer information to appear on your graph.

   • Fill in the date range and intervals in the Dates to Graph area and values to use in your graph in the Value to Graph area.

4. **On the Graph tab, make a few more graph-specific choices, including whether you want a bar or line graph, the graph size, gridlines, the colors used in the graph, or the scaling used in your graph (see Figure 20-10).**

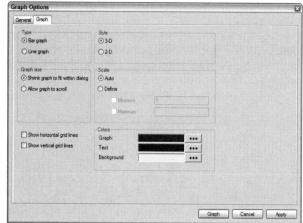

Figure 20-10:
More graph
options.

5. **Click the Graph button.**

   Voilà! Your graph appears before your eyes. Try not to look too surprised. If the boss walks by, you might want to make little grunting noises indicating how studiously you're working on your graph. You can see a sample graph in Figure 20-11.

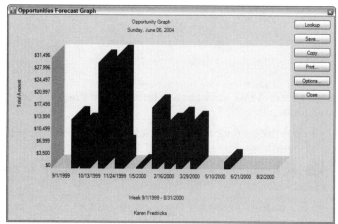

Figure 20-11:
A sample
opportunity
graph.

6. **In the Opportunities Forecast Graph window, you can**

   • **Lookup:** Change the criteria for the contacts that appear in the opportunity graph.

   • **Save:** Save your graph as a bitmap (`.bmp`) or JPEG (`.jpg`) file to preserve your artwork for future generations.

   • **Copy:** Save it to the Windows Clipboard in case you want to perform a little cosmetic surgery on it. After you copy the graph to the Clipboard, you can paste it into your favorite graphics program and change any of its elements.

   • **Print:** Does just that.

   • **Options:** Modify the graph.

   • **Close:** Exit the graph without printing or saving it.

Viewing the opportunity pipeline

A picture is worth a thousand words — or in this case, it might be worth thousands of dollars! Most large sales organizations are already familiar with the concept of a sales pipeline. The ACT! Pipeline graphic represents the number of opportunities at each stage of the sales development process. Each section of an opportunity pipeline represents one of your pre-determined sales stages. Opportunities that are marked as closed, or those that are missing a sales stage, are excluded.

1. **Perform a lookup to find the contacts that you want to include in the opportunity pipeline.**

   Although you don't have to assign a sales stage to an opportunity, only opportunities with assigned stages are included in the opportunity funnel.

2. **Choose Reports⇨Opportunity Reports⇨Opportunity Pipeline.**

   The Opportunity Pipeline Options dialog box opens, as shown in Figure 20-12. Fill in the pipeline options that you want to use in your opportunity pipeline:

   • Select the contacts you want to include in your pipeline from the Create Graph For area.

   • Select the Record Managers whose data you want to include from the Display Data for Sales Managed By area.

   • Select the process that you want to track.

- Color-coordinate your opportunity pipeline by assigning colors to each of your sales stages in the Assign Colors area. If you want to change a color, click the ellipsis button to the right of the color and select another color.

- Fill in the header and footer information that you would like to include with your pipeline.

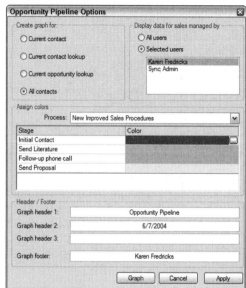

Figure 20-12:
The Sales
Pipeline
Options
dialog box.

3. **Click the Graph button.**

   You are now the proud owner of a beautiful opportunity pipeline (similar to what's shown in Figure 20-13), guaranteed to impress the heck out of your boss and other members of your sales team.

4. **In the Opportunity Pipeline window, you have options similar to those available in the Opportunity Forecast Graph window (see the preceding section).**

   The size of each section is fixed and does not scale based on the number of opportunities at each stage:

   - **Lookup:** Change the lookup criteria for the pipeline.

   - **Save:** Save your pipeline as a bitmap (`.bmp`) or JPEG (`.jpg`) file to preserve your artwork for future generations.

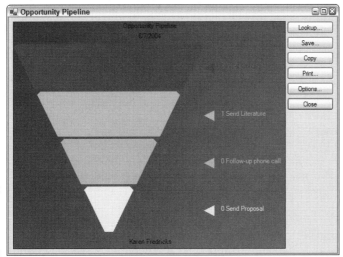

Figure 20-13:
A sales
pipeline.

- **Copy:** Copy it to the Windows Clipboard and later paste it into a graphics program for modifications.

- **Print:** It doesn't get any more self-explanatory than this!

- **Options:** Modify the pipeline.

- **Close:** Exit without saving or printing the pipeline.

Chapter 21

Grouping Your Contacts

. . . .

In This Chapter

▶ Understanding groups

▶ Creating groups

▶ Establishing group rules

▶ Putting groups to work

▶ Utilizing group notes and activities

. . . .

*I*n this chapter, I focus on a very commonly overlooked ACT! feature: the ACT! group. What exactly is a group? Generally speaking, a group is a collection of something. In ACT!, a ***group*** is a collection of contacts. More specifically, a group is a semi-permanent lookup whose contact records you assign to the group by any criteria that you want.

The contact record helps you to keep track of all activities as they relate to an individual; the group allows you to track activities as they relate to an entire group of contacts. So when used correctly, ACT! groups provide you with the potential to increase the overall power and efficiency of the ACT! program.

Throughout this chapter, after explaining all the ins and outs of groups, I show you how to create a group. I then show you how to put groups to work so that you can enjoy all the benefits that groups have to offer. After reading this chapter, you'll become a real group pro — knowing when to use them (and when not to) and how to use them to their greatest potential.

A Few Good Reasons to Create a Group

You shouldn't just create groups willy-nilly without putting some thought into them. If you do that, you're liable to end up with bad groups, which consume your time without offering any real benefits. (See the nearby sidebar "Don't create bad groups!" to see what I mean.) So what exactly makes a ***good*** group, you ask? Here are a few examples of when groups can really make life easy for you:

- **Managing large projects:** Groups are particularly well suited for those of you who work on large projects. For example, if you're building a home, you're involved with any number of people from building inspectors and city officials to subcontractors, your own personnel, and the new home-owner. Assigning all these contacts to a group allows you to easily zero in on only those contacts involved in the project.

- **Tracking real estate listings:** If you're a real estate agent or broker, setting up a group for each listing allows you to track all clients that see a particular property and to list all properties that you show to a particular client.

- **Organizing your classes and seminars:** If you teach classes and seminars, you can set up groups to track all the attendees for each of your classes. Then, when the time comes, you can print out class lists to ensure that you contact all class members. You also have a clear listing as to what classes an individual contact has taken.

- **Focusing on a specific group of contacts:** Say you went to a trade show and came back with 75 good, solid leads — all of which you are determined to call. Your first step is to put all those leads into a group. On Monday, you might call 20 of those leads, moving each one out of the group as you make the call. On Tuesday, your list is down to 55 but maybe you only have the chance to call 5 people. Wednesday finds you putting out fires around your business and you don't have a chance to continue phoning until Friday; you can easily access those remaining 50 contacts and take up right where you left off.

Don't create bad groups!

Here's an example of a *bad* group: I once worked with an ACT! user who had exactly 50 groups — one for each state. He had then sub-divided each group into subgroups representing each zip code within the state. This user had overlooked the obvious — his database already contained fields for both state and zip code. His groups provided him with no more information than he already had — and after he had put all that time and effort into creating them.

Many ACT! users create groups to track contacts for their newsletter or holiday card mailings. Unfortunately, this situation is another poor use of a group; although the user sees who will be receiving the mailing, he doesn't find out who is *not* to receive the mailing. More importantly, he doesn't find out who fell through the cracks and was just overlooked. Setting up a Mailing field allows you to track all three things.

In previous versions of ACT! you might have relied on groups to track members of a large company or account. ACT! 2005 introduces the Companies feature, eliminating the need to use groups to track the companies and/or divisions that you work with. Best of all, if you're using groups to track your companies, you can convert them with a few clicks of your mouse. Chapter 22 shows you the various ins and outs of this new feature.

What All Groups Have in Common

In the preceding section, I provide examples of using groups that surely give you an idea of how you can use groups for a wide range of tasks. Despite the flexibility of groups, however, all groups share a few common elements:

- ✔ **Volatility:** In general, groups and the contacts within them do not have to be permanent. A contractor, for example, replaces subcontractors he works with if they do a poor job. And, after that contractor completes a house, he might no longer need to use the group that he created for the project and may choose to delete it. Also, removing a contact from a group doesn't in turn remove the contact from the database.

- ✔ **No limit to the number of groups:** You're allowed to create as many groups as you want; your only limitation is self-imposed. Working with thousands of groups, however, is probably rather cumbersome.

- ✔ **No limit to the number of contacts that belong to a group:** However, if your database appears as though it has taken a tranquilizer every time you go to the Group Detail window, look at the number of contacts in the first of your groups.

- ✔ **No limit to the number of groups a contact can belong to:** Depending on the type of groups that you set up, you might find that a contact needs to belong to more than one group. For example, if you use groups to help with project management, you might need to include the same subcontractor in several groups.

- ✔ **Relational cross-referencing:** By creating a group, you can easily move between the group as a whole and the individual members within the group. From the Group Detail window, you can see a list of all the contacts that belong to that group; from the Contacts Detail window, you can see all the groups that a contact belongs to.

- ✔ **15 levels of subgroups:** You might be working on a huge project that requires a greater amount of micro-management and consequently more subgroups. Maybe you're a realtor and you want to list each neighborhood you work with and then subdivide that into subdivisions and then subdivide again into individual houses.

Creating a Group

Like most of the other ACT! commands, creating groups is as easy as pie. Just remember that planning is always the first step: If you work in a shared database, all users need to agree on how to use groups *before* creating groups and adding contact records to them.

A group is not meant to be a replacement for the ID/Status field (or any other existing field for that matter; see the sidebar "Don't create bad groups!"). The ID/Status field serves to categorize each contact. For example, you might categorize each contact as a vendor, customer, or prospect using the ID/Status field. Limit your groups to help you accomplish something that *can't* be done through the use of fields.

To create a group, simply follow these steps:

1. **Display the Group Detail window by clicking the Groups icon on the Navigation bar.**

   The Group Detail window should look vaguely familiar — in fact, it's nearly identical to the Contact Detail window. Just like the Contact Detail window, the Group Detail window features tabs along the middle of the screen. And, just like the Contact Detail window, the Group Detail window allows you to choose the layout of your choice. As shown in Figure 21-1, the only differences between the Group and Contact Detail windows are the list of Subgroups appearing in the Subgroups field and the Hierarchy field. If you're creating your very first group, the screen appears to be blank.

2. **Choose Groups⇨New Group.**

   If you prefer, you can right-click in the Group Detail window and choose New Group. Or, feel free to click the New Group icon on the toolbar. We aim to please!

   A new group appears, which is blank and naked as the day it was born.

3. **In the Group field, enter a name for the new group.**

   When you move to another field, the group list automatically updates and your group is saved.

4. **(Optional) Create a subgroup by selecting the primary group, choosing Groups⇨New Subgroup, and then filling in the name of the subgroup.**

   You can have as many subgroups per group as you like. And, you can have up to 15 levels of subgroups; in other words, you can further divide your subgroups into sub-subgroups. And, after you create a group, you can go back to the scene of the crime and add a subgroup at any time.

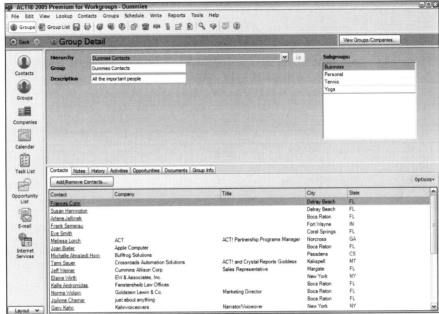

Figure 21-1:
The Group
Detail
window.

5. **Choose Groups⇨Group Membership⇨Add/Remove Contacts and then click the Contacts button to add some contact records to your group.**

   If you prefer, you can also click the Add/Remove Contacts to Group button on the Group Detail window Contacts tab — or even right-click in the Group Detail window and choose Group Membership⇨Add/Remove Contacts.

   In any case, the Contacts dialog box appears (see Figure 21-2).

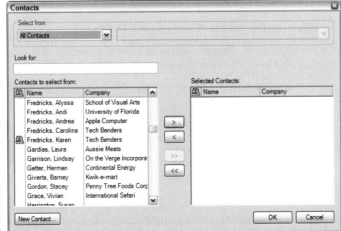

Figure 21-2:
Adding or
removing
contacts
from a
group.

6. **Select the contacts you want to add to your group.**

  • Select the All Contacts, Current Lookup, Groups, or Companies option from the Select From drop-down list.

  • Type in the first several letters of the last name of the contact you want to add to the group in the Look For text box.

  • If you want to search by company name, click the Company column heading in the Contacts to Select From area and then type the first several letters of the company you want to add to the group in the Look For text box.

You'll probably find creating a lookup prior to adding members to a group easier. By creating the lookup first, you can choose the Current Lookup option from the Select From drop-down list and then click the double right-pointing arrows to move all the contacts into your group with a single click. Need a little help in creating a lookup? Skip back to Chapter 7.

7. **Click the right-pointing arrow to add a contact to your group.**

8. **Click OK when you finish adding new contacts to the group.**

Need to remove contacts from your group? Use the same procedure you followed to add a contact to a group — except that you click the left-pointing arrow in the Contacts dialog box!

Adding new contacts to a group does not *remove* existing members of the group — it just adds additional members.

Updating group membership

After you set up your group and throw a few contacts into it, you can easily go back to the group to add — or remove — a few members.

1. **Choose View⇨Group List from any ACT! window.**

2. **Select the group to which you want to add a query, right-click it, and then choose Group Membership⇨Add/Remove Contacts⇨Contacts.**

   The Contacts window opens, ready and willing to help you out (refer to Figure 21-2).

   • **To add a contact:** Select additional contacts from the Contacts to Select From area and click the right-pointing arrow.

   • **To remove a contact:** Select the contact from the Selected Contacts area and click the left-pointing arrow.

3. **Click OK when you finish.**

Adding a single member to a group

In addition to adding or removing several contacts at a time to/from your group, you might want to do it on a contact-by-contact basis. This is easy to do as well.

1. **If necessary, create a lookup for the contact that you want to add to a group.**

2. **Click the Contacts icon on the Navigation bar to make sure you are in the Contact Detail window.**

3. **Click the Groups/Companies tab.**

   The Groups/Companies tab is the home to both group and company information. To make sure that you are viewing group information, make sure that the Show Membership For drop-down list is displaying Groups and Subgroups.

4. **Click the Add Contact to Group button.**

   The Add Contact to Groups dialog box opens.

5. **Select the group to which you want to add the current contact and click OK.**

   Because a contact can belong to more than one group, you can add the contact to as many groups as you like. The contact's Groups/Companies tab displays the groups the contact is a member of.

Setting Up a Group Query Definition

In the preceding sections of this chapter, I show you how using groups in ACT! is a good thing. I show you how to add and remove contacts to groups. By now, you're probably an old group pro, qualified to receive an Official ACT! Groupee certificate. But, like the best-laid plans of mice and keyboards, there is one small hitch to your otherwise perfect world. What happens if you forget to add a contact to a group?

For some of you, forgetting to add a contact to a group isn't a life-threatening event. In other circumstances, however, it might be absolutely crucial that all appropriate contacts are added to the proper group. For example, what if you send a notification to all members of a group about an important meeting, but the CEO isn't included in the group?

Step away from the aspirin — this problem is easily licked with the simple creation of a group definition *query.* A definition query is ACT!'s way of automatically adding contacts to a group based on information in specific fields. Your group rules can be as simple as adding all contacts created by Joe Blow to the Joe Blow Group, or they can be based on much more complex criteria, such as "All customers in the Southwest region managed by Joe, Sue, or Steve belong in the Widgets Group."

A query runs every time you're looking at the Group Detail window. You create a query based on specific field values. For example, you might set up a group rule to find all the *prospects* in *New York* for whom *Mike* is the sales rep; base your rule on the ID/Status, State, and Record Manager fields.

To set up a group definition query, follow these steps:

1. **Choose View➪Group List from any ACT! window.**

2. **Select the group to which you want to add a query, right-click it, and then choose Group Membership➪Add/Remove Contacts➪Edit Criteria.**

   The opening screen of the Group Criteria dialog box opens, as shown in Figure 21-3.

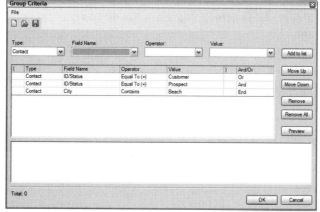

Figure 21-3:
Creating a
group
membership
query.

3. **Fill in the criteria to use to establish group membership.**

   • **Type:** You can query on either Contact or Opportunity fields.

   • **Field Name:** All the fields in your database are included in the Contact or Opportunity field drop-down lists. Select the field that determines the membership into your group depending on the type you selected.

   • **Operator:** Pick an operator from the drop-down list. The choices are fairly self-explanatory with options like Equals, Contains, and Ends With. It might even make you feel like you're playing charades!

   • **Value:** Type in the field value you're looking to match. If you select the State field name, the value might be FL.

4. **Click the Add to List button.**

   Your entry now appears in the table portion of the Group Criteria dialog box, and ACT! is ready and waiting for you to add another criterion.

5. **Repeat the process until you select all the values.**

   For example, if you want the contact record to be in one of a series of states and have an ID/Status of Customer, you can add a second condition.

6. **Change the And/Or indicator as needed.**

   By default, ACT! inserts an And in the And/Or column. That means that a contact must match both criteria in order to become a member of the group. In Figure 21-3, I changed the value to Or indicating that I was searching for either Customers or Prospects.

   If you add a second condition, the contact must match both conditions, not one or the other. For example, if you specify values for both the City and ID/Status fields, all members of the group have to reside in the same city and have identical ID/Status. The only way to avoid this scenario is to change the And/Or value to Or.

7. **Click the Preview button.**

   After a few seconds of contemplation, ACT! presents you with a list of the contacts that match your criteria.

8. **Click OK.**

   If you take a look at the Group Detail window Contacts tab, you'll notice that all of the contacts that appeared in the preview are now members of the group. And those contacts that didn't meet the specifications were sent out in the cold — or at least removed from the group.

Working with Groups

You can customize groups in the same exact way that you can customize the Contact Detail window. You can add new fields, change the layout, and add tabs. You can even do a special Group lookup to search for a group based on the information in any one of the group fields that you've created. For a crash course in adding new fields, scurry to Chapter 15. For a refresher course in customizing layouts, scamper over to Chapter 16.

After you create a group and stick a few unsuspecting contacts into it, things really get exciting. I love to use the phrase "unleash the power of ACT!" — I have this vision of Mr. Clean roaring out of my monitor. Okay, maybe I need to get a life, but I feel that by correctly using groups, you can really get a lot of bang for your buck with the ACT! program. This is how you can fool ACT! into believing it's a relational database. Try not to let too many people in on the secret — it might just raise the price of the software.

Think of your groups as a program within a program. You have nearly the same functionality that you do with the contact portion of ACT! — with one big difference: The activities you create while in the Group Detail window affect the entire group. After you set up a group, you can add group notes, histories, activities, and opportunities for the group in exactly the same way you set them up for a contact. You can even attach a group-specific file to the group Documents tab. This is a great timesaver because information that you input belongs to the group and doesn't have to be duplicated on the contact level.

Using groups to schedule activities

One of the most powerful aspects of ACT! is its ability to associate a contact with an activity. (See Chapter 9 to read more about activities in ACT!.) Many scheduling programs allow you to design beautiful calendars; the problem is that these calendars aren't tied to a particular contact record. For example, if you schedule an appointment to visit Jane Smith and forget the date of the appointment, your only recourse is to flip through your calendar until you find the appointment. After you met with Jane, you have no history of the appointment unless you once again search through your previous appointments.

To take this analogy one step further, suppose that you chair a special committee for your local Chamber of Commerce and need to schedule a meeting. Scheduling the same appointment with each of the twenty-odd participants is very time consuming. Trying to fit each committee member's name on your calendar isn't very practical either. By scheduling the meeting with the group, however, you achieve your goal without the hassle.

Here's how it works:

1. **Click the Groups icon on the Navigation bar.**

2. **Click the Group List button on the toolbar and select the group with which you want to schedule a meeting by double-clicking it.**

3. **Click the Schedule Meeting icon on the toolbar.**

   The Schedule Activity dialog box pops open (see Figure 21-4). The name of the group that you select magically appears in the Associate With field.

4. **Click the Contacts button to the right of the Schedule With field and then click Select Contacts.**

   Here's where you can add any individual contacts that you might want to include in your meeting. When you schedule an activity with a group, the activity appears on each and every contact's individual Activities tabs.

5. **Click OK to close the Contacts dialog box and OK again to close the Schedule Activity dialog box.**

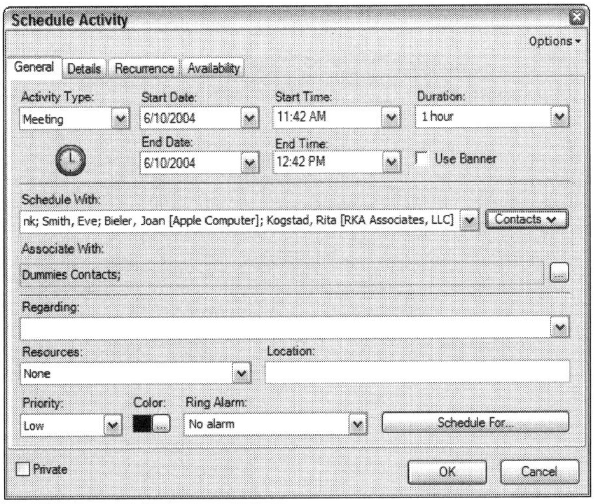

Figure 21-4:
Scheduling
a group
activity.

6. **Flip over to the Group Detail window by clicking the Groups icon on the Navigation bar.**

   Okay, I know I get overly excited about the little things in life, but to me this is way cool. You'll notice from Figure 21-5 that when you schedule an activity with an entire group, our friend the hyperlink shows up in the Schedule With column. By clicking the word "multiple" — which shows up when you schedule a group activity — you're sent to the Contact List where you're rewarded with all the contacts invited to the festivities. Or, if you prefer, look on the Activities tab of any of the individual attendees; once again, you'll notice that "multiple" appears in the Scheduled With column; click it to return to the Contact List to see the list of attendees.

Using notes with groups

You can create a note and assign it to a specific group in three different ways. I describe each of these ways in the following subsections.

Entering a note directly from the Group Detail window

By far the easiest way to enter a Group note is via the Group Detail window. All you need to do is

1. **Choose View➪Group List from any of the ACT! windows.**

2. **Select the name of the group for which you want to enter a note and give it a double-click.**

3. **On the Notes tab, click the Insert Note icon.**

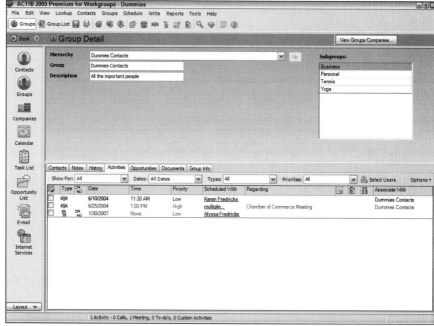

Figure 21-5:
The Group
Detail
window's
Activities
tab.

Entering a note from the Contact Detail window and assigning it to the group

You can also add a group note using the Contact Detail window as your starting point. The drill is just about the same as for adding a regular note, with one extra step.

1. **From the Contact Detail window, create a lookup for the contact record of the group member for whom you want to create a new note.**

   Scratching your head as to how you're going to find that contact? You find the answers to all your lookup questions in Chapter 7.

2. **On the Notes tab, click the Insert Note icon.**

   The Insert Note window pops open. If you want to see a real live picture of this window stroll over to Chapter 8 for a better look. To edit an existing note, give the note a double-click.

3. **Click the Ellipsis button in the Associate With area.**

   For those of you who might not be acquainted with an ellipsis, it's the button decorated with the three little dots.

4. **Select the appropriate group name, click the right-pointing arrow, and then click OK.**

Creating a group history

Another method of adding a group note is slightly more complicated than the other methods. So why, you might be wondering, am I including this in a *For Dummies* book? The reason is that you might find yourself in a situation where you need to designate a note as belonging to a group after you created it. Besides, by now you know that nothing in ACT! is hard once you learn the trick. Here's how you do it:

1. **Choose View⇨Group List to see a list of all your groups.**

2. **Select the group you want, give it a right-click, and select Create Lookup.**

3. **From the Contact List that appears, click the Tag All button.**

4. **Press Ctrl+H.**

   The Record History window opens. You can see what it looks like in Figure 21-6.

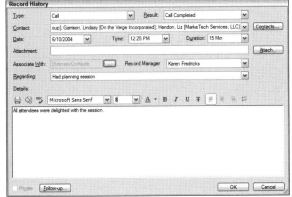

Figure 21-6:
Recording a history for a group.

5. **Fill in your information, making sure that you include the group name in the Associate With field.**

   ACT! grabs a pen and paper and starts jotting that note down for all of the contacts in your group. Well, maybe no pen is involved but you get the idea!

Chapter 22

Joining a Company

. . . .

In This Chapter

▶ Discovering companies

▶ Navigating the corporate maze of divisions

▶ Creating companies

▶ Working with companies

. . . .

*T*he first portion of this book focused mainly on the contact aspect of ACT!; after all, ACT! is considered to be a "contact manager." In Chapter 21, you can find out about groups, which, as the name implies, allows you to group your contacts into more manageable-sized pieces. The company portion of ACT! is new in version 2005 and quite frankly not all of you are going to take advantage of this feature. However, those of you who are working with larger companies and organizations will find this feature invaluable.

In this chapter, I lead you through setting up a company and, if necessary, a division. I show you how to add (or remove) members of a company and how to use the various company features. You even find out about the company reports before all is said and done.

The 411 on Companies

Face it: Bureaucracy is alive and well and living in most civilized countries. Actually, it probably lives in *un*civilized ones as well. Your database might contain the names of the head guy (also know as The Decision Maker), your main point of contact, the guy who signs the checks, and the person who actually does all the work (the Administrative Assistant). Seems easy at first until the head guy gets fired, the check signer takes off for Brazil — and new people replace both of them.

In really large companies (generally those that have their own cafeteria and a lot of cubicles), various divisions within the company often compound this hierarchy. Fortunately, ACT! can accommodate your need to track contacts, companies, and even divisions.

Just like navigating your way around a maze of cubicles can be intimidating, you might be a little hesitant about learning yet another piece of the software puzzle. Relax! A lot of similarities exist between the contact and company portions of ACT!; you can apply most of the concepts that you know about contacts to companies as well. For example,

- ✔ You can add your own unique company fields and associated drop-down lists (see Chapter 15).
- ✔ Companies come with a variety of modifiable layouts (see Chapter 16).
- ✔ You can add company specific documents, notes, activities, and opportunities (see Chapters 5, 8, 9, and 20).
- ✔ ACT! provides you with various customizable company specific reports (see Chapters 11 and 12).
- ✔ You can view, modify, and print a list of all your companies.
- ✔ You can create company-based lookups (see Chapter 7).
- ✔ You can create a mail merge to a specific company (see Chapter 13).

Hey Dude, Where's My Company?

Just like with contacts and groups, ACT! provides you with a whole series of windows that help you manage your companies. Although most of these windows parallel the contact and group windows, you'll soon see that the correct usage of companies can transform ACT! into a highly effective relational database. Although you might find navigating this maze of windows a bit confusing, read on and you'll soon navigate around your companies like a seasoned veteran.

Hyperlinks

The company feature you'll probably like the best is the ability to quickly flip back and forth between a company and the contacts that "belong" to that company. This is done through a series of hyperlinks. When you indicate that a contact is associated with a company, the company name turns to blue; click it and you arrive at the Company Detail window. From the Company Detail window, you see a series of tabs running across the middle of the screen. Click the Contacts tab, and you see a list of the contacts associated with the company. Guess what? All the contact names appear in blue. At first, you might think that this feature is just decorative, but if you venture forth and click a contact name, you'll find that the hyperlink returns you safely to the Contact Detail window of the contact you clicked.

If you're really feeling adventurous, click the company hyperlink one more time. When you see the list of company contacts, click a *different* contact and, *voilà,* you land on that contact's contact record. Even though you'll probably find "hyperclicking" back and forth between the company and its contacts lots of fun, read on to find out even more about companies.

The Companies tab

Sorry to disappoint you, but in ACT! the *Companies tab* doesn't refer to the boss's decision to pick up the check for Friday night's beer bash! The Companies tab actually refers to one part of the Groups/Companies tab in the Contact Detail window. When you click the tab, you have a choice of seeing the membership information for either the groups or the companies that a contact is associated with. The Company List works in much the same way in that it flips you back and forth between your groups and companies; guess you can consider that you're getting two tabs for the price of one!

In ACT!, you can link each contact only to a single company. The Companies tab works a bit differently because a single contact can be a *member* of multiple companies. Sound confusing? Think about it. I am linked to Tech Benders because that is the name of my company. But what if I were a sales rep and assigned to several companies, all of which I like to cross-reference on my contact page? Or what if you have a contractor in your database who works with more than one company? Enter the Companies tab, as shown in Figure 22-1.

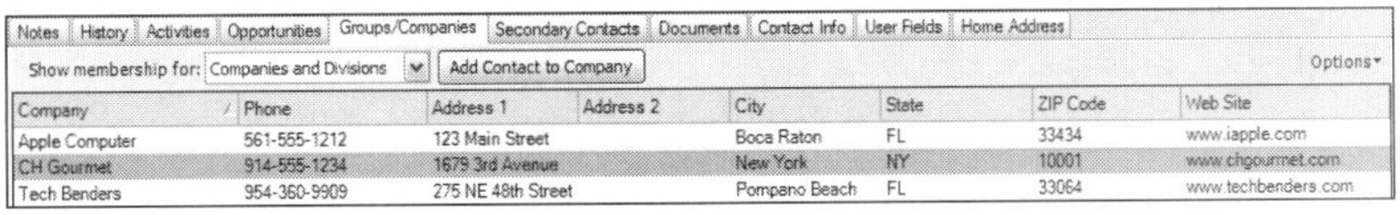

Figure 22-1:
The Groups/
Companies
tab.

Company	/ Phone	Address 1	Address 2	City	State	ZIP Code	Web Site
Apple Computer	561-555-1212	123 Main Street		Boca Raton	FL	33434	www.iapple.com
CH Gourmet	914-555-1234	1679 3rd Avenue		New York	NY	10001	www.chgourmet.com
Tech Benders	954-360-9909	275 NE 48th Street		Pompano Beach	FL	33064	www.techbenders.com

Notes | History | Activities | Opportunities | Groups/Companies | Secondary Contacts | Documents | Contact Info | User Fields | Home Address

Show membership for: Companies and Divisions ▾ | Add Contact to Company   Options▾

The Company List

The Company Detail and Contact Detail windows are two ways you can see company information as it pertains to the individual contact. The *Company List* lets you view a list of all the companies that you have previously created. Like with all lists, you can change the sorting order, add or remove columns, filter the information, and print the list; feel free to review Chapter 5 if you need a refresher course in how to do any of that.

You can access the Company List in a number of ways (see Figure 22-2):

✔ Choose View➪Company List from any of the ACT! screens.

✔ Click the Company icon on the Navigation bar and then click the Company List button.

✔ Create a Company lookup by choosing Lookup➪Companies➪All Companies. If you create a lookup based on any of the individual company fields, the resulting Company List includes only those companies that matched your search criteria.

In addition to allowing you to see a list of all your companies, the Company List allows you to accomplish various company chores, all of which you can access by right-clicking your way to the shortcut menu. As you can see from the shortcut menu in Figure 22-3, your options include

✔ Creating or deleting companies and divisions

✔ Creating a lookup on any of the company fields

✔ Attaching notes, histories, and attachments to a company

✔ Moving that entails demoting a company to division or promoting a division to a separate company

✔ Adding or removing members from a company

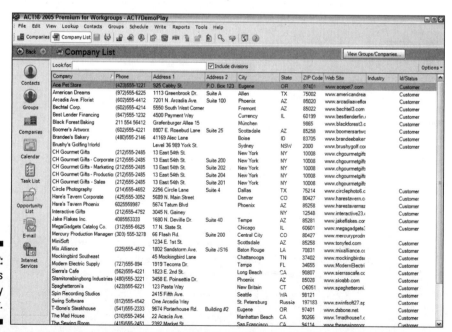

Figure 22-2:
ACT!'s
Company
List.

After you arrive at the Company List, you might find that your visit is somewhat short-lived because you want to zoom in on one of the companies for more details. Not a problem — just double-click the company you want to focus on, and you're transported lickety-split to the Company Detail window.

Figure 22-3:
The
Company
List shortcut
menu.

Knowing the juicy company details

The Company Detail window has many of the same features as the Contact Detail window, such as its own definable fields and layouts, and tabs for adding or removing contacts as members, inserting or viewing notes, histories, activities, and opportunities.

You create and manage companies in the Company Detail window. Not sure how to get there? Just click the Companies icon on the Navigation bar. If you look at Figure 22-4, the Company Detail window looks almost exactly like the Contact Detail window.

Because the Company Detail window is so similar to the Contact Detail window, you may find yourself wandering dazed and confused into the wrong window by mistake. You might think you are entering new contacts, contact details, or contact notes when you are actually entering new companies, company details, and company notes. Just as checking the title bar to assure that you are in the correct database is important, remember to sneak a peak at the Back and Forward bar to make sure you're in the correct view. Believe me, the only thing worse than entering lots and lots of data is deleting it all — and then starting all over again!

At first glance, the Company Detail window looks like a clone of the Contact Detail window. A couple of major differences, however, are

✔ **Division and Hierarchy fields:** You can subdivide companies subdivided into divisions; the Division field allows you to see all the divisions within a company. You can zoom into a division by double-clicking it. The Hierarchy field in Figure 22-4 indicates that you are viewing a division; clicking the Up button returns you to the main company.

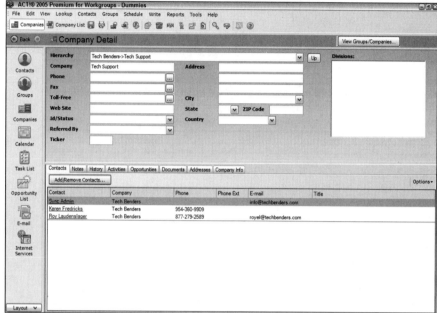

Figure 22-4:
The Com-
pany Detail
window.

> ✔ **The Contacts tab:** There is a certain symmetry here. In the Contact Detail window, you have a Groups/Companies tab; and in the Company Detail window, you have a Contacts tab. The neat thing about the Contacts tab is that you can zoom to any individual contact by clicking the hyperlink attached to the name.

Company Housekeeping

The Company portion of ACT! is at the same time both surprisingly powerful and surprisingly easy to use. Like anything else in life, your companies function best when you give a little thought to their care and feeding. Here are a few of the routine tasks you need to know about.

Forming a new company

When you create a company in real life, you have to hire an attorney and sign a bunch of papers. In ACT! the procedure is a bit simpler, thank heavens! You can add a new company from either the Company List or Company Detail window.

1. **Click the New Company icon on the toolbar of the Company Detail window or the Company List.**

   A blank Company Detail window appears.

   Adding a new company works in pretty much the same way as adding a contact. When that blank screen appears, you are the proud owner of a new, albeit blank, company. You need to start entering in some information. If you clicked the New Company icon by accident, you'll need to delete the company.

2. **Fill all the necessary information into the various company fields.**

3. **Click the Contacts tab, click the Add/Remove Contacts button, and then click the Contacts button in the Add/Remove Contacts dialog box.**

   Whew! I agree, that seems like a lot of steps, but you safely arrive at your destination, which in this case is the Contacts dialog box, as illustrated in Figure 22-5. Type in the first several letters of the last name of the contact you want to associate with this company.

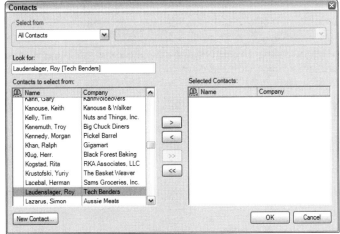

Figure 22-5:
Adding
contacts to
a company

4. **Click the right-pointing arrow.**

   You may add as many names as you like to the company.

5. **Click OK when you finish.**

Creating a division

You might find yourself dealing with companies that vary in size from the sole proprietor who runs his business from his backyard tree house to the Fortune 500 company with locations all around North America — or the world for that matter. You might even find yourself working with a really super-sized corporation — like the federal government. ACT! allows you to create 15 division levels so you can have divisions of your divisions of your divisions. Sound confusing? It is, but then so is the structure of many mega corporations.

The Company Detail window is probably your best source for navigating through the corporate maze. If you are looking at the main company window, you'll notice all the divisions listed in the Divisions field along the right side (refer to Figure 22-4). If you want to home in on a division, just double-click the division name; the company name and path now appear in the Hierarchy field and additional subdivisions appear in the Divisions field. You can keep drilling down through the divisions until you reach the final subdivision or oil — whichever comes first.

To create a new division, subdivision, sub-subdivision, or whatever, follow these steps:

1. **Display the company to which you want to add a division.**

2. **Click the New Division icon on the toolbar.**

   You right-clickers in the crowd can also right-click and choose New Division from the shortcut menu. Either way, a blank Company Detail window appears.

3. **Enter the pertinent info for the division that you are creating.**

   The next time you display the original company, you see the division you added in the Divisions field. Double-click it and you land in the new division. To add members to the division, click the Add/Remove Contacts button on the Contacts tab and add division members just like you add company members.

Deleting a company

I almost hesitate to tell you this one because you could easily delete a company by accident. The good news is that even if you delete a company, the contacts associated with the company are still alive and well and living in your database. The bad news is that all the information from the company fields is lost forever — unless, of course, you have a backup!

1. **Select the company you want to delete in one of the following ways:**

   • Highlight the company from the Company List.

• View the company from the Company Detail window.

2. Right-click and select Delete Company.

3. Click Yes to confirm that you want to delete the selected company.

Converting a group to a company

You might already be an ACT! fanatic and have recently converted from ACT! 6 to ACT! 2005. ACT! 6 users had to be content with groups because the concept of companies was non-existent at that time. You might have set up a group that in actuality is a company. New users in the crowd might set up a group from time to time and find that the group miraculously transformed itself into a full-scale company. By now, you know that ACT! thinks of everything, and this is just one more instance. You can easily convert a group into a company at the click (or two) of a button by following these steps:

1. From any ACT! screen, choose View⇨Group List.

2. From the Group List, select the group you want to convert to a company.

3. Right-click and select Convert to Company.

If you prefer, you can also head up to the menu bar and choose Group⇨ Convert to Company. In any case, the Convert Groups to Companies Wizard appears.

4. Continue clicking Next until you arrive at the last screen; then click Finish.

If you like, I can try to make these instructions a bit more difficult. Basically the wizard is confirming that yes, you want to convert the group into a company. By default, the group name becomes the company name; the group address now is the company address and so on. Feel free to muddle in there if you want, but don't blame me if your muddling efforts are successful!

After the conversion is complete, you might want to race over to the Company List to have a look at the company you just worked so hard to create! You'll also notice that the original group has disappeared — or at least been replaced by the new company.

Following the company rules

Nothing is worse than letting things "slip through the cracks," and ACT! works like a demon to prevent this from happening. Companies are only as good as the contacts associated with them — so what happens when you forget to link a contact to a company? Never fear, once again ACT! is here with a solution. Setting up company rules helps automate the process. That way, whenever you add a new contact to an existing company, it is automatically linked to that company.

To set up a company rule, follow these steps:

1. **Right-click from either the Company List or the Company Detail window and choose Company Membership⇨Add or Remove Contacts⇨Edit Criteria.**

   The Company Criteria dialog box, as shown in Figure 22-6, opens.

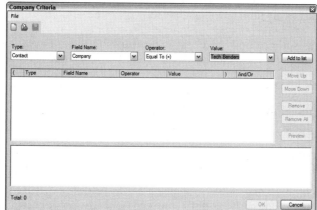

Figure 22-6:
Creating
company
rules in
ACT!.

2. **Indicate the criteria that you're using to determine how the new contacts are automatically linked to an existing company.**

   Nine times out of ten, you base the criteria on the company name so you fill in your criteria exactly as you see it in Figure 22-6. If you're working with a large company with multiple offices, you might need to indicate the city as well. For those of you who always prefer multiple choice to fill-in-the-blank exams, you can choose all the values from drop-down lists so that you can simply select the criteria you want:

   • **Type:** Indicate that you want to match a Contact or an Opportunity field.

   • **Field Name:** Indicate the field you want to use.

   • **Operator:** Typically, you use something like Equal To or Contains.

   • **Value:** Indicate the name of the company or the exact verbiage you want to match.

3. **Click the Add to List button.**

In general, you only add one criterion — the company's name. However, if you need to have more than one criterion, go ahead and add as many as you like. The criteria you select display in the center pane.

4. **Click the Preview button to preview the contacts linked to the company.**

5. **Click OK when you finish.**

The next time you add a new contact and indicate that he works at an old company — or at least one of your existing ones — ACT! automatically links the contact to the company.

Joining the Company Association

The beginning of this chapter concentrates on the company side of things; you can read how to create a company and associate contacts with that company. This section looks at the individual contact and his association with a company. As I mention earlier, there are two ways that a contact can be associated with a company: through the use of a hyperlink in the contact's company field, and by association with a company or companies on the contact's Groups/Companies tab.

A contact can be *linked* to only one company. However a contact can be a *member* of more than one company.

Linking a contact to a company

You have two important concepts to remember before linking a contact to a company:

✔ You can link a contact to only *one* company.

✔ Linking a contact to a company creates a hyperlink from the contact to the corresponding company.

Sound a bit confusing? It is, but here's a way to simplify things. Linking a contact to a company is done using the company field on the Contact Detail window. In general, the contact will be linked to his own company.

Now with those concepts in hand, follow these steps to link a contact to a company:

1. **Create a lookup of the contact that you want to link back to a company.**

2. **Click the Browse button (with the ellipsis) next to the Company field in the Contact Detail window.**

The Link to Company dialog box appears, as shown in Figure 22-7.

3. **Select the company to which you want to link the contact and then click OK.**

   The company name now appears in blue, indicating that a hyperlink is created between the contact and the company.

If you find that you no longer want the link, simply click the Browse button again. ACT! asks you whether it's okay to disable the link. Click OK, and it's history.

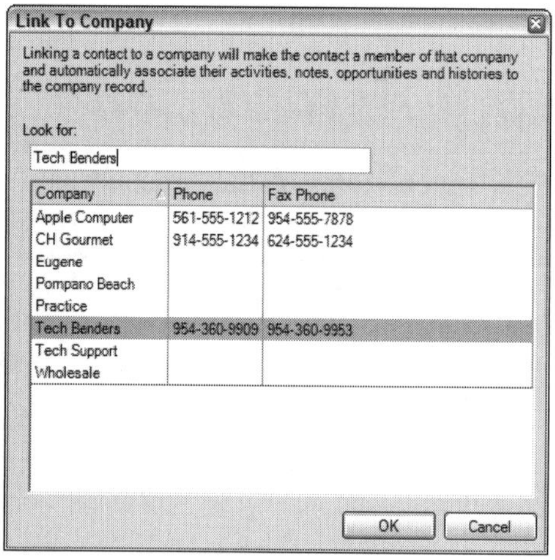

Figure 22-7:
Creating a
hyperlink
between a
contact and
a company.

Link To Company

Linking a contact to a company will make the contact a member of that company and automatically associate their activities, notes, opportunities and histories to the company record.

Look for:

Tech Benders

Company	Phone	Fax Phone
Apple Computer	561-555-1212	954-555-7878
CH Gourmet	914-555-1234	624-555-1234
Eugene		
Pompano Beach		
Practice		
Tech Benders	954-360-9909	954-360-9953
Tech Support		
Wholesale		

OK   Cancel

Adding or removing company members

Just because a contact is *linked* to a company doesn't mean that he is a *member* of that company. I know this seems like fuzzy logic, but this concept ties in to the fact that a contact can be linked to only one company but can be a member of several. You saw earlier in this chapter how you could associate a contact with a company from the Company Detail window. Now you can see how to associate an individual contact to one or more companies from the Contact Detail window.

Don't worry — gaining membership to a company is easy and doesn't require a membership application or initiation fee. You can add new members to the club, er, company from either the Company Detail or the Contact Detail windows. Start with an individual contact and sign him up as a member of the company:

1. **Create a lookup on the contact that you want to add as a member to the company.**

2. **Click the Groups/Companies tab and show membership for Companies and Divisions.**

You'll probably find that last step a bit unnecessary; I do, too. Just remember that Groups and Companies are forced to share the same tab so you have to specify that you are interested in using the Company portion of the tab.

3. Click the Add Contacts to Company button.

The Link to Company window shows up, as shown in Figure 22-7.

4. Select the company you wish to link to the current contact and then click OK.

After you set up a link from the contact to the company, you can also do it from the Company side in pretty much the same way. You might want to add several contacts to the company at once, so now's your opportunity.

1. Create a lookup on the company to which you want to add additional members and click the Contacts tab.

2. Click the Add/Remove Contacts button.

The Contacts dialog box appears (refer to Figure 22-5).

- **To add a contact:** Select a contact from the list on the left and then click the right arrow to move the contact to the Selected Contacts list.

- **To add all the contacts from the current lookup:** Click the double right-pointing arrow button.

- **To remove a contact:** Select a contact from the Selected Contacts list, and then click the left arrow to move the contact to the Contact to Select From list.

- **To remove all the contacts:** Click the double left-pointing arrow button.

3. Continue adding or removing contacts.

Feel free to add as many contacts to a company as you like.

4. Click OK when you finish.

The members of the company now appear on the Contacts tab of the Company Detail window. Feel free to rearrange that tab in any way that you like; if you need help doing that, refer back to Chapter 5.

Working with a Company

You might want to think of a company as a mini "database within a database." The Company Detail window includes the same tabs as other views do — Notes, History, Activities, Opportunities, and Documents. However, it has one major difference: You can filter the Notes, History, Activities, and Opportunities tabs to show just the information that pertains directly to the contact. This feature is very useful and powerful and gives ACT! a whole new dimension.

Jotting down a company note

The concept of company notes is a powerful but confusing one. You might have 12 contacts, all associated with one company. Assume each of those contacts has an average of 20 notes that you've entered. If my math is correct — and it doesn't hurt to double-check me here — the combined total notes for all the company members is 240. Now imagine having to sift through all those notes looking for the one important one. Yikes! That might take a while. Conversely, imagine your company just closed a major deal with the other company; you'd probably find having to enter the same note 20 times, once for each member of the company, repetitious and a huge waste of your time. Enter the company note.

Entering a note from the Company Detail window solves both of these dilemmas: You don't have to enter the note repeatedly and you don't have to search through a mountain of notes to find it.

Entering a company note is as easy as one, two, three:

1. **Click the Notes tab in the Company Detail window.**
2. **Click the Insert Note button.**
3. **Fill in the details of the note and click OK.**

Now comes the fun part. If you look at Figure 22-8, you'll notice the Show For drop-down list. Here's where you can filter the notes to show only company specific notes. You have three choices from which to choose:

- ✔ **All:** Shows both company-specific and contact-specific notes.
- ✔ **Company:** Shows only company-specific notes.
- ✔ **Company Contacts:** Shows only contact-specific notes.

When you enter a note from the Company Detail window, you can only access it from the Company Detail window. If you enter a note from the Contact Detail window of a company member, you can view the note from both the Contact Detail and Company Detail windows.

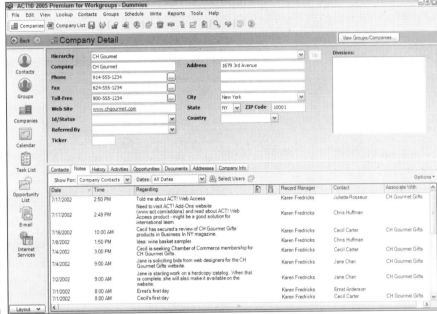

Figure 22-8:
The
Company
Detail
window's
Notes tab.

Associating a note, history, activity, or opportunity with a company

The final piece of the company puzzle occurs when you want to create a note, history, activity, or opportunity with a specific member of a company and you want to make sure that it's easily accessible from the Company Detail window. And, of course, you don't want to have to plow through numerous items just to find the specific note, history, activity, or opportunity that you're looking for. If you were dealing with another Contact Management program, I might just tell you to take a hike; but you're dealing with ACT!, so of course I have a solution for you.

Actually, the solution is a pretty easy one. Any time you create a note, history, activity, or opportunity, ACT! allows you to associate it with a company. By doing that, you take advantage of the Company filter on the appropriate Groups/Companies tab so that you can just view the pertinent information that you want. I show you how to do it for an opportunity, but you can use the same methodology when creating a note, history, or activity.

1. **Create a lookup for the contact with whom you want to create a sales opportunity.**

2. **Click the Opportunities tab and then click the New Opportunity icon.**

3. **Click the Ellipsis button next to the Associate With field.**

The Associate with Group/Company dialog box appears, as shown in Figure 22-9.

Figure 22-9: Associating a note, history, activity, or opportunity with a company.

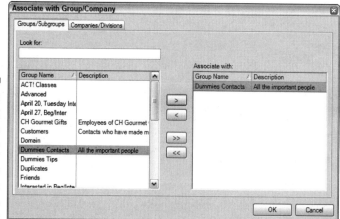

4. **Select the Companies/Divisions tab.**

5. **Locate the company or division from the list on the left, and click the right-pointing arrow to select it.**

The company name now appears in the Associate With list.

6. **Click OK.**

After you associate a note, history, activity, or opportunity with a company, you can view them from the Company Detail window. Filter the History, Activities, and Opportunities tabs exactly the same way as the Notes tab by clicking the Show For drop-down list and selecting your desired filtering option. And, when you quickly find just the item you're looking for in the filtered list, think of me before heading out to the pool!

Accessing the company files

Unlike the other systems tabs, you can't filter the Documents tab. Rather, it sits there like a giant bank vault, just waiting for your deposit. Okay, maybe all this talk about companies has left me with dreams of Monopoly, but you can attach as many documents as you like to the Documents tab of the Company Detail window. This saves you having to hunt through the various company contacts looking for the contact to whom you attached an important file.

Getting the Company Reports

Although ACT! might not be submitting reports to the SEC for you, at times, it seems like it comes pretty darned close. ACT! comes out of the box with five reports, all of which you can clone and customize to fit your needs. If you haven't done so already, you may customize your reports in Chapter 12.

- **Company Membership:** Lists all your companies and their members.

- **Company Summary:** Shows the notes, histories, activities, and opportunities for all companies.

- **Company Comprehensive:** Gives you the complete lowdown on a company. It includes all field information as well as notes, histories, activities, and opportunities.

- **Company List:** Provides you with a list of all your companies including the description, phone, and toll-free numbers.

- **Company Directory:** Lists the regular and shipping addresses, and phone and toll-free numbers for each of your companies.

Part VI
The Part of Tens

The 5th Wave — By Rich Tennant

"Why, of course. I'd be very interested in seeing this new milestone in the project."

In this part . . .

Every *For Dummies* book has a Part of Tens. By golly, this book is no exception to that rule. Think of this as the icing on your ACT! cake. Here's where I've put some ways to make a good program like ACT! work even better:

- First, I give you a rundown of the coolest new features that ACT! 2005 offers.

- Next, I offer you some hints for improving and beautifying your ACT! layouts.

- Finally, I show you some nifty add-on products that can improve ACT!'s functionality.

Chapter 23

Ten Differences between ACT! 2005 and ACT! 2005 Premium

*B*y now you know about all the neat features in ACT!. Your head is probably spinning and you're feeling like you just can't cram one more piece of information into your addled brain. But wait — there's more! So far, this book has concentrated on ACT! 2005. However, a great universe of ACT! users are part of larger office environments who have been hankering for a larger solution for their contact management needs. Ta-dum (drumrolls, please) — here it is! As I mention throughout this book, ACT! 2005 has a big brother product — its name is ACT! 2005 Premium. In this chapter, I list the differences between the two products.

ACT! 2005 Premium includes all the features of ACT! 2005 . . . and then some.

Sharing Databases between the Two Versions

Realizing that the two versions of ACT! represent totally different products is important. You can't install ACT! 2005 and ACT! 2005 Premium on the same machine; to upgrade to ACT! 2005 Premium, you have to uninstall ACT! 2005 before installing ACT! 2005 Premium. You also need to register the product.

If you have multiple users on your network, they must all be using the same version of ACT!; ACT! 2005 can't read ACT! 2005 Premium information and vice versa. You also can't synchronize information between the two versions.

You can easily convert ACT! 2005 databases to the ACT! Premium format. However, ACT! 2005 cannot open or convert ACT! Premium databases, though the Premium version does allow you to save a database in the 2005 format.

SQL Versions

SQL is the language that is used to create the latest versions of ACT!. This is a good thing because it makes ACT! much more robust than previous versions: Your database now supports more users, contacts, and fields. It's also good because developers can develop products that integrate with ACT!.

If you want to appear to be particularly knowledgeable at the next cocktail party, you'll want to throw around the word *SQL* a few times — and realize that it doesn't apply to the latest Oprah selection. SQL is the abbreviation for *structured query language.* In order to avoid embarrassment, pronounce it as either *SEE-kwell* or S-Q-L.

ACT! 2005 automatically installs the Microsoft Desktop Edition (MSDE) of SQL on your computer. The installation CD includes the MSDE version of SQL.

Depending on your operating system, ACT! 2005 Premium installs either the MSDE or the Microsoft SQL Server 2000 Standard Edition. If you are using Windows XP Home, XP Professional, or 2000 Professional, ACT! 2005 Premium automatically installs the MSDE version of SQL on your computer. Microsoft SQL Server 2000 Standard Edition is installed if ACT! 2005 Premium detects that you are running Windows 2000 Server, 2000 Advanced Server, or Server 2003. The full-blown version of SQL is included with your ACT! 2005 Premium purchase; however, because this version of SQL is so large, you receive a second CD that you're prompted to install.

You can't specify which version of SQL you want to install on your computer. ACT! automatically installs either the MSDE or Server Standard Edition based on your operating system.

You might be thinking that because you already own SQL licenses you don't have to purchase additional licenses. Because ACT! 2005 Premium comes packaged with its own OEM version of SQL, you must still pay the full price for the software. The ACT! versions of SQL are read-only; you can export information out of the SQL tables, but you can't change the structure of those tables.

System Requirements

The minimum system requirements for ACT! 2005 and ACT! 2005 Premium running the MSDE version of SQL are exactly the same:

- ✔ A Pentium III-or-higher processor
- ✔ 512MB RAM
- ✔ A hard drive with 300MB of available space
- ✔ The Windows XP, 2000, or Server 2003 operating system
- ✔ A CD-ROM drive
- ✔ SMTP/POP3, Outlook, Outlook Express 5.5 or higher, or Eudora 5.2 or higher as e-mail
- ✔ Internet Explorer 5.5 or higher

When you move up to running ACT! 2005 with Microsoft SQL Server 2000, you need to bump your system up slightly to include

- ✔ A hard drive with 350MB of available space
- ✔ Windows 2000 or 2003 Server as your operating system

These system requirements are the minimum necessary to run either version of ACT! 2005. In this case more is, well, more! Don't be afraid to double up on your RAM memory — you can never have too much of a good thing.

Scalability

Scalability is a popular buzzword that refers to how well a hardware or software system can adapt to increased demands. For example, a scalable network system is one that starts with just a few workstations but can easily expand to thousands. Scalability can be a very important feature because it means that you can invest in a system confident that you won't outgrow it.

ACT! 2005 has a size limitation of 2GB per database. As your database approaches that size — and believe me, I'm talking about one huge database — you'll probably experience a decrease in performance. ACT! 2005 Premium is a more scalable database; it does not have any size limitations.

Number of Users

Ten is the magic number. If you currently have ten named users in your ACT! database, you can use ACT! 2005. This restriction is very specific. You can't, for example, have 20 users in your database and just let 10 of them use your database at one time; ACT! 2005 actually restricts the number of users that you can add to your database.

 One way to limit the number of users in your database is to make users who are no longer accessing your database inactive. Make any users inactive who never access your database or who left the company. Chapter 3 tells you how to designate a user as inactive.

ACT! 2005 Premium lets you have over 10 users accessing your database. In fact, you can have 100 if you like. Because of ACT! 2005 Premium's scalability, it doesn't have a hard and fast limit on the number of users. However, the developers recommend that you limit yourself to 100 concurrent users.

Limited Access Contacts and Teams

In ACT! 2005, the only way you can limit access to a contact record is by designating it as private; the Record Manager can only view private records.

ACT! 2005 Premium takes the issue of security one step further by adding a third level of contact access — *limited access.* Database Managers and Administrators can allow users to access these limited access contacts on a contact-by-contact basis.

In addition to designating a contact as having limited access, ACT! 2005 Premium also introduces the concept of *teams.* Teams are basically groups of users; Managers and Administrators can assign limited access contacts and resources to teams in order to grant access to several users all at the same time.

Group Invitations and Scheduling

ACT! 2005 Premium includes the ability to send formal invitations to activities out to the other members of your organization. Don't get too excited — these invitations are not engraved on vellum but arrive in the shape of an e-mail. If you are the proud recipient of one of these invitations you have the option to accept, tentatively accept, or decline the invitation. After you make that life-shattering decision, two things happen: A notice goes out to the person who sent you the invitation informing them of your decision and, if you accepted the invitation, ACT! automatically adds it to your calendar.

Scheduling Resources

Imagine working in a large company and scheduling a meeting with several of your largest prospects only to find that someone else was using the conference room. Or what would happen if you were scheduled to travel across the country to give a presentation — and the LCD projector was nowhere to be found? ACT! 2005 Premium considers items, such as conference rooms and audio/visual equipment, as *resources*. More importantly, you can check the availability of these resources exactly like you can check the availability of a co-worker. This doesn't sound like a big deal — until you hold your next meeting in the hall closet because someone else had boogied into the conference room ahead of you!

Synchronization

In ACT! 2005, you can only synchronize to another database if the master database is open. Not so with ACT! 2005 Premium; an independent sync service sits around waiting for the syncs to appear even if ACT! isn't open.

ACT! 2005 can only synchronize through a separate service, such as VPN or Terminal Services. Although ACT! 2005 Premium can also make use of those services to sync, you can also configure it to work via an IIS Service.

Pricing and Availability

ACT! 2005 is available for purchase at literally all software and office supply stores as well as on most Internet sites that sell software. ACT! 2005 Premium is available only through volume licensing. That means you can't cruise over to your local Software 'R Us store and pick up a copy; ACT! 2005 Premium is available only through special volume license distribution channels. Volume licensing is available to users needing ten or more seats of ACT!. The good news is that you can order just the number of licenses that you need for your business. Need 18 seats of ACT!? No problem. Need 18 and a half? Well, *that* might be a problem!

Your best bet to order volume license software is to contact an ACT! Certified Consultant. All certified consultants sell volume licenses of ACT!. In addition, you might ask if the consultant is a *platinum* level reseller; platinum resellers offer you the very best prices.

Great things don't come without a price, and ACT! is no exception. The MSRP for ACT! 2005 is $229, although you can expect to pay somewhat less than that at most retail and Internet sites. You're probably thinking that because ACT! 2005 Premium does a lot more it costs a bit more. Good thinking — the MSRP of ACT! 2005 Premium is $399.

Chapter 24

Ten Cool New Features in ACT! 2005

*T*here's always room for improvement, and ACT! is no exception. For the benefit of you loyal fanACTics out there who upgraded to ACT! 6 from a previous version — and for the new fanACTics, too — this chapter highlights a few changes that I find particularly useful. So many new enhanced features are in ACT! 2005 that limiting myself to my favorite ten new features was really difficult. But, upgraders take heart; even though ACT! 2005 contains a plethora of new features, the basic look and feel of ACT! is still alive and well.

Sequel

The loyalty of ACT! users never ceases to amaze me. Many ACT! users start off as single users and find their business expanding by leaps and bounds. Other ACT! users move on to larger companies. Ironically, when an ACT! user finds himself in a new working environment, he or she first sharpens a few pencils, hangs a picture or two, and then looks around for the company's ACT!

database. I'd be a very rich person if I had a quarter for every time a large corporation called me in to install ACT! because "the new guy" couldn't live without it. Unfortunately, however, there were times that I couldn't help because the user had simply outgrown ACT!. Well friends, those days are over!

If I were forced to have only one favorite new ACT! 2005 feature, it's a rather intangible one. Previous versions of ACT! were all based on a technology that limited the size of the database. Various factors, including the number of contacts, fields, notes, and histories, all contributed to the size of the ACT! database; when the database got too big, users experienced a drop in performance. Because ACT! 2005 is SQL-based, size limitations are hardware-based rather than mandated by the software. Simply put, you can have a whole lot more contacts in your database than before and you don't have to limit the number of fields you add.

Large organizations demand large or "enterprise" solutions to their computing needs. They want to limit the contacts specific users can access. They want to schedule things such as conference rooms and equipment. And they not only want to see the calendars of their co-workers, they want an easy way to check their availability before they schedule meetings. Finally, with ACT! 2005 Premium Edition, ACT! has a true enterprise version.

Another benefit of SQL is that supplemental files — layouts, reports, and templates — are stored in the database. For some of you, this isn't a big deal, but for any of you that synchronize your database to remote users, this feature is huge. You no longer have to send supplemental files out to your remote users via e-mail or carrier pigeon.

Opportunities

The good news was that ACT! 5 introduced sales opportunities. The bad news was that the feature was not as flexible as most users would have hoped. The bottom line is that the sales opportunities module in ACT! 5 and 6 was a "what you see is what you get" experience; you couldn't customize any of the fields, and many users were frustrated by the lack of functionality they were experiencing. Chapter 20 tells you about all these great new additions to ACT! but I'm so excited about them that I just have to mention a few of my favorite improvements to the opportunities area again:

- Customize eight opportunity user fields
- Include multiple products in a sales opportunity
- Transfer your opportunity information directly into a customizable Word quote template

✔ View a list of all your current opportunities, zoom in on any given item, and send the entire list over to Excel if you so desire

✔ Choose from many new sales reports

✔ Create a lookup by opportunity fields or products

New and Very Much Improved E-Mail

One of the exciting things about ACT! is that over the years it has slowly evolved into a better and better program. Sometimes the little things just make a program that much easier to use. A case in point is three minor, but much needed, improvements to ACT!'s e-mail features:

✔ **Multiple e-mail address fields:** Just as most people have multiple telephone numbers, more and more people have multiple e-mail addresses. They may have a personal e-mail address and a business e-mail address. ACT! now allows you to add multiple e-mail addresses for each contact — and use all of them.

✔ **Lookup by part of the e-mail:** In earlier versions of ACT!, the e-mail field wasn't actually a field — it was a table. Although this didn't cause much of a problem most of the time, it did cause a number of minor irritations. One of them was that you could only search by the beginning letters of an e-mail address. Now, because the e-mail field is a real, live field, you can search for any part of the e-mail address when using a keyword search.

✔ **Alphabetical sort by e-mail:** Another frustration many ACT! users experienced in previous versions was the inability to create an alphabetized list of e-mail addresses. Again, this was caused by the fact that e-mail addresses were stored in a table and not a field. Guess what folks — because of the new improvements to the E-mail field, you can now get that list.

Cool New Field Types

Most of you old-timers have discovered how easy modifying fields is in previous ACT! versions. And, you had a variety of different field types to choose from. For most of you, this ability was what made ACT! so appealing. ACT! 2005 expands the list of field types by adding six new field flavors to the mix:

✔ **Yes/No:** With all due respect, I would have named this field Check Box because that's exactly what it does — creates a check box, allowing you to indicate "Yes" or "No" with the simple click of the mouse.

New to ACT! 2005 is the ability to easily choose several items from a drop-down list. In previous versions of ACT!, you could do this if you played around in the program a bit — or found someone willing to show you the trick.

✔ **Memo:** Most of the time, you want to put your long winded explanations on the Notes tab; however, sometimes you may want some very specific note information to appear on your layout rather than getting buried under a mass of other notes.

✔ **Pictures:** After all, they're worth a million words. So if you want to include contact specific pictures on a contact record, you can.

✔ **Address fields:** You just have to love this new feature. Many of you like to add new addresses for shipping or billing information. In previous versions, you had to add each new field for the address, city, state, and zip code individually. The new Address field feature automatically adds these additional fields for you.

✔ **E-mail:** I mentioned it before and I'll mention it again: ACT! 2005 allows you to track more than one e-mail address for each of your contacts. And, best of all, you get to send e-mail to any of those addresses.

✔ **Decimal:** This field allows you to specify a field as a number and include decimal places.

ACT! 2005 has another new feature that isn't a new field type exactly, but rather an embellishment of an existing field. ACT!'s Contact field has traditionally been two fields rolled up into one: a First Name field and a Last Name field. This was generally a good thing because it allowed you to look for a contact by either his first or last name. At times, however, this was a bad thing. If you were looking for Tom Smith, you had a choice of searching for either "tom" or "smith". Either way, you probably ended up with a long list of matching contact names, which you then had to hunt through to find the smith among the toms, or the tom among the smiths. ACT! 2005 has introduced the Lookup by Contact, which allows you to search for the entire name at one time. And the contact field now includes a specific area for a middle initial.

The All New Documents Tab

There's a new tab in town, and it's called the Documents tab because it lets you store all your contact-related documents on one tab. In ACT!'s prior versions, there was a Notes/History tab. The good news was that it was a great place to record notes and histories about your interactions with a contact. You could even attach a file to a note, which allowed you to access saved files in a jiffy. The bad news was that as time marched on, the number of entries on the Notes/History tab became larger and larger until you reached the point where you just couldn't find anything anymore.

ACT! 6 introduced the Library tab, which seemed a great idea at the time; you now had a tab dedicated solely to your saved files. And, so the theory went, you could open those files right inside of ACT!. Unfortunately, the Library tab proved to be a little flaky; the files were slow to open and, if not closed again, ACT! started to crash and burn. ACT! 2005 still lets you attach files to the History tab. However, I suspect that you'll soon be spending a lot of time on the Documents tab. Unlike ACT! 6's Library tab, documents opened from the Documents tab open in their appropriate programs. For example, an attached spreadsheet opens in Excel, and word processing documents open in Word. In Chapter 5, I give you the full skinny on the Documents tab.

Consistency of Templates

In ancient times, or at least in the earliest versions of ACT!, there lived an ACT! word processor. This was a good thing because some ACT! users didn't own a word processor and were thrilled beyond words to receive one with ACT!. Documents created using ACT!'s word processor received the `.tpl` extension, which stood for template. As Word became more and more popular and most ACT! users started using it, ACT! allowed you to decide whether you wanted to use Word or the ACT! word processor; if you chose to use Word, your templates were given the `.adt` extension. Then, to confuse you further, ACT! 6 added an e-mail template with the extension `.gmt`. And of course, these templates had no compatibility; you couldn't e-mail a template created in Word or merge an e-mail template with your word processor.

ACT! 2005 has decided to end the confusion by allowing you to save documents in various formats no matter what your word processor preference. And, your documents are now multi-tasking because they'll work equally well on paper or as e-mail templates. If you think this idea sounds good, head to Chapter 13, where you find all the pertinent details.

Prior to ACT! 2005 you received letterhead, fax, and memo documents that you could customize and this was a good thing. Now, however, ACT! comes equipped with a whole bunch of sales and marketing templates as well as several newsletter templates.

All the News That's Fit to Print

Rumor has it that all of you loyal ACT! users love to print reports. And, a few of you more adventurous people even like to customize the format that these reports use. Those of you who are into creating reports are just going to love the new ACT! reporting features.

Quick Print

One of the features many ACT! fanACTics found to be particularly useful was the ability to print out any of the ACT! list views. Chapter 5 talks about list views and shows you how easy they are to customize. Although this feature has always been integral to ACT!, the ability to print these lists out with customizable headers and footers is a new ACT! 2005 feature. ACT! users can now create "quick and dirty" reports on the fly — all the while producing a professional-looking product.

Redesigned Report Writer

For years, loyal ACT! users struggled with the creation of customized reports. Most of you found it to be confusing at best and a downright pain at worst. Although creating customized reports is still a feature best left to the more advanced users of ACT!, the new Report Writer is much more intuitive than the old one. And you can add a much wider variety of fields to your reports. When created, save your reports in either HTML or PDF format. If you want to become better acquainted with the new Report Designer you might want to scurry over to Chapter 12.

Improved Activity Series

Although prior versions of ACT! included the activity series, ACT! 2005 has added several much needed improvements. After you create a series, the individual activities in the series are linked together so that when one activity in the series is rescheduled or removed you're prompted to change the rest of the series accordingly. For example, you may have a whole series of steps that you run through each time you encounter a potential customer. But suppose that the prospect loved you from the get go, rendering the last sales steps unnecessary. When you delete or change one of steps, ACT! asks you what you want to happen with the remaining activities.

And, unlike in prior versions, you can now assign each step in the series to unique members of your organization rather than having to assign the entire series to the same person.

Grouping by Company

The Group feature has always been one of my favorites because it allowed you to tap into one of the most powerful ACT! elements: the ability to create a "one to many" relationship. For example, you might use a group if you are a contractor building a house and you needed to be able to find all the sub-contractors involved in the project. The new Company feature takes that idea a step further. You might be working with several contacts in a large organization but not be able to remember which exact person you spoke with. Or, the company may relocate and you find yourself having to change the addresses for the 25 company employees. You might even need to further group the company members into subgroups or divisions so that you can easily find all the members of the sales or IT departments. You can accomplish all this and more through the use of companies, and Chapter 22 shows you how to do it.

Cool New Look and Feel!

All right, I know it's not one of the more crucial new features, but ACT! underwent a radical facelift with the advent of ACT! 2005. I like to tell upgraders that it's kind of like buying a new car. It feels strange at first, especially that first time you have to turn on the lights or the windshield wipers. Just take a deep breath and realize that the lights do work — you just don't turn them on the way you did before!

Although the icons are still located exactly where you expect them to be, they're updated to give them a slightly more modern look. ACT! now has more of a Windows feel to it; you can navigate in ACT! to return to the previous window just like you do in your Internet browser. You'll also notice that the Navigation bar on the left side of the screen has a bit more flexibility than it did before. You'll particularly want to use the Nav bar to take you to two of the exciting new additions: Companies and Opportunities.

Being left-handed, I'm often accused of doing things backward. However, I think we're all in agreement that, generally speaking, slapping a label on the top of something makes more sense than on the bottom. After all, who ever heard of putting a file folder label on the bottom of the folder? In previous versions of ACT!, the tab labels were placed beneath the tabs; in ACT! 2005 they've been moved up to the top of the tabs where they belong.

Despite the many changes in ACT! 2005, you should find most of the original features that have been around since the earliest editions of ACT!. And, with the introduction of several wizards throughout the program, you should find that some of the more advanced areas — such as creating a new database or adding customized fields — are easier to manipulate than before.

Chapter 25

Ten Tips to Make ACT! Work Better

*B*y now, you know about the various powerful and timesaving features that you find in the ACT! program. But I believe that you can never have too much of a good thing. With that thought in mind, I give you ten suggestions that allow ACT! to work even better — if that's possible. Some of my suggestions include products that are available for purchase; other suggestions are free to one and all.

If you're looking for more information about any of the items I list in this chapter, please visit my Web site at `http://techbenders.com/act4dummies.htm`. Because something new is always on the horizon, check back often to find out about the latest and greatest ACT! products, enhancements, and tips.

Refreshing Your Data

It seems like everyone is in a hurry these days, and ACT! users are no exception. In order to get the optimum performance in ACT!, screens don't necessarily change "before your eyes." This is the same thing you experience when looking at a Web site; the stock quote you're looking at might change after five minutes and you need to refresh your screen to see the "latest and greatest."

Most of the time, ACT! refreshes automatically when you move on to another screen. However, if you make a change in ACT!, such as adding a new layout, and find that the change didn't seem to happen, you need to refresh your current screen with a simple Ctrl+F5.

Linking Your PDA

Who doesn't use a handheld these days? They're great for people on the go — and ACT! lets you take your database along with you. And, if you believe that the best things in life are free, you'll be happy to know that ACT! 2005 includes both the ACT! Link for Palm OS and the ACT! Link for Pocket PC right on the installation CD.

The links allow you to sync your ACT! information (including notes and history) with your handheld device in just seconds. Your ACT! information synchronizes to the basic fields that are included with the Palm or Pocket PC.

ACT! links allow you to

- Map basic ACT! Contact fields including phone numbers, snail mail, and e-mail addresses, several custom ACT! fields, and the ID/Status field.
- Synchronize ACT! contact notes and histories for each ACT! contact.
- Synchronize a select group of contacts if you are using the Group feature in ACT!

In addition, mini-versions of ACT! are available for Palm, Pocket PC, and Blackberry handheld devices. These mini-versions of ACT! allow you to view your customized ACT! fields. You can schedule activities and create notes exactly as you do in the full-blown version of ACT!.

Linking Your Accounting Software

Most of you business owners out there need at least two pieces of software to run your business: database software to keep track of customers and to market to potential customers, and accounting software to help you keep an eye on your bottom line. Unfortunately, a piece of software that does it all often comes with a whopping price tag and a very steep learning curve. As a result, maybe you've chosen to use ACT! for your contact management and Peachtree or QuickBooks for your accounting. If you have larger accounting needs you might be using MAS 90, 200, or 500.

Accounting links are available to link your accounting software to ACT!. These products eliminate the need to enter your contact information into both applications. You can enter the contact information into either ACT! or the accounting software and then synchronize the information between the two. The link inserts a new accounting tab into ACT!, showing all the pertinent Accounts Receivable and Payable information for any linked contact in ACT!. This feature allows your sales team access to invoice and payment history without sharing the rest of your confidential accounting information.

Sharing Your Database over the Web

For the past 15 years, ACT! users everywhere have been relying on ACT! to take care of their contact management needs. During that same time, reliance on the Internet has increased dramatically. Maybe you've contemplated using an online calendaring system, such as the one that Yahoo! provides, just so that you could access your calendar while away from the office. If you choose that solution, however, you lose some of the functionality that makes ACT! so appealing in the first place. Keeping your calendar in an online program other than ACT! essentially cripples ACT!'s power.

One of the greatest strengths of ACT! is the ease in which you can enter notes and other pertinent data into a database. Better still, if your database is located on a network drive, you can share all that information with the other members of your staff. However, many salespeople find that they are not in the office on a regular basis yet want to share updates with the home office. One way to share information is by using a Web-based product.

Using an online product allows you to access, update, and share ACT! information via the Internet. Best of all, the information is in real time. You can perform lookups, run reports, and work on the Web-based version of ACT! just as if you're working back in the main office.

There are several huge benefits of having your ACT! database on the Web:

- All users can access the database on a real time basis.
- Unlike other Web-based CRM solutions, you still deal with ACT!.
- The Web-based version of ACT! offers good security options to limit which users have access to your database and which contacts they're allowed to view and edit.
- A remote user isn't able to "take the database with him" should he leave your company.

So why isn't everyone using a Web-based version of ACT!? Well, the service does have its limitations:

- ✔ **You must have access to the Internet.** If you like to work from various client locations or even on an airplane, you likely don't have an Internet connection, limiting when you can use the Web-based version of ACT!.

- ✔ **You must purchase the Web-based version of ACT!, which is slightly more expensive than the ACT! program itself.** Each of your remote users also must purchase the Web-based version of ACT! rather than the traditional version even if they already own a regular ACT! license.

- ✔ **You need a Web server with IIS installed at the site where your ACT! database resides, a licensed copy of ACT!, and a Web site.** This limitation doesn't mean, however, that you have to host your own Web site. What it does mean is that you must buy a fully licensed copy of ACT! for both your Web server and anyone wanting to access ACT! offline.

Several Web-based versions of ACT! are on the market. Although not available in retail stores, they are available for purchase directly from most ACT! Certified Consultants. Talk to one of them to help you decide which product is best for you.

ACT! Add-Ons and Enhancements

There were probably over 300 add-on products that worked with ACT! 6. As of this writing, developers were scrambling to rewrite their existing products — or create new ones to fill a perceived gap in ACT!. Here are a few of my favorite products.

ASDS

Steve McCandlish of ASDS Computer in Denver believes if it ain't broke, fix it anyway! He racked his brain and came up with several housekeeping solutions that really make most offices purr along quite nicely. A few of my favorites include

- ✔ **MigrateAdmin:** After you discover all the cool new features of ACT! 2005, you'll be kissing other contact management products good-bye. MigrateAdmin converts data from other sources, such as GoldMine and Access, into ACT!. MigrateAdmin converts all basic contact data as well as custom fields, histories, notes, activities, and sales data.

- ✔ **DocAdmin:** Allows you to scan documents onto the Documents tab of ACT! 2005 with a single mouse click. It automatically names the file and attaches it to the ACT! contact record in PDF format, making the documents extremely portable. A DocAdmin license is needed only for the workstation that does the scanning; all other users can automatically see the document.

- ✔ **FaxAdmin:** Unlike earlier versions, ACT! 2005 no longer supports WinFax. FaxAdmin allows you to fax right from within ACT! 2005 via WinFax and MS Fax. Using this tool, you can easily write letters and send them via fax, send fax cover pages, send quick faxes, and do a mail merge and fax.

- ✔ **MedleyAdmin:** Includes a series of custom controls for enhanced layouts including tabs within tabs, a personal dashboard of critical daily information, and an automatic fill of city and state upon zip code entry. Also included with the product are a series of tools that include Group/Company tree views, a Group/Company Calendar window, Multi-Group lookups, and lookups of who is not in a group.

The New Hampton Group

Sometimes it's the little things in life that prove to be the most annoying, whether it's the missing cap on the toothpaste tube or ACT!'s inability to quickly copy field information from one field to the next. Geoff Blood of The New Hampton Group is a real "do-it-yourself" kind of guy. I can just imagine the type of things he was creating with his erector set when he was a little boy. The last time I checked his Web site he had over 20 "enhancements," as he calls them, that help with many of the minor, albeit annoying, little things that ACT! just can't do. My personal favorite TNHG enhancements include

- ✔ **Sales Dash Board:** Provides you with a "Tachometer" display of sales performance-to-quota for the week, month, quarter, and year.

- ✔ **Schedule Board:** Displays a grid, with each column representing a user (or resource), and each row representing a time-slot. You can quickly see who is busy and when.

- ✔ **AutoFill ACT! Fields:** Automatically loads any number of ACT! fields with values determined by the contents of another field.

Northwoods Software

Some of you may feel that there is no such thing as a free lunch. Well, for many years now the nice folks at Northwoods Software have been providing ACT! users with free ACT! add-ons. These add-ons consist of various free enhancements to ACT!. As of this writing, I don't know how many of these products will be updated to ACT! 2005, but, knowing those prolific folks, they'll probably be updating a bunch of them.

Northwoods also produces several fee-based products. Among my favorites are

- ✔ **Sales Automation Mania:** Allows you to define and automate your standard sales processes. The program literally prints your mail merges or sends your birthday newsletters in the middle of the night.
- ✔ **Mail Merge Mania:** Sends mail merge blasts that avoid ISP limitations and allows you to insert ACT! fields in both the body and the subject line of an e-mail template.
- ✔ **Web Prospect:** Reads the mail you receive from your Web site registration forms and creates contacts in ACT!, saving you hours of re-typing.

Reporting Software

ACT! comes with an amazing array of reports right out of the box. And, if you read Chapter 12, you see how easy you can tweak those reports. Because variety is the spice of life, you might find yourself wanting to wander "outside the box" and hankering for a different report. Unfortunately, ACT!'s Report Designer can be somewhat limiting when designing complex reports that involve multiple levels of grouping, filtering, and sorting.

Most report writing software requires an in-depth knowledge of tables and queries. However, the folks at Stonefield Query have taken a relatively difficult process and made it pretty much "dummy proof." Reports are created using a wizard that lets you pick from all the available fields in your database, decide how you want to use those fields, and then preview your results. Reports that used to entail hours of programming can now be created in minutes, passed on to the other folks in your organization, and used over and over again.

E-Blast Software

Chapter 13 talks about mail merging and mentions some of the pitfalls you might encounter when attempting an e-mail blast. One of biggest problems you might encounter is your ISP's reluctance to let you send more than 50 or so e-mails at a time. Another common problem is knowing how to create a cool-looking HTML template. Well, worry not my friends. A multitude of products are available to help speed you on your way — or to at least speed your e-mail blast on to your customers.

E-blast software comes in three flavors that I like to refer to as small, medium, and large. The small products are the least expensive and offer less functionality; the large products are designed for those of you who are basing your marketing efforts on e-mail and are willing to pay for it.

✔ **Small:** Helps you overcome the limitations set by your ISP by sending out your mailing in a series of smaller blasts. These products are generally good for people who want to send out text e-mail messages rather than the more graphical ones. Small products generally run around $100. My recommendation is MergeMaster! Pro by GL Computing.

✔ **Medium:** These products generally include templates for the HTML-challenged members of the crowd who want to send out snazzy looking e-mail blasts. These products usually cost you slightly more money but are well worth it. My favorite is Ace Mailer by Visual Data Integration.

✔ **Large:** If you are marketing to a database with over 1,000 contacts, you're faced with a whole new set of challenges. You'll want to be able to track your "opt-outs" so as not to violate any spam laws. You might also want to track how many people actually open your e-mail message or who they forward it on to. Several products can do that for you — and more. These products are generally subscription-based and generally set you back $20 to $100 a month; however, when you consider the cost of printing, folding, labeling, stamping, and sending via snail-mail, the price is a bargain. I highly recommend Swift Page Email if you do large scale e-blasting.

As of this writing, software developers were scrambling to rewrite their existing products to work with ACT! 2005. Check the *For Dummies* page on my Web site at `http://techbenders.com/act4dummies.htm` to find out more about the various products as they become available.

Tips from the ACT! Guru

I am very fortunate to have had Mr. Roy Laudenslager as the Technical Editor of this book. Roy spent over 10 years assisting befuddled ACT! users in his capacity as senior support specialist at Interact, Symantec, and then Best Software. If you ever had an ACT! support incident "escalated" to the highest level of support, you probably had the good fortune to have spoken to Roy. And, if you've ever read any of the Knowledge Base articles at `www.act.com/search`, there's a good chance that Roy wrote it!

Roy's mind is amazing — he has an encyclopedic memory when it comes to any and all things ACT!. He tackled learning ACT! 2005 and immediately came up with a few tips that I want to pass along:

✔ Roy likes to view the mini-calendars by pressing the F4 key from any ACT! screen. After he's there, he right-clicks a day to see all the pertinent details. If you double-click a day, you land in your daily calendar. You'll notice, by the way, that any days with scheduled activities are bolded.

✔ In Chapter 16, I mention how you can use an anchor field to determine the width, height, and alignment of other fields in your layout. Identify the anchor field by the solid handles on the field. When you select multiple fields, ACT! automatically decrees that the last field selected is the anchor field. To designate another field as the anchor field, press the Ctrl key, click the field once to deselect it, and then click it a second time to make it the anchor field.

✔ Some of you multi-taskers like to view several ACT! screens at the same time. For example, you might want to view the Contact Detail window and the Daily calendar at the same time. Roy searched until he found an obscure setting to enable him to do just that. From any ACT! screen, choose Tools➪Preferences➪Startup Tab and check the Open Each View in Its Own Window option.

✔ Roy's favorite shortcut is to create a lookup on any field simply by right-clicking the field in the Contacts Detail window and choosing Lookup. In fact, Roy makes a habit of right-clicking throughout the ACT! program looking for shortcuts along the way.

Thanks for sharing, Roy!

Hiring an Expert

I like to say that ACT! is kind of a "good news, bad news" product. The good news is that ACT!'s MSRP is fairly inexpensive; the bad news is that ACT!'s MSRP is fairly inexpensive. You might *assume* that because the software price is low, it is a fairly easy product to master.

My mother told me that the word *assume* has a special meaning. Not sure what it is? Write to me at dummies@techbenders.com!

People who have been using ACT! for over 10 years often come out of my classes shaking their heads and muttering, "Gee, I didn't know that!" In fact, many consultants have been known to mutter, "Gee, I didn't know that," because part of the fun of ACT! is discovering an unknown shortcut or feature.

ACT! Certified Consultants make their living by helping ACT! users discover the full power of the program. You can find a local consultant by choosing Help⇨Service and Support⇨ACT! Consulting from any ACT! screen. Can't find a consultant nearby? Many ACT! consultants like myself use tools that allow us to remotely access your computer.

Your local IT person might claim to "know" ACT!. To me, that's kind of like taking an anatomy class and claiming to "know" surgery. Because of the complexity of ACT!'s file structure, save yourself time, money, and aggravation by going directly to an expert.

Some ACT! consultants also have an additional certification. ACT! Premier Trainers (or APTs) not only help you customize your database, they help you learn how to use it. You find a list of ACT! Premier Trainers by going to www. act.com/partners/apt/.

I could buy a scalpel, but I don't think you'd want me to perform brain surgery on you! So it goes with ACT! — save yourself a lot of time and frustration and let an expert help you to get up and running quickly.

Joining a Users Group

John Kaufman of Compass Technology LLC is an ACC who runs the South Denver ACT! Users Group. Regular attendees find the information that they learn there about ACT! and ACT! add-on software invaluable. They also get tips and tricks from other ACT! software users. Attendees find John's Users Group to be a really great way to stay updated on new and innovative ways to use the ACT! software for their businesses and to test drive some of the add-ons before actually purchasing them.

Don't live in Denver? I run the ACT! Users Group of South Florida where 75 ACT! fanatics regularly hang out to learn more about ACT!.

Don't live in Colorado or Florida? Don't worry, Users Groups are in virtually every state of the union. To find a local Users Group, go to http://act.com/ community/usergroups/find.

Index

• G •

• H •

FOR DUMMIES®

The easy way to get more done and have more fun

PERSONAL FINANCE

0-7645-5231-7

0-7645-2431-3

0-7645-5331-3

Also available:

Estate Planning For Dummies
(0-7645-5501-4)
401(k)s For Dummies
(0-7645-5468-9)
Frugal Living For Dummies
(0-7645-5403-4)
Microsoft Money "X" For
Dummies
(0-7645-1689-2)
Mutual Funds For Dummies
(0-7645-5329-1)

Personal Bankruptcy For
Dummies
(0-7645-5498-0)
Quicken "X" For Dummies
(0-7645-1666-3)
Stock Investing For Dummies
(0-7645-5411-5)
Taxes For Dummies 2003
(0-7645-5475-1)

BUSINESS & CAREERS

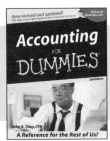
0-7645-5314-3

0-7645-5307-0

0-7645-5471-9

Also available:

Business Plans Kit For
Dummies
(0-7645-5365-8)
Consulting For Dummies
(0-7645-5034-9)
Cool Careers For Dummies
(0-7645-5345-3)
Human Resources Kit For
Dummies
(0-7645-5131-0)
Managing For Dummies
(1-5688-4858-7)

QuickBooks All-in-One Desk
Reference For Dummies
(0-7645-1963-8)
Selling For Dummies
(0-7645-5363-1)
Small Business Kit For
Dummies
(0-7645-5093-4)
Starting an eBay Business For
Dummies
(0-7645-1547-0)

HEALTH, SPORTS & FITNESS

0-7645-5167-1

0-7645-5146-9

0-7645-5154-X

Also available:

Controlling Cholesterol For
Dummies
(0-7645-5440-9)
Dieting For Dummies
(0-7645-5126-4)
High Blood Pressure For
Dummies
(0-7645-5424-7)
Martial Arts For Dummies
(0-7645-5358-5)
Menopause For Dummies
(0-7645-5458-1)

Nutrition For Dummies
(0-7645-5180-9)
Power Yoga For Dummies
(0-7645-5342-9)
Thyroid For Dummies
(0-7645-5385-2)
Weight Training For Dummies
(0-7645-5168-X)
Yoga For Dummies
(0-7645-5117-5)

Available wherever books are sold.
Go to www.dummies.com or call 1-877-762-2974 to order direct.

WILEY

FOR DUMMIES®

A world of resources to help you grow

HOME, GARDEN & HOBBIES

0-7645-5295-3

0-7645-5130-2

0-7645-5106-X

Also available:

Auto Repair For Dummies
(0-7645-5089-6)

Chess For Dummies
(0-7645-5003-9)

Home Maintenance For Dummies
(0-7645-5215-5)

Organizing For Dummies
(0-7645-5300-3)

Piano For Dummies
(0-7645-5105-1)

Poker For Dummies
(0-7645-5232-5)

Quilting For Dummies
(0-7645-5118-3)

Rock Guitar For Dummies
(0-7645-5356-9)

Roses For Dummies
(0-7645-5202-3)

Sewing For Dummies
(0-7645-5137-X)

FOOD & WINE

0-7645-5250-3

0-7645-5390-9

0-7645-5114-0

Also available:

Bartending For Dummies
(0-7645-5051-9)

Chinese Cooking For Dummies
(0-7645-5247-3)

Christmas Cooking For Dummies
(0-7645-5407-7)

Diabetes Cookbook For Dummies
(0-7645-5230-9)

Grilling For Dummies
(0-7645-5076-4)

Low-Fat Cooking For Dummies
(0-7645-5035-7)

Slow Cookers For Dummies
(0-7645-5240-6)

TRAVEL

0-7645-5453-0

0-7645-5438-7

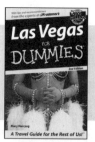

0-7645-5448-4

Also available:

America's National Parks For Dummies
(0-7645-6204-5)

Caribbean For Dummies
(0-7645-5445-X)

Cruise Vacations For Dummies 2003
(0-7645-5459-X)

Europe For Dummies
(0-7645-5456-5)

Ireland For Dummies
(0-7645-6199-5)

France For Dummies
(0-7645-6292-4)

London For Dummies
(0-7645-5416-6)

Mexico's Beach Resorts For Dummies
(0-7645-6262-2)

Paris For Dummies
(0-7645-5494-8)

RV Vacations For Dummies
(0-7645-5443-3)

Walt Disney World & Orlando For Dummies
(0-7645-5444-1)

Available wherever books are sold. Go to www.dummies.com or call 1-877-762-2974 to order direct.

FOR DUMMIES®

Plain-English solutions for everyday challenges

COMPUTER BASICS

0-7645-0838-5

0-7645-1663-9

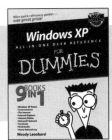

0-7645-1548-9

Also available:

PCs All-in-One Desk
Reference For Dummies
(0-7645-0791-5)

Pocket PC For Dummies
(0-7645-1640-X)

Treo and Visor For Dummies
(0-7645-1673-6)

Troubleshooting Your PC For
Dummies
(0-7645-1669-8)

Upgrading & Fixing PCs For
Dummies
(0-7645-1665-5)

Windows XP For Dummies
(0-7645-0893-8)

Windows XP For Dummies
Quick Reference
(0-7645-0897-0)

BUSINESS SOFTWARE

0-7645-0822-9

0-7645-0839-3

0-7645-0819-9

Also available:

Excel Data Analysis For
Dummies
(0-7645-1661-2)

Excel 2002 All-in-One Desk
Reference For Dummies
(0-7645-1794-5)

Excel 2002 For Dummies
Quick Reference
(0-7645-0829-6)

GoldMine "X" For Dummies
(0-7645-0845-8)

Microsoft CRM For Dummies
(0-7645-1698-1)

Microsoft Project 2002 For
Dummies
(0-7645-1628-0)

Office XP For Dummies
(0-7645-0830-X)

Outlook 2002 For Dummies
(0-7645-0828-8)

Get smart! Visit www.dummies.com

- **Find listings of even more *For Dummies* titles**
- **Browse online articles**
- **Sign up for Dummies eTips™**
- **Check out *For Dummies* fitness videos and other products**
- **Order from our online bookstore**

Available wherever books are sold. Go to www.dummies.com or call 1-877-762-2974 to order direct.

FOR DUMMIES®

Helping you expand your horizons and realize your potential

INTERNET

0-7645-0894-6

0-7645-1659-0

0-7645-1642-6

Also available:

America Online 7.0 For Dummies
(0-7645-1624-8)

Genealogy Online For Dummies
(0-7645-0807-5)

The Internet All-in-One Desk Reference For Dummies
(0-7645-1659-0)

Internet Explorer 6 For Dummies
(0-7645-1344-3)

The Internet For Dummies Quick Reference
(0-7645-1645-0)

Internet Privacy For Dummies
(0-7645-0846-6)

Researching Online For Dummies
(0-7645-0546-7)

Starting an Online Business For Dummies
(0-7645-1655-8)

DIGITAL MEDIA

0-7645-1664-7

0-7645-1675-2

0-7645-0806-7

Also available:

CD and DVD Recording For Dummies
(0-7645-1627-2)

Digital Photography All-in-One Desk Reference For Dummies
(0-7645-1800-3)

Digital Photography For Dummies Quick Reference
(0-7645-0750-8)

Home Recording for Musicians For Dummies
(0-7645-1634-5)

MP3 For Dummies
(0-7645-0858-X)

Paint Shop Pro "X" For Dummies
(0-7645-2440-2)

Photo Retouching & Restoration For Dummies
(0-7645-1662-0)

Scanners For Dummies
(0-7645-0783-4)

GRAPHICS

0-7645-0817-2

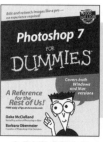

0-7645-1651-5

0-7645-0895-4

Also available:

Adobe Acrobat 5 PDF For Dummies
(0-7645-1652-3)

Fireworks 4 For Dummies
(0-7645-0804-0)

Illustrator 10 For Dummies
(0-7645-3636-2)

QuarkXPress 5 For Dummies
(0-7645-0643-9)

Visio 2000 For Dummies
(0-7645-0635-8)

FOR DUMMIES®

The advice and explanations you need to succeed

SELF-HELP, SPIRITUALITY & RELIGION

Sex FOR DUMMIES
0-7645-5302-X

Parenting FOR DUMMIES
0-7645-5418-2

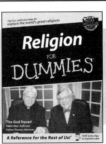

Religion FOR DUMMIES
0-7645-5264-3

Also available:

The Bible For Dummies
(0-7645-5296-1)

Buddhism For Dummies
(0-7645-5359-3)

Christian Prayer For Dummies
(0-7645-5500-6)

Dating For Dummies
(0-7645-5072-1)

Judaism For Dummies
(0-7645-5299-6)

Potty Training For Dummies
(0-7645-5417-4)

Pregnancy For Dummies
(0-7645-5074-8)

Rekindling Romance For Dummies
(0-7645-5303-8)

Spirituality For Dummies
(0-7645-5298-8)

Weddings For Dummies
(0-7645-5055-1)

PETS

Puppies FOR DUMMIES
0-7645-5255-4

Dog Training FOR DUMMIES
0-7645-5286-4

Cats FOR DUMMIES
0-7645-5275-9

Also available:

Labrador Retrievers For Dummies
(0-7645-5281-3)

Aquariums For Dummies
(0-7645-5156-6)

Birds For Dummies
(0-7645-5139-6)

Dogs For Dummies
(0-7645-5274-0)

Ferrets For Dummies
(0-7645-5259-7)

German Shepherds For Dummies
(0-7645-5280-5)

Golden Retrievers For Dummies
(0-7645-5267-8)

Horses For Dummies
(0-7645-5138-8)

Jack Russell Terriers For Dummies
(0-7645-5268-6)

Puppies Raising & Training Diary For Dummies
(0-7645-0876-8)

EDUCATION & TEST PREPARATION

Spanish FOR DUMMIES
0-7645-5194-9

Algebra FOR DUMMIES
0-7645-5325-9

The ACT FOR DUMMIES
0-7645-5210-4

Also available:

Chemistry For Dummies
(0-7645-5430-1)

English Grammar For Dummies
(0-7645-5322-4)

French For Dummies
(0-7645-5193-0)

The GMAT For Dummies
(0-7645-5251-1)

Inglés Para Dummies
(0-7645-5427-1)

Italian For Dummies
(0-7645-5196-5)

Research Papers For Dummies
(0-7645-5426-3)

The SAT I For Dummies
(0-7645-5472-7)

U.S. History For Dummies
(0-7645-5249-X)

World History For Dummies
(0-7645-5242-2)

FOR DUMMIES®

We take the mystery out of complicated subjects

WEB DEVELOPMENT

0-7645-1643-4

0-7645-0723-0

0-7645-1630-2

Also available:

ASP.NET For Dummies
(0-7645-0866-0)

Building a Web Site For
Dummies
(0-7645-0720-6)

ColdFusion "MX" For
Dummies (0-7645-1672-8)

Creating Web Pages
All-in-One Desk Reference
For Dummies
(0-7645-1542-X)

FrontPage 2002 For Dummies
(0-7645-0821-0)

HTML 4 For Dummies Quick
Reference
(0-7645-0721-4)

Macromedia Studio "MX"
All-in-One Desk Reference
For Dummies
(0-7645-1799-6)

Web Design For Dummies
(0-7645-0823-7)

PROGRAMMING & DATABASES

0-7645-0746-X

0-7645-1657-4

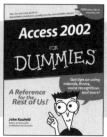

0-7645-0818-0

Also available:

Beginning Programming For
Dummies
(0-7645-0835-0)

Crystal Reports "X"
For Dummies
(0-7645-1641-8)

Java & XML For Dummies
(0-7645-1658-2)

Java 2 For Dummies
(0-7645-0765-6)

JavaScript For Dummies
(0-7645-0633-1)

Oracle9i For Dummies
(0-7645-0880-6)

Perl For Dummies
(0-7645-0776-1)

PHP and MySQL For
Dummies
(0-7645-1650-7)

SQL For Dummies
(0-7645-0737-0)

VisualBasic .NET For
Dummies
(0-7645-0867-9)

Visual Studio .NET All-in-One
Desk Reference For Dummies
(0-7645-1626-4)

LINUX, NETWORKING & CERTIFICATION

0-7645-1545-4

0-7645-0772-9

0-7645-0812-1

Also available:

CCNP All-in-One Certification
For Dummies
(0-7645-1648-5)

Cisco Networking For
Dummies
(0-7645-1668-X)

CISSP For Dummies
(0-7645-1670-1)

CIW Foundations For
Dummies with CD-ROM
(0-7645-1635-3)

Firewalls For Dummies
(0-7645-0884-9)

Home Networking For
Dummies
(0-7645-0857-1)

Red Hat Linux All-in-One
Desk Reference For Dummies
(0-7645-2442-9)

TCP/IP For Dummies
(0-7645-1760-0)

UNIX For Dummies
(0-7645-0419-3)

Available wherever books are sold.
Go to www.dummies.com or call 1-877-762-2974 to order direct.

WILEY